AF529485

Women Empowerment

Women Empowerment

R K Dutta

Reference Press
4831/24, Ansari Road
Darya Ganj
New Delhi-110 002
Phone: 3260807
Fax: 3274173
E-mail: essess@del3.vsnl.net.in

© Publisher

First Published 2003

ISBN: 81-88583-05-7

Price: Rs.650/-

All rights reserved. No part of this publication may be reproduced,stored in a retrieval system or transmitted in any form or by anymeans, electronic, mechanical, photocopying, recording or otherwise without the prior written permission of the copyright holder

Published by:
Reference Press
4831/24, Ansari Road,
Darya Ganj,
New Delhi-110 002.
Phone: 3260807
Fax: 3274173
E-mail: essess@del3.vsnl.net.in

Printed in India by:
Mehra Offset Press

Contents

Preface

1. Women Movements **1-77**

The Empowerment Wing

The Growth of Movements

Women's Participation in Politics

Development of Women

Role of Movements in Violence Against Women

The Status of Women in India

2. Higher Education of Women **78-145**

Professional Colleges

Oriental Colleges

Women's Studies

Inequality of Opportunity for Higher Education

Equality of Rights

'Outside' and 'Inside'

The Dead Band of the Past

Economic and Social Consequences

Special Scheme for Girl's Education

Integrated Child Development Programme

Functional Literacy Programme

3. Women Empowerment in Islam **146-212**

Condition of Muslim Women in India

Protest Against Shariat Laws

Expansion of Judicial System

Purday-Izzat and Variations

Marriage System for the Muslims

Initiation of Marriage Proposal

Istikhara and Imam-Zamin

Mangni (Betrothal)

4. Women in Society **213-267**

Changing Theories

5. Women's Employment **268-288**

Status of Employment

6. Development of Women **289-304**

Women's Cells in Ministries/ Public Sector Undertakings

Women and the Electronic Media

Women and the Print Media

Plan/Strategies for Women's Education
Women Headed Households
Trends in Female Employment
Women in Unorganised Sectors
Women Belonging to Scheduled
Caste Communities
Women Belonging to Scheduled
Tribe Communities
Suggestions for Improving
the Status of Women
In Backward Groups
Index

Preface

Society is generally sensitised to the injustice perpetuated on the women over the centuries. The problems of women reared in a traditional set-up and ethos remain even when they take up employment. The face of the managerial superiority of the father, brothers, or the husband is so deep-rooted in the society that even though a young-woman becomes the bread winner or one more earning member of the family, she does not enjoy the economic independence that ought to be hers by right.

Women are by nature more pliable and less ruthless. The society's expectations from working woman at the domestic front remain the same as those from a non-working woman. So strict and well-defined is the socialisation of boys and girls into the stereotype patriarchal sex-roles that the girls automatically own up the domestic chores as they grow up while the boys feel that they are meant only for the outer spheres. Therefore, even when the woman in the house has a job outside the house too, her first responsibility is considered to be towards her family while there is no concession for her in the office work for her being a woman.

The exploitation of women, in terms of more work and less wages should come to an end. The eve-teasers should be adequately punished and the molestation and rape of girls should be dealt with strictly. Ensuring security of girls and women during the working hours should be the responsibility of the employers and they should listen sympathetically to the genuine complaints of women. Law must provide equality to women in practice not in abstraction, and special cells for the redressal of women's grievances must be set up and made really functional. Legislation and social reforms can provide strength to a woman to fight against all types of evils and discriminations.

To awaken women to their rights, powers and potential is the foremost need of the hour, because injustice against them will continue as long as they remain reconciled to the myth of femininity. Women have to be awakened to the fact that their inferiority is not ordained in heaven and that they are capable of falsifying the male definitions given to them. Women must form solid groups to fight out their common problems. It is heartening that some such groups have come up and their number is increasing but much still remains to be done to activise these groups as well as to give them wide publicity. Women, even the illiterate ones, must have information regarding the hopes they have from such groups.

This book intended to provide a detailed account of women's problems, discusses the strategies for their empowerment and tries to awaken them to work for their rights, powers and progress. It is hoped that this book will be beneficial for scholars, activists and policy makers in the field of women's rights and education.

1

Women Movements

This chapter briefly introduces the structure and goals of the movement, and presents a theoretical approach to answering both a prior question and a subsequent one that is at the heart of this book. First, how does one define a movement and judge whether or not it exists: is there indeed a women's movement in India? Second, how should an analyst go about predicting what a movement will (or will not) be able to accomplish? Some additional questions are necessary to answer the latter question: How is the structure of a movement related to its outcome? And in what arenas do we judge movement results: movement results with relation to what? The first question is necessary because women who are politically active on behalf of women's causes in India often demur when asked if there is an Indian women's movement, The question seems to them to imply a singular, unified entity, perhaps with one guiding ideology and a compact leadership group.

Such a phenomenon certainly does not exist. A movement, however-vibrant, energetic, and multi-faceted—does. That its parameters are difficult to pin down and that its tactics and leaders are many and varied make it no less a movement. Indeed, this chapter begins to argue that the decentralized structure of the Indian women's movement and its resulting capacity to engage simultaneously with many levels of government and society marks a strength, not a weakness, in its capacity, to build the rights, economic and political power, and status of women.

A movement is a collective effort to seek change. Political scientists have generally attended only to the latter aspect. But many women are prevented by social constrictions from significant participation in the economy and in politics. In defining the parameters of a women's movement, then, one must make the connection between the private, or social exercise of power, and its public, or political exercise.

A movement may aim to overthrow the state, to transform it, or just to get something from it. Although it was once thought that movements were symptoms of anomie and irrationality, movements in democracies are now generally seen more prosaically as a means of aggregating and articulating interest in order to affect state policies! Movements, like interest groups, are contenders for influence.

In India many organizations within the women's movement have as their goal moving the state to action; it is primarily the government, they believe, that should provide women with equal rights and economic opportunity. But other organizations, instead of or in addition to targeting the government, strive to improve women's lives within the context of movement participation itself. The goals of economic cooperation and development, greater autonomy within the family, and access to participatory, democratic decision making are pursued within the movement's own activities.

A movement can target society, particularly with regard to social consciousness or ideology; it acts to influence the state; and it can act on participants within the movement itself. A movement is not a mob, but neither is it an interest group. The former is completely anarchic; the latter is characterized by stable bureaucratic organizations and formal interaction with government. A movement is ordinarily somewhere in between.

Within a movement, there may be a number of movement organizations with identifiable leaders and members, as well as unaffiliated individuals "who sympathize with the goals of such organizations,' and who may intermittently contribute time or money, or be mobilized by those groups for particular political actions: demonstrations, letter writing campaigns, and the like. Thus Indian women activists are mistaken when they think that the decentralized character of their activities constitutes a movement; that quality is, in fact, more typical of movements than not.

Movements are not content merely to influence the behaviour or thinking of the already converted. Movements are by their nature evangelical; they seek to convert--to move--people both to new consciousness and to action. The desire and ability of movement organizations to mobilize new constituents is a key aspect of what distinguishes a movement from an interest group.

If they fail to grow, movements may instead become more formally organized interest groups seeking only to protect or further the interests of their existing membership. Movements, on the other hand, seek to persuade, to mobilize, to build. If, as Mao said, a revolution is not a dinner party, so a movement is not a meditation or, for that matter, a colloquium. A movement agitates and acts: it mobilizes people to attack and transform power relations in their social and political lives.

In response to Mancur Olson's suggestion that rational individuals will participate 6 in movements only if they receive some selective, or individual, reward, a number of resource mobilization theorists have argued convincingly for the importance of ideological belief as a factor in movement emergence. For example, in his discussion of the causes of the 1960s U.S. antiwar movement, Perrow maintains that self-interest is an inadequate explanation: the war, he argues "was an issue with youth because it was seen as immoral." Similarly, her study of the U.S. feminist movement brings Carden to conclude that ideological incentives motivate most members, who "enjoy working for a cause in which they believe." In short, people may join a movement not because they have rationally balanced the selective rewards that participation will, bring them against the collective rewards they can reap by letting someone else do it; people may join a movement because they feel ideologically committed to changing society and because they will find it hard to live with themselves if they don't.'

One of the main tasks of a movement, then, is to develop and disseminate ideas that challenge the status quo and suggest more satisfying alternatives. This need not be a fully developed ideology that comprehensively analyzes society's problems and gives specific, detailed guidelines for action, although this, and the charismatic leadership that sometimes accompanies it, may be the best mobilizers of movements. The belief may instead be a more vague sense that a wrong needs to be righted, and that it can be righted. Movement organizations and movement members will agree about some things, disagree about others, come together when they agree, diverge when they disagree. As long as the broad goals--such as greater equality for women--remain the same, there is a movement.

There are limitations to the existing theoretical approaches to answering the question of what movements can accomplish, but there are some useful analytical insights.

It is helpful to view movements, as Alberto Melucci does, as "action systems operating in a systemic field of possibilities and limits." What a movement can accomplish, in other words, is substantially influenced not only by what resources the movement brings to the battle, but by the strength of those institutions with which it contends.

Thus, to the extent a movement's goals include the changing of state policy or action, the analyst must explore why the state is disposed to facilitate or to hinder the movement's achievement of its goals and what resources it can bring to bear to enforce its desires. Similarly, one must examine the strengths of other movements or interest groups that are in alliance or in contention With the movement for influence and power.

In evaluating the possible outcomes of the Indian women's movement, then, one line of questioning has to concern what groups oppose its goals, and what are their relative strengths. Similarly, it is necessary to ask two questions about the state: What incentives does it have and what capacity--economic and political--does it have to respond positively to movement demands?

Centralized movement organizations are thought to be more successful in the short run in influencing established institutions of government because they can coordinate the support that exists and can provide the type of technical expertise to which bureaucratic government institutions respond.

On the other hand, grassroots mobilization and ideological innovation seem to be better accomplished by smaller organizations that can more precisely fulfil the individual desires of prospective members for such selective incentives as direct participation, consciousness raising activities, the learning of new skills, and the development of interpersonal bonds and thus group solidarity. A number of small organizations linked together loosely are better able than one hierarchical organization to embrace a diversity of ideological beliefs and choice of tactics; this characteristic, too, makes them better suited to mobilizing the grass roots.

Movements come in diverse structural forms--some, like the Indian nationalist movement, centralized with a single organization and authoritative leadership at their core; others, like the U.S. feminist movement that began in the late 1960s, characterized by a large number of organizations (some with identifiable leadership; others more collective in nature) that share related goals.

An assessment of how promising is a movement's overall structure therefore requires an examination not only of the type of organizations within the movement, but also of the nix of organizational structures and how well it corresponds to the goals of the movement, There may be, within a movement, a role for organizations that concentrate on persuading government to institute or implement law (much as the Women's Equity Action League acts in the U.S.), while other groups contribute to the development of ideology and mobilization at the grass roots (as U.S. "radical feminist" organizations have done). Indeed, it can be hypothesized that a friendly alliance among Such structurally disparate groups provides a strong model for a movement with broad aims. As will be discussed below, the women's movement in India is characterized by such a structure of alliance; this book's conclusion will revisit the question of how promising this structure is.

The above contributions aside, theorists of movements have devoted too little attention to the question of what movements can accomplish. Having overcome the prejudice of the collective behavioural school of the 1950s and early 1960s that movements are a social pathology, resource mobilization theorists have gone too far in the direction of seeing movements as merely contenders for influence with regard to state policy. In their efforts to legitimize movements, they have rendered them one dimensional. Whether or not movements have some unique qualities that provide opportunities--personal or political--that other institutions do not is not a question that resource mobilization theorists ask.

"New social movement" theorists do ask if movements have special qualities, and find that they do." Unfortunately, they concern themselves only with advanced capitalist societies characterized by great wealth and highly developed technologies.

Specifically they argue that the new social movements, such as European and North American feminist, peace, human rights, and environmental movements, are a response not to class issues, but rather to political systems that are overly hierarchical, centralized, bureaucratized and unresponsive. In the absence of meaningful avenues of participation provided by the state, these movements attempt to create channels for participatory democracy, It is within the context of the movement itself that activists (who are of at least middle-class status, because only they have the time and material resources to support their activities) find the rewards of community, personal autonomy, access to decision making, and growing self-esteem.

Thus, while such movements attempt, in part, to have an impact on state policies, their concern is as much to recapture from the state a space within civil society in which there can be meaningful participation and thus personal and community empowerment. This requires resisting the expanded capacity of the industrialized state to control social and cultural life and regaining from the state the means of production of "symbolic goods of information and images, of culture itself." By so doing, the movements hope to alter public opinion and public demands, to change the way people perceive their society and their government.

This study of the Indian women's Movement will show that some of the impulses and some of the potential that new social movement theorists find in movements in advanced capitalist society exist in movements among women, including the very poorest women (who do indeed have class issues), in one of the world's poorest nations. The assumption is incorrect that movements that value the means of direct democratic participation and access to cultural production as much as the ends of moving the state are products of advanced capitalism.

In India, too, tile desire tor participatory democracy, for individual and group autonomy, for a redefinition of politics to include the production of cultural norms are present. For some parts of the women's movement--what I call the "empowerment wing"--the drive to create them constitutes as important a part of potential movement achievement as winning concessions from the state.

The movement has an environment internal to itself. To fully judge a movement's achievements one therefore must also evaluate its interaction with individual movement participants and groups. This study refers to those organizations within the women's movement whose central goal is moving the state to protect and enhance the rights and opportunities of women as the "rights wing" of the movement; the exploration of its strengths and weaknesses constitutes a major portion of the analysis that follows. But the state does not exist in a vacuum, and these organizations are keenly aware of that. An analysis of their activities leads in the direction, too, of looking at the interaction of the movement not only with the state but with society.

For while to be sure many policies of the Indian state inhibit the growth of women's equality, participation, and development, and while it has resources that could be put to better use, it is not an all-powerful state. Instead, the state is but one of several institutions, including religion and the family, that are rightly seen by movement participants to construct culture and limit women's access to meaningful decision-making about their own lives. The women's movement thus hopes to transform social consciousness: to name and analyze the problem of women's inferior status and power, and to point the way toward their transformation.

In thinking about what a movement may accomplish, one needs, then, to think about state power, but also about social power and ideology, and about the ways in which they intersect and uphold one another. As the women's movement in India shows, both areas may be targets for movement action. And, this study will suggest further, if women are to experience meaningful change toward equality, both of them should be targets. Additionally, to understand what a movement does, one must ask what happen, to people during their participation in the internal environment to the movement. This is particularly so for less empowered people and especially women in the third world, whose opportunities for political participation in traditional political institutions are normally limited, and for whom movement participation is therefore the first, or the most involving, political action in which they have engaged.

Women can learn skills and gain self-confidence that are in turn essential to increasing, their economic and political power. Thus the resource mobilization theories that look for movement causality and movement results only in the field of play outside the movement miss a major part of the story of what a movement can achieve.

The interplay of the various types of power mentioned above is complex: without economic power, women have a hard time exercising power within their families and communities. When they are plagued by poverty, malnutrition, ill-health and illiteracy, they are destined to be politically and socially negligible, So movements that seek to empower women attempt to make concrete changes in their material lives.

But at the same time, unless women have some autonomy and power within their families and communities, some capacity for direct community participation and decision making, they cannot develop economically and politically. Attacking patriarchal institutions that proscribe women's lives is thus an activity of instrinsic importance to the furtherance of women's status and power. It is a task to which movements, by virtue of their ability to generate and disseminate new ideologies, change consciousness, and provide support to individuals, are better suited than political institutions that operate from above, such as legislatures, bureaucracies and courts.

By empowering women economically and socially, movements provide a bridge between institutions of the state and people who heretofore have lacked access to political power or a political voice. The empowerment of women privately"--within the family in particular--is a prerequisite for their participation in public life. They must have some control over their own lives, some confidence in their own powers, some sense of personal efficacy, some freedom from physical violence, some alleviation of malnutrition and disease if they are to engage in politics.

'Thus movements, far from being the anomic enemies of democratic systems depicted by some political theorists," can, in fact, serve to educate, mobilize and empower the disaffected and disempowered for participation in democratic processes at local and national levels. Whereas Samuel Huntington, for example, sees "the highly institutionalized political party" in developing countries as the institution that best functions "to organize participation, to aggregate interests, to serve as the link between social forces and the government," this writer sees in India a case where parties have increasingly failed to fulfil this function and where movements, including the women's movement, can and have served it.

In India, the movement is composed of uncountable organizations in both cities and rural areas; it claims participants who are wealthy, who are middle class, who are poor; who are communist, socialist, or resolutely nonideological; who are members of parties or who hold political parties in contempt as elitist, opportunist or corrupt. Although the movement organizations are many, and the web of communications that connects them informal, this study sees two major ideological and organizational tendencies within the movement (although each of them is further subdivided by disagreements over the proper relationship of the movement to the state).

One, which is largely urban-based, focuses on issues of rights and equality; the other, with both urban and rural components, emphasizes empowerment and liberation. "Tendencies" or "emphases" are more accurate descriptions than "divisions" or "splits" because while different movement organizations devote their energies to different tasks, the activities are in many respects complementary rather than conflictual, and there are many individuals and groups whose loyalties and actions appear to crosscut the differences in emphasis.

Additionally, the two wings of the movement share a desire to transform the consciousness of women and men, first to understand that women in contemporary India occupy an interior position relative to men economically, socially and politically, and then to realize that this position is unjust, unacceptable, and alterable.

Women's rights advocates see women's concerns as issues of human tights within the secular democracy that India's constitution proclaims. Their demand is for equality for women under the law; they see themselves as modernizers and social democrats seeking basic human rights, rather than as "feminists" pressing a radical social agenda.

The rhetoric of rights groups refrains from positing a conflict between women and men; it does not even present itself as a challenge to gender roles, fearing that such an attack would mark the movement as overly influenced by the West, I's and as attacking the family (which, in India, enjoys a place on a high pedestal). They are determined to be in the mainstream of an attempt to modernize India without sacrificing essential Indian culture or values except insofar as those values violate women's rights as human beings and as equal citizens.

Rights groups urge the state to pass and implement laws that give women equality in those family matters subject to legislation (such as inheritance, marriage, divorce and child custody); to act to improve women's health and access to education; to move toward equality in employment; and to pass and implement legislation with regard to rape and dowry that will free women from violence.

The diversity of the roots of different movement organizations has led to differences in their structures, modes of operation, and particularly in their degree of cooperation with political parties and electoral Politics 20 Some of the groups that operate within this wing of the movement were born from opposition political parties and generally act in concert with the politics of those parties. These include the Janata Party's Mahila Dakshata Samiti, the Communist Party of India's National Federation of Indian Women, and the All India Democratic Women's Association and All India Coordinating Committee of Working Women, both of which are affiliated with the Communist Party of India (Marxist). It may seem ironic that those parties rhetorically committed to communism operate, at least in part, within the "rights" wing of the movement. But in. India, the CPI and CPM have resolved to work within the parliamentary system; that the women's organizations associated with them share this strategy is therefore not surprising.

Other groups within the rights wing of the women's movement include venerable independent social service agencies, such as the All India Women's Conference, which has historical connections to the Congress Party, and the Young Women's Christian Association, These have a long history of action on behalf of women and, influenced by the broad feminist stirrings that have taken place since the 1975 Emergency, are now becoming increasingly radicalized.

With the exception of the Mahila Dakshata Samiti, which is based in New Delhi and has affiliated groups in only a few states, all of the above organizations are national in scale, have local chapters, and are organized hierarchically with the national leadership based in the capital. They are mobilizational organizations with large memberships. NFIW, for example, claims 800,000 members, while AIDWA claims 115,000 are enrolled in its branches.

The YWCA has 67 branches all over India and considerable financial resources. Along with their access to and skill in using media, the ability of these organizations' leaders to mobilize large numbers for agitational purposes confers on them considerable political clout; they have entree to high government bureaucrats and to elected officials, including the prime minister.

Differences within the rights wing. Party affiliation versus autonomy. The divide in the rights wing comes between those organizations with ties to political parties and those that reject any direct connection to electoral politics and to the parties, which they regard as elitist and opportunist. The latter, "autonomous" groups are generally small, with a strong emphasis on internal participatory democracy. Both in this emphasis and in their efforts to raise consciousness and to empower individual women through personal support, they share much with the "empowerment" wing of the movement.

Examples include Sahel! ("sister") in New Delhi and the Women's Centre in Bombay, both of which provide informal counselling and some material support (including temporary housing) to women faced with a variety of problems, particularly domestic violence, but also health and employment concerns. However, while the internal democracy, counselling, consciousness raising, and support activities mark these autonomous organizations as empowerment groups, they also engage in agitational political activity (sometimes in cooperation with party-affiliated organizations) designed to pressure the government to change laws or implement existing laws.

Such organizations tend to have few members--Saheli, for example, has 25 to 30 active members at any given time--but unlike the mass organizations in which members are mobilized by the leadership for political activities, members of the autonomous organizations tend to be personally active in both policy making and implementation.

Since, by definition, the autonomous organizations are small, localized, and unaffiliated with any larger group, it is impossible to get an accurate count of how many exist. However, they do appear to exist in most parts of India; a 1985 national conference of autonomous women's organizations attracted 85, groups from 15 cities and states, while a 1988 conference drew 750 representatives, with 8000 attending its final rally.

The rights wing of the movement is largely urban. Its and the participants in the collectively-operating autonomous organizations, are generally middle-class, highly educated, and Hindu; while there is also representation from the small Indian Christian and Parsi communities, only a very few are Muslim. The leaders often have prior experience working within the political, system, either as members of opposition parties or as intellectual leaders who have contributed to govern men sponsored studies or forums.

While, measured on a standard scale of left-wing to right-wing politics, they represent a range of ideological beliefs, they have nonetheless been able to adopt common demands for legislation with regard to dowry and dowry deaths, inheritance, police brutality, and other matters upon which the government can act. Organizations spanning the ideological spectrum from the women's wing of the CPM to the YWCA have formed coalitions around such issues and acted in unison to build public opinion and bring pressure to bear on parliament and government bureaucracies to act.

They share in common a strategy of trying to move the government. This should not be taken to mean that the rights wing of the movement places unending faith in the capacity of government to provide sufficient redress for women; but activists do recognize that government has resources and powers-to create law, to police the law, and to expend large sums of money-that are unique. They attempt, then, to push the state apparatus for all it is worth, but not necessarily to become a part of it. Those who operate within opposition parties obviously believe that the strategy of pushing government from within parliamentary structures is the most efficacious; there is no doubt, too, that organizations attached to parties of the left hope to build their parties' strength by mobilizing women voters around women's issues. That strategy offends many other activists, who see the parties--both Congress and parties of the left--as opportunistic and corrupt. The nonparty activists thus do not engage in electoral politics themselves, but instead lobby members of government and build public opinion through agitation and publicity. Still, this does not negate the fact that their goal, too, is government action to bring about and guarantee rights for women.

The empowerment wing

The "empowerment" wing, aims at the personal and community empowerment of poor women in both urban and rural areas. Not infrequently (and this is why the common categorization of the movement as divided along urban/rural lines is incorrect) it is educated, middle-class city and town dwellers who are instrumental in organizing the rural and urban poor; the largest organizations are headed by educated, urbane women with extensive prior experience in politics whose backgrounds are strikingly similar to those of leaders in the rights wing. Their leadership has been the most vital resource in the establishment of empowerment groups; poor, illiterate women do engage in spontaneous protest, but cannot sustain an organization without the help of educated activists.

In the empowerment wing, there is also a notion of rights, but the goal is economic and social rights--the right to a livelihood and to determine one's own future. These require both political empowerment at the local level and access to the tools of economic well-being. The search is for empowerment from below, not the conferring of rights or economic development from above.

Typically, the organizations mobilize poor women to seek expanded economic opportunity. In rural areas, this may involve seeking land ownership or improved agricultural wages. In both rural and urban areas, the creation of small cooperatives, sometimes linked together through a parent organization, is a staple of women's organizing.

Economic development is just one aim of such movement organizations. There is also a self-conscious attempt to create organizational forms in which women become empowered psychologically and socially. Participating in decision making and in the implementation of decisions; raising consciousness about the situation of women in the family and community; creating mutual interdependence and group solidarity developing skills, self-confidence, and assertiveness: All these are seen as integral to the process of empowerment. The small local groups that form the grass roots of these movements foster economic growth, but become more than that. They are support groups that emotionally and intellectually empower, the location of access to local political participation I as well as the aggregators and articulators of political interests vis-a-vis the state.

The empowerment organizations emphasize self-help and the power of the local community, most are not averse to seeking and accepting resources both from international donors (including development agencies such as the Ford Foundation, organizations affiliated with the United Nations, and bilateral aid from friendly governments, including several Scandinavian countries) and from the Indian government to assist in organizing or in implementing the economic development schemes they pursue.

However, some of the empowerment organizations, motivated by a socialist disdain for the existing parliamentary system and for international capitalism, do not seek any such outside intervention, which they regard as inherently co-optative. Thus, within those organizations that seek empowerment, a distinction must be drawn between those that view the state as an enemy with which they must inevitably clash, and those that see the state as a potentially and store of resources.

While the truly rural-based movements tend to be small and localized, some of the urban-based organizations are very large and have expanded into rural areas. For example, the Self Employed Women's Association has over forty thousand members in Ahmedabad and its chapters in several states, the Working Women's Forum has forty thousand women in the city of Madras and in rural areas of Tamil Nadu, Andhra Pradesh and Karnataka; and the Annapurna Mahila Mandal has some fifteen thousand members in Bombay.

To distinguish between the "rights" and "empower-ment" wings of the movement will be helpful as a way of marking differences in priorities but, on the ground, the barrier between the two is a fluid one. The emphases are different but not mutually exclusive, and often a single organization will engage in both types of activities simultaneously. Thus, for example, the women's wing of the CPM, the All India Coordinating Committee of Working Women, not only engages in demonstrations and lobbying aimed at influencing legislation on such "rights" issues as dowry and changes in law regarding Muslim women's right to receive maintenance upon divorce but also organizes working women within the rubric of the CPM sponsored labour union, CITU.

Urban "think tanks" such as the Centre for Women's Development Studies in New Delhi or the Research Centre on Women's Studies of SNDT University in Bombay will provide scholarly support for legal arguments made by groups attempting to influence legislation. They will also sponsor study groups--or even entire projects--directed at organizing and empowering poor rural women. By the same token, SEWA and Working, Women's Forum, as they work to empower women, continually interact with government agencies to obtain resources, ease police harassment, or make labour laws more responsive to the needs of the self-employed.

In situating the women's movement within the context of Indian politics, we suggest two meanings of movements in democratic political systems. First, a growth in movements and movement participation marks a belief that existing political institutions cannot produce desired remedies. In polities characterized by political repression, movements provide one of the few avenues of political participation. When movements appear in democracies, it is a sign that political channels that should provide meaningful opportunities for participation, such as electoral politics, parties, and interest groups, are inaccessible to movement participants or are ineffective.

The dramatic growth since the 1970s in the number and type of political movements in India--including the women's movement, subnationalist movements, caste movements, poor peasant movements, middle peasant movements, tribal movements and others indicates a growing failure of state institutions to incorporate and expand grassroots participation and respond positively to demand. A second meaning of movement emergence is that participants believe that the state is not the only appropriate arena in which to resolve their grievances.

Because movements can target and alter social consciousness, and because they can provide within themselves a new supportive community that can itself transform economic, social and political aspects of people's lives, movements provide possible venues for problem resolution apart from state influence or control. In India, the women's movement has been part of an explosion in the number of nonparty affiliated, ideologically left-of-center movement organizations, known variously in India as "nonparty formations', non-governmental organizations," and "action groups."

Their goals include the types highlighted by new social movement theorists: decentralized political decision making, women's rights, civil liberties, the achievement of economic power at the grass roots, the right to a safe environment, to education and health care, and a growth in personal and small group autonomy. At the heart of all these movements is a concern with empowering those who lack power to make decisions affecting their own lives By and large, the movement organizations have focused on the economically deprived, but powerlessness and underprivileged are also associated with non-

Hindu ethnic minorities, including Muslims and the scheduled tribes; with the lower castes (thus the movements seeking Dalit rights and development) and with the female sex (thus prompting the women's movement). While seeking rights suggests the need to push for state action--either to insure rights or to refrain from violating them--the movement itself can provide the space in which to achieve some of the goals mentioned above. A movement can create access to decision making, heightened autonomy and some economic development within the context of the movement itself. It can transform consciousness about self-worth and heighten self-confidence.

One of the factors motivating the formation and growth of movements is a belief that movements can perform this function better than political parties, which are normally thought to be appropriate aggregators of interest and mobilizers of democratic participation.By the mid-1970s it had become evident that the state was in crisis. It had failed to integrate large sections of the Indian population into the political process and the benefits of economic development, and it seemed unlikely to do so in the near future. Incumbent governments at the national level and in many states appeared corrupt and intent on destroying democratic liberties.

The growth of movements

Movement politics became an alternative to party politics, The growth the number and size of nonparty organizations seeking rights and empowerment for the powerless developed from the belief that existing state structures--bureaucracy, parliamentary bodies at state and national levels, national and state executives, the Planning Commission and opposition political parties--could create neither meaningful economic development nor more political power for the poor and those who, like women, exercised less political influence than their numbers would seem to warrant. This discontent with government and with opposition political parties, discussed in the sections that follow, led activists away from institutional politics as they searched for other ways to empower the powerless.

Thirty years after independence, India had made progress in combatting poverty and increasing access to political power, but, in the eyes of many Indian citizens, not nearly enough. Poverty still appeared to be intractable. The community development schemes of the 1950s and the green revolution of the 1960s had failed to close the gap between rich and poor. India's cities were becoming a refuge of last resort for the rural poor at a rate that far outstripped the capacity of urban governments to provide jobs, housing, sanitation or transportation. Except in government rhetoric, the poor were being left farther and farther behind.

The generation that came of age towards the end of the nationalist struggle put its trust in parliamentary procedures and specifically in the Congress party. But the generation coming of age thirty years later had not been part of the independence struggle and did not share the same loyalties with equal certitude. Trust in the Indian state was replaced by impatience and skepticism. As the "revolution of rising expectations" began to give way to what Robert Hardgrave calls a "revolution of rising frustrations," movement organizers, often middle-class, urban and educated, worked to aggregate and articulate the demands of women, of the rural and urban poor, and of the scheduled castes and tribes, to bring pressure to bear on the state from outside the party structures.

For most activists, the critique is much deeper than that of particular politicians Or parties; it is a critique of the model of development that has been pursued by the Indian state. "Development" has meant not a decrease, but an increase in the gap between rich and poor, and between those with social and political power and those without. Those concerned with empowerment recognize that efforts to have an impact on government policy can bear only limited fruit since the government does not control the means of social transformation; resources and authority are predominantly in the hands of dominant elites. Thus, action within or aimed at government cannot be enough; movement organizations must also aim to challenge the structure of the economy and the "sociocultural" barriers that prevent the poor and powerless from taking purposeful action.

However, although government is neither the entire problem nor the entire solution, organizers and "activist theorists" of the nonparty movements do accuse the political system of not providing opportunities for genuine participation as opposed to "rituals of plebiscitary democracy. Elections, they argue, only result in the replacement of one block of elites with another, each "equally antagonistic to the peoples' interests."

As any investment the poor might make in electoral politics yields little in the way of concrete returns, participation becomes ever more demoralizing. Neither the opposition parties discussed below, nor the Congress party, particularly following the deinstitutionalization that took place under Gandhi, are seen as offering any room for the genuine involvement of most people in meaningful political decisions crucial to their own existence.

In addition, then, to the goal of mobilizing outside pressure to move the state, the agenda of the nonparty organizations is like that of the "new social movements" in more economically advanced countries: They want to create alternative political spaces in which the powerless can learn to organize and act politically, and in which they can exercise self-determination immediately.

In terms of building the self-esteem of the participants, the practice of independent decision making ,within the groups is intended as an end in itself. Indeed, at the core of these movements is the effort to build empowerment through the creation of consciousness and the reconceptualization of politics as something deeper than the exercise of influencing state power.

Some women's groups do work with or are part of, political parties. However, members of autonomous organizations go so far as to lay the blame for the crisis in politics and in development not only on the government, but on what they see as the failure of organized political parties, trade unions and other traditional forms of opposition to the ruling elite. The growth of nonparty movements thus results in part from widespread dismay with "the continuous limitation and failures of Left parties: the Communist Party of India (CPI), the Communist Party of India Marxist (CPM), the Communist Party of India Marxist-Leninist (CPML) and with Janata, the inheritor of the socialist party mantle. Criticisms of the left parties include charges of opportunism: that parties organize the poor primarily in order to generate electoral support for their own bids for office. In addition, activists reject the left parties' hierarchical style; criticisms of the "bureaucratic" and "vanguardist" structures and principles of the political parties are common.

At the heart of these tensions are differing views of what constitutes genuine progressive change and how best to achieve it. Both the CPI and the CPM seek elective office, a strategy that from the perspective of the nonparty movements is too narrow and too elitist. The parties, they believe, seek to mobilize votes, not to transform consciousness. Such a transformation, movement participants argue, is a prerequisite for lasting change. For example, one activist in an autonomous women's organization, the Forum against the Oppression of Women, has found the left parties' attitudes towards women to be "instrumentalist." While acknowledging, she said, that violence against women is a problem, the left parties maintain it is primarily a law and order issue. Once a communist party I's elected, they argue, the problem will be solved."

Activists of the women's and other nonparty movements feel instead that creating real social change is much more complicated and difficult. Change must come from below, not be instituted from above by those who believe their party line is scientific and thus infallible.

From the time of its founding in 1928, the CPI was closely associated with Moscow. Nevertheless, it took a benign view of parliamentary democracy and capitalism in India, viewing "the bourgeois democratic state" as "a historic advance." The CPI believed that it must assist the bourgeoisie to complete the capitalist stage of development. Its selfassigned task was to organize the working class, so that the party could first share power with the bourgeoisie and then lead the bourgeois-working class alliance. To this end, the CPI pursued two complementary strategies: the organizing of trade unions and the pursuit of electoral alliances with what it believed to be progressive elements of the nationalist bourgeoisie, or, most particularly Congress. At the time of the Congress split in 1969, the CPI allied itself with Indira Gandhi; it remained loyal to her throughout the emergency. To those who, like most activists in the nonparty movement sector, found the rule of Congress and Indira Gandhi during the 1970s to be wanting, CPI strategy appears to be part of the problem rather than the solution.

The CPM, which split from the CPI in 1964, seeks to replace the present "antidemocratic and antipopular government" with one composed of "democratic, antifeudal and anticapitalist forces." While the CPM does not believe that parliamentary politics can create revolutionary change, it nonetheless considers the pursuit of office at state and national levels to be a worthy tactic: communist governments can help to solve local problems, "bring greater morale to the democratic masses," and "intensify the struggle" between progressive and reactionary forces within the ruling Congress party. As a step towards these goals, the CPM organizes "mass struggles" among trade unionists and peasant groups. The mobilization of the peasantry is a priority, a fact which distinguishes CPM strategy from the proletariat-centered strategy of the CPI. But unlike the CPML, which hoped to generate peasant-based revolution, and which was crushed in Bengal in 1967 by a CPM-led state government, the rural mobilizations sponsored by the CPM are conducted so as to enhance the party's electoral performance. How well this serves the peasants is a question answered with skepticism by many nonparty movement critics.

Neither party has met with much electoral success on the level of national politics. The CPI has not had much influence in state elections either; only in Bihar does it enjoy concentrated support. The CPM, though, has several times been able to govern in West Bengal, Tripura and Kerala. However, the communist movement has been unable to expand beyond these regional bases, and it has lost support in Andhra Pradesh and the Punjab. In the judgment of one scholar, "Communism in India is stagnant, and there is no state where support for either the CPM or CPI is growing."

Their inability to move forward at the polls and to claim the loyalty of much of the organized working class does not inspire confidence in those not already converted to the communist cause. Still, it is not their electoral weakness that earns them the distrust of those in the autonomous movements. More fundamental are questions about means and ends, about how a movement should proceed and what it should achieve.

Movement activists are particularly critical of the hierarchical structure of the communist parties, and of any suggestion of the party as "vanguard." These result, they assert, in a lack of flexibility, and an unwillingness to learn from the masses. The accuse party members of having an 'egotistical attitude with respect to their own fallibility" anti reject the communists' alleged "objectivity," Movement activists believe the parties rely too heavily on the Marxist canon, isolate themselves from the knowledge that might flow from below, and thus separate theory from practice.

The disagreement is about means rather than ends, for most groups who seek to empower the poor and powerless hold to a vague socialist notion of a classless society.' But the nonparty movement participants favour a non-hierarchical, collective style of work. They value the encounter between middle-class activist/ intellectuals and the poor, and the learning that comes to each from this interaction." Rather than approaching those they hope to organize with a detailed blueprint of an anticipated revolutionary outcome, nonparty movement activists believe instead "that the awakened people will mould the socioeconomic system according to their needs and it is not necessary to insist on loyalty to everything that goes under the Marxist label.

Another difference between the communist parties and the nonparty activists is that the latter have rejected any insistence that class is the sole determinant of revolutionary preparedness. Their writings repeatedly take the communist parties to task for their adherence to ideological doctrines evolved in a different cultural context and historical condition. Whereas the parties focus most attention on organizing labour, the nonparty movements target "groups and strata considered unorganisable for social transformation... in conventional Marxist theory." Their reason for this is twofold. First, theorists involved with the new movements see the poor as hampered not only by a lack of wealth, but by a culture that separates them from the "world of development." Thus revolutionary strategy must include a fight for social and cultural uplift, for the conferring of a sense of empowerment and confidence on those who have been vulnerable because of their gender, caste, or ethnicity. Furthermore, the poor and powerless are divided by a myriad of cultural, ethnic, caste and gender differences; these separations, theorists of the nonparty sector behave, make class organization impossible. Thus, organizing within groups hampered by their "sociocultural" position--tribals, backward castes, dalits and women--is a necessary precursor to class-based organizing.

They reject, too, the idea that the capture of the state is a prerequisite for societal change. The nonparty movements believe the reverse is true. In fact, they argue for a "redefinition of politics" that moves beyond the question of whõ controls the state to the issue of how the process of social transformation will occur, It is in the process of transformation, in which democratic decision making and collective action are the desired means, that the nonparty movements feel that empowerment will first be realised. Thus it is not Lenin and Mao who are frequently cited by nonparty movement theorists, but rather Paulo Freire and Saul Alinsky on the importance of community organising and conscientization.

Indeed, at the core of these movements is the effort to build empowerment through the creation of consciousness and the reconceptualisation of politics as something deeper than the exercise of capturing state power. The most important step, virtually all nonparty movement theorists agree, is to "awaken critical consciousness among the poor. From this, the capture of state power might logically seem to be a possibility, but that is not what is emphasized by the nonparty groups. When the state is engaged, it is generally addressed on local issues, or issues of enforcement--such as a demand that the minimum wages act or land ceiling laws be implemented--but the purpose of such actions seems always to be twofold. To move the state to action is half the agenda; the other is to build political awareness and a sense of political empowerment among those not accustomed to demanding their rights or exercising power.

The dismay that participants in nonparty movements feel, then, with regard to the left opposition parties, derives from profound differences over the desirable relationship between means and ends. Theirs is a fundamentally different approach to how political change, even revolutionary change, is to occur. While to the communist parties the capture of state power is a necessary prerequisite to social transformation, the nonparty movements adopt the position that social transformation must occur "from the bottom up through organizations of the people." A revolution is seen not as a seizure of power, but as a transformation in people's ability to exercise power over their own lives.

Thus, the agenda of the nonparty movements is twofold. They seek to counter a culture of despair and hopelessness with one charged with purposefulness, self-esteem, self-reliance, and power. This is seen as a necessary precondition for the meaningful participation of the poor or powerless in their own liberation. But most nonparty organizations pursue this strategy, too, in order to have an impact on the government and those private citizens with economic power. The nonparty movements aggregate and articulate interests; they increase the bargaining power of the less powerful.

The Lok Sabha has 545 members elected from single-member constituencies based on population. Of these, 119 seats are reserved for members of the "scheduled" tribes and castes, the groups that historically have been the most marginalized members of Indian society. These reserved seats are divided among the states by the proportion of their population that falls into these categories. The majority of the 250-member Rajya Sabha are elected by the state legislatures, with 12 of its members nominated by the president. Although the Lok Sabha and the Rajya Sabha have similar powers, the membership of the prime minister in the Lok Sabha and its control over money bills means that the Lok Sabha is the primary arena of governmental decision making. Since independence India has mostly been ruled under democratic procedures. The sole exception was from June 1975 through February 1977, when then Prime Minister Indira Gandhi, faced by Jay Prakash Narain's "total revolution" mass movement and the High Court judgment declaring her election null and void, declared a state of emergency.

Although India ostensibly has a multiparty system, the Indian National Congress, now often called Congress (I)—an outgrowth of the Congress movement that led the fight for independence—has controlled the central government and dominated national politics for most of the period since independence was achieved; only twice, in 1977-79 and 1989-91, has there been a non-Congress government. Currently there are four other major political parties. The Janata Dal, a centrist anti-Congress (1) coalition, is generally regarded as the second most powerful political party. To the left and less influential are two communist parties, the Communist Party of India (Marxist) and the Communist Party of India. The major party emerging on the right is the pro-Hindu nationalist Bharatiya Janata Party. There are also several regionally based parties that challenge the Congress (I)'s hegemony at the state level. The most powerful of these are the All India Anna Dravida Munnetra Kazhagam in Tamil Nadu, Telugu Desam in Andhra Pradesh, the Shiromani Akali Dal in Punjab, the National Conference in Jammu and Kashmir, and Asom Gana Parishad in Assam.

The political parties have for the most part been supportive of women's rights. Congress (I), however—because of the tradition of the freedom struggle and the early liberal leadership of Mahatma Gandhi and Jawaharlal Nehru, as well as because of its greater strength overall—has been more effective both in terms of increasing women's representation in elected positions and in terms of policy initiatives specifically geared to women's interests.

India's status as a developing nation has also played a central role in shaping Indian women's political engagement. The country had a per capita annual GNP of U.S. $340 in 1989; nearly one-third of its population subsists below the poverty line set by the national government; and one in ten infants dies within a year.' These statistics present a vivid picture of the human costs of "developing nation" status. Poverty and the high infant mortality rate—together with a rate of population growth that threatens to make India the most populous country in the world by the year 2000, widespread malnutrition, and an economy that is 70 percent dependent on agriculture—have profoundly shaped the daily life experiences of Indian women. For the past 20 years the inclusion of women in governmental development programs has understandably been a primary concern for Indian women.

Society and culture are multilayered, multistructured, multireligious, and multilingual owing to uneven development, incomplete detribalization, and a constant influx of outsiders. Over the centuries a composite culture has evolved, even though fanatics, trying to use religion as a tool of power politics, also try to make religion a point of discord. The Indian population is 82.4 percent Hindu, 11. 7 percent Muslim (the fourth largest Muslim population in all the countries in the world), and Buddhist, Jain, Sikh, and Christian in significant numbers. Fifteen constitutionally recognized languages and over 1,600 dialects add to the rich cultural mosaic. Among the Hindus a four-tiered caste system, which has also affected other religious groups, makes for a highly stratified society. Caste and class are inextricably intertwined and complicate simple sociological formulations. The experiences of Indian women and the forms that their political engagement takes have varied according to caste, class, region, and religious and ethnic group. Yet the national tradition of the freedom movement has led in some instances to consensus about certain national objectives and the primacy of certain women's issues.

Cultural diversity has also influenced women's engagement in politics indirectly through its effects on governmental policy. Notwithstanding the Hindu majority, the commonly applicable penal code, and increasingly vociferous demands for a uniform civil code, all religious and ethnic groups and tribes have their own separate personal laws.

Though under heavy attack in recent years, this government policy of separate personal codes has minimized open conflict among the different sectors of the diverse population. It has also limited tile number of national political issues, often paradoxically shifting the lines of conflict from community against community to conflicts within and across sectors of society, setting Progressives in the same or different religious sects against traditionalists or fundamentalists. The state's efforts to defuse violence and tension also have often adversely affected women's efforts to achieve equality, for keeping fundamentalists of the various religions at peace has been important for the state.

The gender relation of dominance and subordination is a political relation that derives material sustenance from conditions and structures of production and that derives its legitimacy from a tradition and culture that uphold subordination. Still, gender relations are only one of several forces that have shaped the context of women's lives.

Women's life experiences and their ensuing political engagement must also be understood within the context of a colonial past and a present as a developing nation; a sharply stratified society with ongoing caste and class conflicts; paternalistic religious cultural traditions imposed on the elite class within the heartland but leaving much greater freedom in peripheral territories and among the productive masses, with their mother-cult practices; and the interconnections and conflicts that exist among all these forces. We argue that without first placing Indian women's experiences within the context of these other forces—which have both enabled and constrained women's attempts to better their life conditions through political action—women's oppression on the basis of gender relations can be neither understood nor finally eliminated.

Because of the diversity of their life experiences, Indian women have been politically involved in myriad issues since the 1970s as the women's movement has grown. Three policy questions have become identified as women's issues: women's representation in government; the inattention to women in the development process; and violence against women, especially in relation to the resurgence of Hindu and Muslim fundamentalism and the concomitant attacks on women's rights. Although Indian women have been involved in many other issues, these have been the primary focus of women's organizations in the Indian women's movement.

Women's participation in Politics

Indian women's involvement in politics in the modern era started in the late eighteenth and early nineteenth centuries. Although British imperialism profoundly influenced the political engagement of both elite and nonelite women during this period, its impact on the character and purposes of their engagement was very different.

Nonelite women fought against the British colonialists. Moved by the hunger of their children, the British confiscation of their land (their means of livelihood), and oppressive British taxes, women, along with men, participated in "famine revolts" in the late eighteenth and nineteenth centuries and other revolts in the nineteenth century.

Elite women were mainly involved in the Indian Renaissance—the social reform movement of the nineteenth century. The main goals were to do away with what were to elite women the most offensive of traditional Indian practices through the abolition of female infanticide, *sati,* child marriage, and laws prohibiting widows to remarry.

The women in this movement also campaigned for women's education. Although high-caste women composed the main body of the movement, high-caste, Western-educated men led it. The emphasis was not on women's equality but, rather, on the separateness and complementarity of the roles of women and men in society. The movement was an attempt to make women into better mothers and wives for progressive, Western educated men by promoting women's education and eliminating what these men saw as backward and degrading practices like sati.

The elite women's movement did not threaten the traditional family structure and the perception of women's role in society and the home, some men supported them, and proponents were able to enact some of the reforms. In contrast, because the political efforts of tribal and peasant women were ranged against the exploitive colonial system, they had no such success.

With the beginning of the twentieth century a number of organizations exclusively for women appeared among high-caste or elite women. Beginning in 1913, Saroj Nalini Dutt, the educated daughter of a high-caste Hindu in the Indian civil service who was married to an officer of the same class and caste, founded mahila samitis in many towns. She also started women's institutes in Bengal.

In 1910, Sardadevi Choudhurani, also married to an officer of the same class and caste, founded the Bharat Stree Mahamandal to assert women's independent identity. She explained her frustration with other women's organizations: "They are the so-called social reformers. They advertise themselves as champions of the weaker sex; equal opportunities for women, female education, and female emancipation are some of their pet subjects of oratory at the annual show. They even make honest efforts at object lessons in the above subjects by persuading educated ladies to come up on their platform and speak for themselves. But woe to the women if they venture to act for themselves.

In 1917 the Women's India Association (WIA) was founded in Madras by Annie Besant, the Irish theosophist who urged Indian women to join the Home Rule League and the Swadeshi movement. The National Council of Women in India was founded in 1925 by Lady Aberdeen, Lady Tata, and others; and the All India Women's Conference (AIWC) was founded in 1927 through the efforts of Margaret Cousins, and others. Muthulakshmi Reddy, a high-caste highly motivated Tamilan woman doctor, became one of the first female legislators.

As the independence movement moved forward, the elite women's movement stood at a crossroads. Both the WIA and AIWC vacillated on the issue of participation in the freedom movement, even as their activities increasingly addressed political issues. In 1917, when Lord Montague came to India to discuss Indian demands for political representation, the WIA raised the issue of women's suffrage. Its lobbying was somewhat successful and influenced the passage of the 1919 Government of India Act, which granted a restricted franchise to women, such that the right to vote in elections for the provincial assemblies was based on wifehood, property, and education.

The Congress movement pledged itself to principles of sexual equality and adult suffrage after independence at its annual meeting in Karachi in 1931. Many members of the AIWC and the WIA would have liked their organizations to confine themselves to the narrow issues of legislative representation of elite women, property and marriage law reforms, and social and educational reforms specifically geared to the interests of upper-class and upper-caste Hindu women, instead of participating in nonviolent mass movements like the civil disobedience movement and the Salt Satyagraha movement of 1931.

Kamla Devi Chattophadhya, a socialist and an activist in Gandhi's mass movement, spoke powerfully to the difficult choice then faced by the elite women's movement as represented by the AIWC: "Though the Women's Conference had originally stated it would not participate in politics, it realised that it would have to concern itself with politics in its wider term, without alignment to any particular political party.

While it accepted as members women from any party, it took a strong nationalist stand, and demanded equal rights for women to enable them to play their full and legitimate role in the national affairs; otherwise all other rights might become illusory." However, under the leadership of the great patriot Sarojinj Naidu, Congress president in 1925 and leader of AIWC, a section of elite women not only built support for their cause of women's equality but also formed an alliance with the nationalist movement for the ouster of the British by linking freedom for women with freedom for India.

The independence movement brought the two streams of politically involved women together—the elite and the masses, who both participated in the struggle for independence. They were nonviolent soldiers in Gandhi's army of liberation in the

1919 protest movements against the promulgation of the Rowlatt Acts—which strengthened control over the press and legalized internment without trial for suspected subversives—and against the Janian Wala Bagh massacre. Their support was vital in Gandhi's 1921-22 Non-Cooperation Movement, the Khalifat Movement, the civil disobedience movement of 1930-31, the Salt Satyagraha of 1931, the Individual Satyagraha Movement of 1941, and the Quit India Movement of 1942.

Women wore the handspun and handwoven *khadi* cloth as a uniform, and they made salt and did not pay salt taxes in defiance of the oppressive Salt Laws. They also picketed liquor and foreign clothes shops, burned foreign clothes, braved *lathis* and bullets, and went to jail. Nearly 10 percent of the prisoners in the independence movement were women with babies in their arms. Other women who did not go to jail or were not directly involved in the activities of the Congress movement shouldered the burden of supporting their families while their men were in jail. During lulls in the struggle for independence, women devoted themselves to developing alternative lifestyles and socioeconomic structures based on the Gandhian philosophy of sustainable development.

The Tebhaga movement in Bengal and the Telengana movement in Andhra Pradesh were launched to obtain a more equitable distribution of land. In both movements women formed "women's brigades" to protect villages, homes, and children against police atrocities and were given guerrilla training for self-defence. These two movements led to the passing of *zamindari* abolition acts in many states in the early 1950s, which granted some rights to the tillers of the land.

The second and third decades of the twentieth century also saw the emergence of an armed struggle by enthusiastic, patriotic young men and women, mostly belonging to the upper strata of society. They were all labeled terrorists by the British and the historians of their empire. The Chittagong Armoury case—with Kalpana Dutta, Kanaklate Barua, Preetilata. Wadedkar, and other women associates—the Lahore and Kakori case, and many others involved women directly as makers and throwers of bombs and indirectly as helpers and givers of refuge to the male patriots.

By the time of independence the elite women's movement had won the battle of the franchise, the partnership of a few women's organizations and the Congress movement had been established, and women from all sectors of society had participated in politics. Direct political participation promoted women's confidence and self-reliance and broke the barriers of the public-private dichotomies in their lives. Yet on the issue of women's roles in society, an ideological conflict continued between those who looked to the pristine purity of an idealized past, when women and men had separate but complementary roles, and those who saw the reality of women's multidimensional roles.

In sum, five factors shaped the similarities and differences in the organizational and political form and substance of women's political engagement prior to 1947: colonial exploitation and the early mass protest movements; the primarily elite origins of the leading participants in the women's movement and male leadership of the early social reform movement; the nonviolent national mass movement under Gandhi; the marginalized militant movement; and the absence of a radical onslaught on the patriarchal basis of Indian culture and society.

Independence brought women constitutional guarantees of justice, liberty, equality, and dignity for the individual in the form of the Fundamental Rights and Directive Principles of the constitution.

These guarantees signaled a shift in the emphasis of women's organizations. Underlying the new constitution was the desire of the mostly male framers to create a new sociopolitical order and a liberal, democratic polity. This desire on the part of liberal men like Nehru for a new Indian sociopolitical order was supported by the AIWC and the women who would soon form the National Federation of Indian Women.

The NFIW was formed in 1954 by active leftwing members of Aiwc, who struggled for egalitarian and socialist structural changes in the socioeconomic sphere, conceptualized women's roles as multidimensional, and demanded a network of support services for working women in urban and rural areas. Women peasants, agricultural labourers, and workers in factories, the service sector, schools, and offices joined in large numbers.

Here, too, the leaders were highly educated, progressive minded elite women, but they were closely connected with the masses, of women and vocalized their marginalization, poverty, and oppression through the legislative bodies and protest movements. The NFIW's affiliation with the Women's International Democratic Federation, made them aware of global trends and the thrust of the first U.N. Development Decade.

Together these women and progressive men lobbied for reform of the personal laws relating to marriage, divorce, and property rights. Their efforts were opposed by Hindu conservatives, as well as by elements within the Congress movement who were hostile to any legislation that threatened male supremacy in personal and familial matters. In spite of this opposition, the efforts of progressive men, the AIWC, and the NFIW eventually led to the passing of the Hindu Code Bills in 1954 and 1956. After the fierce fight for the Hindu Code Bills, many of the leaders of the established women's organizations turned their focus away from further legislative lobbying for equal rights, settling down instead to implementing social welfare measures created by the Congress government—such as consciousness raising, skill training, creation of support services, child welfare and nutrition, condensed courses for school dropouts, and working women's hostels.

While these established women's organizations attended to implementation of these programs women's representation in the political power structure remained low. Even though more than

10 percent of the Indians who went to prison in the struggle for independence were women, since 1952, the year women were first allowed to stand for election, women's representation in the Lok Sabha has never risen above 8 percent. The cause of this low level of representation does not lie in women's non-participation in politics. Historically men have been more likely than women to vote; but between 1952 and 1984 the difference between men's and women's voting participation was cut in half, from 17.9 to 9.6 percent.

Several factors have contributed to women's low levels of representation. For the most part the women who have been elected to the Lok Sabha have been Congress members. As a result, the defeats of Congress at the polls in 1977 and 1989 led to declines in women's representation in the Lok Sabha. In 1977 and 1989, respectively, only 3.4 and 5.2 percent of the Lok Sabha were women.

The paradox of the Indian polity is that with the passage of time rightist parties like the Bharatiya Janata Party and regional ones like the Akali Dal have been fielding and getting more and more women elected while the non-Congress (I) centrist and left parties have successfully fielded negligible numbers. Women candidates have increased gradually in number, from 51 in 1952 to 164 in 1989. With the exception of 1967 and 1977, however, the overall percentage of candidates who are women has remained between 2.7 and 4.3. At the same time, the women's wings of the parties have been marginalized for the most part, leaving women outside the party power structures.

Under the Congress governments of Indira Gandhi, women's lack of formal participation in politics came to be seen as a problem, with the 1971 census revealing the limits to women's gains. A comparative time-series analysis shook the complacency and false optimism generated by the constitutionally guaranteed rights, the legal reforms, the educational advances for women, the entry of women into the public service, and women's token ascension to governmental and elected power in the previous 20 years. In response to these alarming figures, a Committee on the Status of Women was appointed in September 1971 to investigate the condition of women. The committee's report, "Towards Equality," published in December 1974, heralded the International Women's Year, for it showed how far women in India had come toward equality since independence and how much effort was still required to bring Indian women true equality in fact as well as in words.

Reviewing women's political participation in its report, the committee concluded that women had a negligible impact on the political process—that though they constituted a numerical majority, they were slowly acquiring the features of a minority group because of inequalities of status and political power. To make women's political rights more functional and to give women more opportunities to participate in the formal political process, the committee recommended that political parties set a quota for women candidates.

In the meantime, as a transitional measure it proposed allotting a block of seats to women in the municipal councils. As a second transitional measure it advocated the establishment of women's *panchayats* at the village level, directly elected by village women. These women's panchayats would have autonomy and resources of their own for the management and administration of women's and children's welfare and development programs.

The committee also recommended the creation of permanent independent commissions on women at both state and national levels, with the power to collect information from government agencies on issues of concern to women, to evaluate existing programs and laws that affected women, and to recommend new laws and programs. To ensure that the recommendations would be followed, the committee stipulated that the government would be legally bound to follow its recommendations.

Over the course of the U.N. Decade for Women, some of the committee's more general recommendations were taken up. The Equal Remuneration Act, which guarantees women equal pay for equal work, was passed in 1976; and a women's department in the Ministry of Labour and Employment and a Coordinating Bureau for Women in the Ministry of Welfare were created.

The Congress (I) and Janata Dal did set a 30 percent quota in their election manifestos in 1989, but the provision was not implemented. The National Commission for Women Act was passed in 1990; the commission, however, has yet to be set up. The Panchayat Bill has been passed, but the recommendation of a women's panchayat was not accepted. A bill to allot a block of seats to women on municipal boards is still pending in the Parliament.

The very process of writing the report "Towards Equality" brought together many committed academics, administrators, parliamentarians, and others propounding the women's cause. The impact of the International Women's Year and the Women's Decade and the associated imperative for the government to report to the U.N. Commission on Women at Vienna gave rise to the women's studies movement in India in the mid 1970s, with the establishment of the Centre for Women's Studies at SNDT University, Bombay, the Centre for Women's Development Studies, Delhi, and the Indian Association for Women's Studies. The movement is a vigorous one, combining academism, activism, and commitment. It is a great help to the women's movement and part of it.

An increasing incidence of violence against women, in spite of the climate of the Women's Decade, caused many new organizations of women to be formed in the late 1970s and early 1980s. These new organizations are affiliated with various political parties. Two important ones are Mahila Dakshata Samiti and the Joint Women's Programme. The All India Democratic Women's Association, another leftwing organization, was founded in 1981 and has been active since then, with more or less the same emphasis as that of the NFM. Another important women's group, the Working Women's Forum, arose out of concern for women in the unorganized sector.

Many groups that are autonomous from the parties but were also established at this time—like Samata Manch, Stree Sangharsh Samiti Stree Mukti Sangathan, Feminist Network Collective, Stree Shakti Sangathan, and Purogami Sangathan represent a new awareness of the situation of women and the necessity of organized struggle against social in justices to ensure the achievement of the goals of the Women's Decade. Whereas the new women's associations with political party affiliations are mainstream organizations with an all-India scope, the autonomous groups are basically locale specific, militant groupings of young women fighting oppression and violence against women generated by the system itself. Most of these autonomous groups are led by educated, urban, and vocal young feminists who have worked with women in rural areas, slums, and trade unions and created awareness and organization among them.

Some groups, like the AIDWA and Stree Sangharsh Samiti, have concentrated on issues of change in the socioeconomic system and opposed anti-democratic measures like the amendment to the Industrial Disputes Act and to the Hospitals and Other Institutions Bill, which proposed to limit the rights of workers to organize. There has also been an unprecedented flowering of joint actions by women's groups in response to specific actions of violence against Women.

These efforts of independent women's groups and the scope of the problems that they have addressed have encouraged some groups to renew the demands made in 1974 for a 30 percent women's quota in the Lok Sabha. Before the 1989 elections all the bourgeois parties promised 30 percent of their seats to women. After the election they reneged. To attain the goal of larger representation, efforts are being made to widen the base of the women's movement through grassroots organizations and greater participation of women in trade unions. Larger groups of women's organizations such as the All Gujarat Social Organizations Interventionist Central Organization are also being created to build a greater awareness of women's issues among voters and to contest elections on women's issues. They also give financial help to women candidates.

No women's organizations specifically focus an getting women elected at the national level. Unlike the earlier elite women activists, most women have not had the economic freedom to choose their life and career. The material circumstances of their upbringing have made their choices for them and inhibited their participation in formal politics. Women's cultural socialization and the fear of unsettling the family and their position in it—the family is considered women's domain—have also lessened many women's desire to participate in politics.

Many unattached young women may be politically active, but once married, they disappear from the political scene. In spite of the progress since independence, lack of education and lack of knowledge about the intricacies of party politics among many nonelite women have limited their participation in the formal political arena. The role of money, the corruption of politics, and growing violence against women have also constrained many potential activists.

In numerous ways, Indira Gandhi has been the archetype for women who are trying to obtain not only political representation but also a place in the power structure in postindependence India. A symbol of both accomplishments and contradictions, she represents the tokenism in women's ascent to power and the underlying limits of the efforts of the women's movement to attain equality and political representation. Her rise to power was due less to the strength of the women's movement than to a combination of other factors, such as her family background in the nationalist movement and the Congress (I)'s need for a compromise candidate, Up to now, almost all other women's efforts in the political arena have been affected by similar forces.

Development of Women

Since independence national development has been premised on an understanding of development primarily in terms of economic growth. Though achieving a modicum of growth and increased industrialization, India has nonetheless failed to achieve "growth with justice." A central example of growth without justice has been the way that development has totally bypassed the needs of Indian women.

While the per capita GNP has risen, the health and educational and economic status of women have remained much worse than men's, or even declined. In response, during the 1980s women, with the help of the government, have organized to create independent local development projects specifically geared both to meeting women's material needs and to increasing women's voices in national development planning and implementation. This approach augments the social service efforts of the government and women's groups to ameliorate the immediate problems of poverty and economic marginality.

Women's generally poor health is indicated by the declining sex ratio and their higher mortality rates. The ratio of women to men has decreased from 972 females per 1,000 males in 1901 to 926 per 1,000 in 1991. In spite of the increase in women's life expectancy from 44.7 years in 1971 to 56.2 in 1981-86, age-specific death rates for female children and young women for every five-year cohort up to 35 years of age are higher for women than for men. The reasons lie in excessive child-bearing, female infanticide and feticide, and lack of proper nutrition and medical care.

Development has also bypassed women in the crucial area of education, The diffusion of progressive ideas notwithstanding, the majority of the population still consider girls to be unwanted burdens. Among the poorest masses, girls have hence been required to help support their families and look after siblings from an early age. Education has not been considered a priority. As a result, even though the overall literacy rate improved from 28 percent to 52 percent between 1961 and 1991, women's literacy rate rose much less: from 15 percent to only 39 percent. Girls' school enrolment figures partly explain this low literacy rate. Whereas 99 percent of the boys between six and eleven were in primary school in 1981, only 66 percent of the girls in the same age-group were enrolled. Nearly 56 percent of the dropouts at the primary level and almost 78 percent at the middle level were girls.

Women's employment outside the home has also been adversely affected by development. Their participation in the paid labour force, instead of increasing with economic growth, has been on the decline. In 1961, 28 percent of the main workers to total population were women; by 1981 only 14 percent of the main workers were women. 14 A lack of technological education and training means that most women who have jobs are forced to do low-paying manual work. The modernization of agricultural techniques and the rapid growth of the organized industrial sectors of the economy have caused a decline in cottage industries, which are dominated by women. Unskilled women workers have very little place in the technologically advancing economy.

Without trade unions or organizations of any kind, the 94 percent of the women in the labour force who are in the unorganized sector of the economy face serious exploitation. They have not been paid wages equal to men's and have often been held in bondage as indentured servants. They also suffer sexual harassment at the hands of their (male) employers. Even the women who work in the organized sectors of the economy have encountered hardships. In spite of the existence of the Equal Remuneration Act, women have generally been paid less than men except in the service sector. In many factories and firms, labour laws have not been followed consistently, nor have the male-dominated trade unions made elimination of discriminatory practices against women workers a priority.

The Committee on the Status of Women concluded in its 1974 report that many of the inequities that women faced in the traditional economy were aggravated by the process of development. In spite of their legal equality and regardless of whether they were far above or far below the poverty line, their status in every sphere of life remained unequal.

In the late 1970s, following the release of the report, many more women's organizations became involved in bringing women into development. Taking a grassroots approach to the problem, they have focused on the organization and integration of poor rural women—particularly from the scheduled tribes and castes—into development programs. One organization, the Self-employed Women's Association, a trade union and cooperative for poor working women in the city of Ahmedabad, has provided credit for poor women.

Working Women's Forum, with members in many southern states, and Annapurna Mahila Mandal, a Bombay-based organization, both work on behalf of self-employed women and those in the unorganized sector, taking joint economic and social action to win loans, impart entrepreneurial skills, and achieve empowerment for their members.

The government now consults more actively with women's groups and includes them more in advisory activities. Beginning with the framing of the Fifth Five-Year Plan in 1973-74, a central concern of the government's development effort has been an effective attack on the negative side effects of growth: poverty, unemployment, and inequality. Nonetheless, not until the late 1970s did the efforts of women's organizations to shape development programs to meet women's needs bear fruit.

The government adopted a grassroots approach, urging the use of *mahila mandals* and other voluntary women's organizations as intermediaries for government funded programs providing wages and self-employment for women in rural areas. It recommended the provision of appropriate technology for upgrading women's existing skills, as well as wage law reforms. One radical suggestion was to confer joint titles on both husband and wife for a development activities involving the transfer of assets and the distribution of land and house sites.

Women were also given priority as beneficiaries of government aid programs in rural areas. The Integrated Rural Development Programme accorded preference to women heads of household. Under another program, Training of Rural Youth for Self-employment Management, over 38,000 women, constituting almost 37 percent of the total number of beneficiaries, were trained in 1986 and 1987.

In 1982 and 1983 a Development of Women and Children in Rural Areas project was started as a pilot project in 50 blocks around the country. Women below the poverty line, its special targets, were organized into groups of 20 to 30. Each group was provided training in a chosen economic activity, such as weaving, fish vending, broom and rope making, brick making, and pickle making. Between 1983 and 1985 over 2,772 of these groups were formed and trained, benefiting over 36,000 women. The Seventh Five-Year Plan had much the same focus as the sixth. It emphasized facilitating women's access to resources like loans, credit, and land.

One program set up women's corporations to employ poor women and made women-headed households a priority in the distribution of surplus governmental lands. The plan also focused on upgrading women's skills and at the same time de-emphasized technologies that displaced women in the labour force. It included an important symbolic step forward with the recognition of the worth of women's work within the home: it acknowledged the long hours spent by masses of women in collecting fuel, fodder, and water, as well as their time labouring on the family farm or in family businesses. Supportive services in these essential areas and for maternal and child care were to be offered as a package. Attempts to compute women's hitherto largely invisible labour, however, did not come about until the discussions for the Eighth Five-Year Plan began with women's groups in 1990 and 1991.

In the second half of the 1980s the government began to use other policy mechanisms to promote women's integration into development. Since the middle of the 1960s education had been conceived of as an instrument of social transformation. Not until the debate on the New Education Policy in 1985, however, was the question of education for equality, specifically women's equality, addressed at the national level. Almost all the women's organizations and the women's studies activists worked together to create a new policy document, "Education for Women's Equality." In compliance with this policy there were efforts to implement reorientation programs for teachers and administrators to eliminate sex bias and efforts to redesign courses and curricula.

Since 1985 nearly 25 universities and 12 departments or colleges have started centers or cells in women's studies. The thrust of the program was decelerated for political reasons, with the new government in 1990 appointing a "review committee." Women's organizations and groups have thus been able to get the state to acknowledge the importance of bringing women into development, and a small number of women have been affected by the public programs.

Advocates of inclusion have been less successful in changing the reality that development bypasses women. Funds earmarked for women's development programs have often not reached the target groups because of governmental and bureaucratic corruption. At the same time, the vicissitudes of the industrial economy have often resulted in a poor domestic market and little export potential for products manufactured by women. The majority of women have consequently experienced little benefit from development programs.

Role of the Movements in Violence against Women

The primary focus of women's efforts to end violence against women have been two other throwbacks to the past, rape and dowry deaths. Mass rapes during periods of political instability, like rapes of women as the *devidasis,* or slaves, of the gods used to be common occurrences. Today women face large-scale "eve-teasing" and an increasing incidence of rapes of all kinds—individual, custodial, and gang rapes, According to the minister of state for home affairs, 8,706 rapes were reported in 1988; the number was tip to 9,517 in 1990-21 Sadly the problem of rape is even larger than these figures indicate. Given the symbolic importance attached to women's physical purity among both Muslims and Hindus, rape is incredibly devastating to women and their families. Because of the stigma and social ostracism that rape victims undergo, most rapes go unreported. When cases are reported and heard by the courts, all too often the victim is blamed and the perpetrator(s) go free.

The rape of women from the lower classes, the scheduled castes, and tribes is especially common. Because of the increased caste conflict that has come with the end to the formal suppression of the scheduled classes and castes, gang rapes of these women have also been on the increase. The greatest threat of rape for women today, however, is from those who are supposed to protect them that is, the police and the guardians of girls and women. Police and custodial rapes are among the most common forms of rape in India today.

Civil rights groups began to protest the incidence of custodial rape in 1977, but women's organizations did not initiate the anti-rape movement until 1980 with the public outcry following a custodial rape. Mathura, a 15-year-old girl and member of a scheduled caste, was raped by two policemen at a police station. The policemen were acquitted by the Sessions Court on the grounds that "there was no rape because there was no proof that Mathura had resisted." Although on appeal the decision was reversed by the Bombay High Court, the Supreme Court again acquitted the policemen, holding that Mathura's story of stiff resistance was false and that the intercourse was a "peaceful affair."

In addition, on Women's Day in 1980 thousands of women—groups of women students from major universities, the women's wings of left political parties, housewives, professional women, and women's organizations of varving political traditions—came together in the cities of Ahmedabad, Nagpur, Pune, Bombay, and Delhi to protest the court's decision and demand a reopening of the case. In Bombay and Nagpur a series of rallies, seminars, marches, sit-ins, and street plays by women's the ater groups were also held, and a woman's organization that specifically focused on ending tape, the Forum Against Rape, was founded.

The Supreme Court took heed and agreed to review its decision, but ultimately stuck to its verdict. Pressure from this campaign meanwhile affected the recommendations of the Law Commission of India, so harsher legal penalties for rape were recommended in the Criminal Law Amendment Bill of 1980, which was passed by the Parliament in 1983. The punishment for custodial rape is now ten years in prison. More important, the onus of proof in rape cases is now on the accused, not the victim.

Marriage without dowry was part of the Gandhian and left ethos during the nationalist movement and continues to be part of the Congress (I) philosophy even today. Though illegal since the passing of the Dowry Prohibition Act in 1961, the practice of dowry is still quite common and increasingly costly. Rising costs have led to an increasing number of "dowry deaths" in the past 15 years, as well as predowry suicides singly and collectively by young women who are financially unable to marry. Dowry deaths, or more accurately dowry murders, have also mounted because of greed and the desire for status symbols like televisions and VCRs, which grooms and their families demand before marriage. In 1988, according to the minister of state for home affairs, there were 2,209 dowry deaths reported; in 1989, 4,324; and in 1990, 4,952.

Women's large-scale organizing against dowry began around 1977, when the Mahila Dakshata Samiti organized to ensure prosecution of the Sudha murder case in Delhi: a well-placed government doctor dissatisfied with his wife's dowry murdered her for another woman and threw his wife's body in the Ganges River in Kanpur. The death remained a mystery for a long time, but the husband was ultimately nabbed and punished. Since then, nearly all women's organizations, both separately and in coalitions in major cities, have been organizing protests against the in-laws, the lawyers, and the police officials involved in arranging, committing, and not investigating dowry deaths. Women's organizations have also engaged in consciousness-raising about the practice,

The efforts of these women's groups and women MPs like Pramila Dandavate and Geeta Mukherjee have brought about the amendment of the Dowry Prohibition Act of 1961 in 1984 and again in 1986. In these amendments the burden of proof was shifted to the accused, and the language prohibiting dowry giving was broadened to include requests for gifts, not just before marriage but also after it. The effects of these amendments on the incidence of dowry and dowry deaths are not yet clear.

From early on, because of the influence of Western education, the social reform movement, and the nationalist reformism of leaders like Gandhi and Nehru, the male elite and the few educated women adopted the cause of women's equality. Set in opposition to this progressive movement since its inception, however, have been the forces of Islamic and Hindu fundamentalism, which have tried to keep traditional patriarchal mores and practices alive.

This conflict between the forces of progress and fundamentalism simmered beneath the surface of the Indian cultural political life during the nineteenth century and the beginning of the twentieth century; mainly because of the strength of the nationalist Congress movement and the central government, it did not erupt into a visible conflict of interest at any level until recently. Since the nineteenth century legal reforms of some of the traditional practices most oppressive to women have come easily. Sati was banned in the nineteenth century. The Sharda Act, outlawing child marriage, was passed in 1929. The Hindu Code Bills were passed in 1954 and 1956 despite opposition. Since roughly 1975, however, the weakness and instability of the national government and the formerly hegemonic Congress party have allowed the resurgence of both Islamic and Hindu fundamentalism and the surfacing of this conflict.

Symptomatic of dangers that resurgent fundamentalism poses to women's rights is the Shah Bano case of 1985 and the attendant furor. A 60-year-old Muslim woman, Shah Bano, was granted alimony by the Supreme Court over the protests of her advocate husband, who had divorced her. The husband, who had already married a much younger woman, appealed to Muslim religious leaders on the grounds that the courts were interfering with Muslim personal law as enunciated in the sharia. Muslim religious leaders raised a hue and cry and threatened the government. In an attempt to appease the Islamic fundamentalist forces and ensure political stability, the Congress (I) government introduced the Muslim Women's Act in 1986, confirming the primacy of Muslim personal law for Muslim women.

Women's organizations and activists protested this legislative measure. Educated Muslims demonstrated against it. Over 100 distinguished Indian Muslims from all walks of life, both men and women, petitioned against it together. Arif Muhammad Khan, a Muslim member of the Central Council of Ministers, resigned.

For the sake of political expediency the government passed the act, which pushed Muslim women back by two centuries. For women the danger and the implications of the act were clear, giving as it did a "new lease of life to religious fundamentalists and obscurantists who now perpetrate injustice on women in the name of religion with impunity." Promila Dandavate, president of the Mahila Dakshata Samiti and a former member of Parliament, further warned Prime Minister Rajiv Gandhi when she and a group of Muslim divorcees called on him to plead for the dropping of the bill that "if the government succumbs to the pressure of the Muslim fundamentalists now, the day is not far when a section of the Hindu fundamentalists will come forward to demand the right to burn widows on the pyre of their husbands in the name of the religious freedom."

Within a year Dandavate's prediction was proven true, for Hindu fundamentalists began to press for their right to practice sati. In September 1987 at Deorala, a young widow, Roop Kanwar, was burned to death on her husband's funeral pyre in the presence of thousands of people. Although there had been other instances of sati prior to this and a number of sati temples still stood in different parts of the country, this incident, coming as it did right at the end of the U.N. Decade for Women and the Shah Bano case, caused a stir.

The response was strong on both sides, Thousands of men and women in Jaipur marched with bare swords in support of sati, treating it as a matter of cultural and family right. Women's organizations and intellectuals condemned it outright as inhuman and culturally oppressive. Many investigative studies were conducted, which led to a nationwide debate on the practice of sati and the sanctity of traditions of cultural groups that were oppressive to other members of society Mass meetings and marches were held all over the country.

The major women's organizations, including the National Federation of Indian Women, the All India Women's Conference, the All India Democratic Women's Association, the Young Women's Christian Association, and the joint Women's Programme, participated in this movement and together formed the Joint Action Committee Against Sati.

Responding to this pressure from Indian women, the government enacted the Commission of Sati Prevention Act in 1987 not only to provide more effective prevention of sati but to stop its glorification. The act defined sati comprehensively, and the death penalty was prescribed for persons inducing or encouraging it, participating in sati processions, or preventing the widow from saving herself Persons convicted but not sentenced to death under the act would be disqualified from contesting elections under the Representation of People Act of 1951 from the date of such conviction and would continue to be disqualified for a further period of five years after release.

Act or no act, many attitudes did not change. The Shankrachaya of Puri came out in defence of sati, saying that a woman who commits sati "earns salvation for the families of her father and her husband." Vijaya Raje Scindia, the queen dowager of Gwalior State, a senior leader of the Bharatiya Janata Party and a sitting member of the Lok Sabha, strongly defended sati at a function of the BJP Mahila Morcha. The Dharma Raksha Samiti (Save Religion Organization) asserted that sati was part of their traditional Rajput caste culture and identity. Others argued the economic benefits of sati, which frees the in-laws from the burden of supporting the widow and can in fact add to their wealth.

Thus, in the name of supporting traditional law and custom, Muslim and Hindu fundamentalists have tried to reinforce the loosening shackles of medieval paternalistic morality and preserve male supremacy. Although fundamentalists have so far been only somewhat successful, their power is increasing. This resurgence, coupled with the desire of the central government to maintain political stability at all costs, means that the influence of progressive and secular women is likely to be less powerful on this issue than on others.

The Indian women's movement is now in transition. Feminism has not yet become the voice of anger that it has become in other parts of the world. Indian women's reaction to the patriarchal forces in their society is complex. While acknowledging the existence of these forces, most do not view men as their oppressors. They have not yet asserted their right to complete in dependence from the traditional Indian understanding of women's role. Although the legal changes of the 1980s have been victories for the women's movement, the outcome of the battle for equality has not been decided. Some trends noticeable today are clear setbacks for the women's movement.

Huge processions of Muslim and Hindu women marched in favour of the retrograde Muslim Women's Act of 1986 and in favour of sati. Some *BJP* women leaders have supported sati.

The progress of the women's movement toward socioeconomic justice and the end to women's subordinate status are seriously threatened by the fundamentalist and communal backlash. To succeed, the women's movement will have to go beyond fighting for women's issues alone and fight against broader issues like communalism. It will have to fight for distributive justice and the minimum needs of the wider masses of women and men alike.

The success of the Indian women's movement will depend a great deal on the strategy that it adopts. To attain long-lasting structural change, feminist activists need to develop both political visibility, including media exposure, and political clout—the capacity to deliver or withhold a significant block of votes. Dependence on political parties, ideologies of female subordination, the reluctance of male party leaders to include women, and corruption currently limit this approach.

Women will also have to give up their reluctance to be involved in party politics as it is practised and turn the women's wings of the parties into more active participants in party power structures, As the political clout and visibility of the women's movement increase so, too, will its stature and its capacity to initiate long-lasting changes.

Another factor that will help determine the future of the Indian women's movement is the balance of other political forces. If the strength of forces hostile to women, such as Islamic or Hindu ftindamentalism, continues to grow, the women's movement will probably be in jeopardy, because these forces divert attention from basic development issues and other issues important to women. On, the other hand, if the political balance of power remains the same and women can continue to tie the interests of the Congress (I) and left parties to theirs, they will almost certainly reap benefits. The form that this alliance should take is not yet apparent, but that there must be an alliance is clear: the Indian women's movement cannot and will not succeed unless it is backed by an already established political player.

So far, nonelite women have with virtually no exception stayed out of formal party politics, but there are some signs that this non-involvement may be coming to an end. In November 1984, disturbed by the decreasing number of women in Parliament and the legislative assemblies, about 150 women's organizations met under the auspices of the Akhil Gujarat Samajik Sanstha Madhyasthta Mandal and drew up a manifesto for the 1984 parliamentary elections. The manifesto, which detailed women's political, economic, and social rights and included a list of demands, was sent to all the parties and candidates participating in the election, Meanwhile, these urban women's organizations also made efforts to increase women's political awareness of their rights and their ability to pressure the government by voting for candidates who supported the manifesto.

There is also some evidence that coalition building among different women's organizations is increasing. Coalitions emerged in the 1970s to celebrate International Women's Year and the U.N. Decade for Women and formed around the Mathura rape case in 1979 and the Roop Kanwar sati case in 1987. These coalitions are trying to keep women's issues and their solutions above petty party politics.

What is needed is women's widespread involvement in decision making, both within the family and outside it at all levels of government The key to the quest for power and equality is the empowerment of the masses—of both women and men. The women's movement cannot cut a furrow on its own but must be part of wider efforts. The basic issues of sustainable development, the nonexploitation of nature and human kind, and the prevention of Mother Earth's being blown up arc fundamentally linked to women's equal rights, not to mention their very survival. Above all, if the Indian women's movement is to become a viable, recognized, and important political actor, it must not isolate itself either from the diversity of India or from the myriad other social and political movements within the country It must find a way not only to respect the diversity of India but also to establish itself as an important part of that diversity.

The existence of grievance, or, put differently, a sense of injustice, while not alone enough to spark a movement, is a critical prerequisite to movement emergence. The belief that something is wrong, and that individuals acting alone or collectively must do something, must at minimum go on record in protest, prompt movements to begin. The government crisis of the early 1970s that provoked the anti government movements in Gujarat and Bihar prompted a gendered response in parts of India afflicted by a declining standard of living.

The Anti-Price-Rise Movement originated in Bombay to protest economic problems with particular resonance for women: scarcities and sharply rising prices of consumer goods, including food and clothing. The Anti-Price-Rise movement drew attention to the possibilities for organization and coalition-building among women, and mobilized many women for the first time around issues presented as gender specific.

Movement activity was directed against government, wholesale traders, and black marketeers, all of whom were held responsible for contributing to the economic decline. The problem was felt especially keenly in Maharashtra, because of several years of drought in that state, but movement protest soon spread to urban areas outside the state, including New Delhi.

Demanding price-cuts, unadulterated food-grains and increased rations at government stores, women took to the streets in the tens of thousands, gheraoed numerous public officials and important businessmen, and utilized agitational tactics of particular symbolic importance to women: one march consisted of a thousand women carrying small stoves to represent their lack of food; another featured women loudly banging spoons on *thalis* (the steel plates on which meals are served); and a third had as many as 20,000 women marching through the streets of Bombay shaking their wooden rolling pins, which became the symbol of the movement.

The movement was made possible by the existence of leadership and women's organizations already in place; these organizations were not the autonomous ones that were to spring up in the late 1970s and early 1980s, but rather were associated with political parties. Bombay not only had women's organizations attached to each of the two national communist parties, it also had a strong organization of socialist women, the Samaj-wadi Mahila Sabha (Socialist Women's Group). Together, these three groups led the series of demonstrations that constituted the movement.

The coalition was initiated by the CPI-associated women's group, the National Federation of Indian Women. At the September 1972 meeting of the Bombay unit of NFIW, its president, Aruna Asaf Ali, called for a united fight against the rising prices of daily necessities. A meeting held soon afterward resulted in the formation of the joint Action Committee of Women for the Resistance of Price Rise. For most of the next three years ' the committee was led by a Socialist, Mrinal Gore, and included other women from the Samajwadi Mahila Sabha, most prominently Pramila Dandavate and Mangala Parikh; as well as CPI women from Shramik Mahila Sang (Toiling

Women's Group, the local branch of the NFIW), including Manju Gandhi, Sushila Gokhale and Prerna Purao; and CPM women of Maharashtra's Shramik Mahila Sabha (Toiling Women's Organization), most prominently Ahilya Rangnekar.

The Anti-Price-Rise movement focused on an issue that in many times and places (including the French and Russian revolutions) has politicized women: the demand for adequate, affordable food on the family table. It was an issue of deep concern around which thousands could be readily mobilized. The movement was a response, expressed in feminine terms, to the structural crises facing the nation. Whether the movement could have broadened its concerns and developed into a sustained movement attentive to other issues important to women is unclear, because Indira Gandhi's 1975 declaration of emergency was followed by the imprisonment of most of the movement's leaders. In fact, the coalition that led the movement had begun to fall apart just prior to this.

While the Socialist and CPM women were supportive of the concurrent antiCongress movements taking place in Gujarat and Bihar, the CPI women, in keeping with CPI policy, were not. The leaders of the Shramik Mahila Sangh withdrew from the movement as Gandhi's hold on power became increasingly tenuous and the CIII called for support for the Congress government This action, which betrayed a loyalty to heeding the party line, even at the expense of continuing agitational activity that privileged the needs of women, was one that contributed to the distrust of party-related women's organizations by those beginning to turn to autonomous groups.

Nonetheless, despite its limitations, the Anti-Price-Rise movement was politicizing; it raised the consciousness of many women, and many women leaders, about women's issues and the possibilities for further organizing. At the end of the emergency, many of these leaders re-emerged at the head of new movement organizations, or became active in parliamentary politics on behalf of women.

Not all the events that helped to promote new consciousness about women's problems and thus, eventually, movement activity were products of internal change or activity: many activities to enhance women's status in India have been prompted, ideologically and materially, by international feminism. One critical event in the emergence of the movement was the direct result of such international influence.

In 1967 the United Nations General Assembly adopted the Declaration on the Elimination of Discrimination Against Women. It followed up the Declaration with repeated requests to member states to submit reports on the status of women in their countries. In response, the Government of India constituted the Committee on the Status of Women (CSWI) in September 1971. The release in May 1975, just prior to the emergency, of the Committee's report, Towards Equality, created an effect similar to that experienced in the United States in 1961 with the creation of the President's Commission on the Status of Women. Just as in the U.S., the President's Commission had created a "climate of expectations"' that something must be done to help women achieve full equality in American society; so, in India, Towards Equality sparked immediate demands for government action. The data it compiled on women's inferior position in religious and family life, in health care and in law, and with regard to economic, educational and political opportunity served as a jolt to the consciousness of many educated and politicized Indians, both women and men, and helped spur their activism in a new direction.

Much of the document is a call for vigorous governmental action to improve the status of women. Significantly, the authors of the report located their advocacy of equality for women not only within the moral scheme of "social justice" but squarely within the developmental needs of the nation as a whole. Women's equality, they argued, is "a basic precondition for [the] social, economic and political development of the nation" and thus should be a governmental priority.

In addition, they argued that their suggestions for the uplift of women are consistent with the goals of the nation as articulated in the constitution. The Indian constitution, they reminded readers, is more than a prescription of rights; it is a social document embodying the objectives of a social revolution to be attained "by making deliberate departures... from the inherited political and social systems". The report praises the constitutional protections for women that were instituted at independence. Article 14 guarantees equality before the law for all citizens, while Article 15 prohibits discrimination on the grounds of sex. Additionally, the Directive Principles section of the constitution, which articulates state goals and acts as a guideline to policy, guarantees to both women cind men a right to an adequate livelihood, to equal pay for equal work, and protection of the health of all workers, including, for women, maternity leave.

Since the government alone cannot alter cultural patterns and social structures that uphold women's inferior position in the family and in the economy, the CSWI, in addition to detailing actions that government should take, called specifically for movement activity. The report urges 11 community organisations, particularly women's organisations" to "mobilise public opinion and strengthen social efforts against oppressive institutions like polygamy [and] dowry" and to "mount a campaign for the dissemination of information about the legal rights of women to increase their awareness". The uplift of women must be the joint task of an educated and committed government, and a social movement that would enlighten and inspire.

Thus, while some within the women's movement concentrate their political efforts on moving government to pass and implement improved legislation and others focus their attention on empowering women at the grass roots, the two are not contradictory. In Towards Equality, the first document of the contemporary movement, there is certainly faith in parliamentary procedures; but there is also a recognition that the transformation of cultural norms and the empowerment of women at the grass roots is critical to the mobilization of interests necessary to move government, and to be ready to receive governmental assistance when it is offered.

Towards Equality constituted an important ideological first step in mobilizing educated activists. Today, movement activists frequently cite the report as a critical factor in raising their consciousness and motivating them to act.' The bulk of the 480 page report is devoted to documenting women's inferior position in society and analysing its causes; in its scale and comprehensiveness, it is a moving, often depressing indictment of a socioeconomic and political system that pervasively discriminates against women. However, as the report was published just prior to the emergency, its recommendations languished. Along with other concerns about human rights, this was one of the frustrations that burst forth at the emergency's close.

The status of women in India

Drawing on Towards Equality and other studies, governmental and private, this section briefly expores the status of women in India during the 1970s and 1980s, This survey will provide a sense of what grievances have sparked, and continue to inspire, movement activity. The substantive portion of the report opens with a brutal fact: from 1901 on, each census has recorded a decline in the ratio of females to males in the population. In 1901, for every 1000 males in India there were 972 females; by 1971, there were only 930 females for every 1000 males. In contrast, most other countries, both in the "developed" and "less developed" worlds, have a higher percentage of women than men in their population."

The Committee also reported that while life expectancy for all Indians had increased dramatically over the previous fifty years, the gap in the number of years of life expectancy at birth had widened between women and men in the years since 1921, from a difference favouring men of 0.3 years to a difference of 1.5 years. These patterns together suggest that the "neglect of women in India is a persistent phenomenon".

The CSWI deplored the lack of reliable information on the causes of these disparities, but suggested among its hypotheses the marked preference for sons and consequent neglect of female infants; the general neglect of women at all ages; and the adverse impact of frequent and excessive child-bearing on the health of women.

In 1985, a document produced by the Indian government to mark the close of the international decade of women made a more succinct analysis: "The problem of overwork for underfed women," it said, "seems to be responsible for female mortality."

Towards Equality's demographic survey also reported that despite the Child Marriage Restraint Act which designated fifteen years as the minimum legal age for marriage, the marriage of young girls was still common." The 1961 census revealed that in more than one-third of the districts in India, the average female age at marriage was below fifteen. In 1971, in rural India, 13.6% of the girls in the age group 1014 were married and 0.1% widowed; in urban India 3.9% of the girls in this age group were married.

The CSWI expressed regret that there were no data about marital status for girls aged nine and below, since, in the Committee's travels, members had come across a number of married girls in that age group.

As recently as 1986, the Health Minister of Uttar Pradesh found that the state contained villages in which all girls over the age of 8 were married; the girls' parents explained that the dowry expected at the marriage of an eight year old was only five hundred rupees, as compared to the fifteen to twenty thousand rupees expected after puberty.

The CSWI found that family planning is practiced by only fifteen perccritot couples in the reproductive age group, and that the level of education and fertility are inversely related; this finding provided one argument for the need to educate women.

That need was made further apparent in the 1971 census, which recorded that while the urban female literacy rate is 42.3%, in rural India the female literacy rate was only 13.2%; the nationwide total of 18.7% female literacy compared to the nationwide total of 39.5% literacy for males. Even these figures are wildly exaggerated: among those females counted in the census as literate, 40.3%, had less than a primary school education. Only 7.8% had completed a secondary education and 1.4% had graduated from a higher educational institution. Thus, the Committee was quick to point out, the women in India who hold high positions in government and intellectual life constitute a small, elite group and do not reflect the position of the enormous majority. By the 1981 census, the percentage of females who were literate had increased to a nationwide total of 24.8% (48% urban literacy and 18% rural). However, the rate at which women's literacy increased slowed between 1971 and 1981, as compared to the rate during the previous two decades.

The Committee understood that social structures are critical determinants of women's troubled status. Acknowledging that many structures of inequality such as caste, community, class, and geographic setting create different problems for women of different spheres, the Committee began by considering the impact of religion.

Religion in India is pertinent not only to the cultural valuation of women, but to their legal position. In India, religion is also law. In most matters pertaining to family life-marriage, divorce, inheritance, guardianship of children--religious law is recognized by the state. Modern India continues the practice adopted by the British of letting Hindu law govern the Hindu community and Muslim law the Muslim community; the state also recognizes Christian, Parsi and Jewish law. The CSWI lamented this tradition. The British policy of general noninterference in personal law had the effect, the CSWI argued, not only of encouraging the dangerous feeling of separation that exists between India's two largest communities, the Hindus and the Muslims, but also of preventing the evolution of personal law. Even as society ' v underwent enormous socioeconomic changes during the two hundred years of British rule in India, personal law stagnated. Despite the constitutional guarantee in Article 114 of the equality of the sexes before the law. Toward Equally finds that some aspects of every religious community's law--laws that are still recognized by the courts today--discriminate against women.

The CSWI's argument for a uniform civil code that would eliminate all such gender discrimination in personal law and would end, too, the discriminatory practice of citizens of the same country being governed by entirely different sets of laws has proved to be one of its most important and certainly most controversial recommendations. The CSWI placed its opinion squarely within the logic of "secularism, science and modernisation," stating that the continuance of various personal laws that accept discrimination between men and women not only violates the Fundamental Rights section of the constitution but is also "against the spirit of national integration and secularism."

The movement in the 1980s has shown ambivalence about the feasibility of a uniform civil code in light of increased communal tensions in India. To many Indian citizens a call for a uniform civil code appears to be a call for the extension of Hindu law to all, and thus even those feminists who hope for a uniform civil code have tended to back down from their demands, preferring to wait rather than give the appearance of abetting Hindu chauvinism or fanning the flames of communal discord.

Of course, no one in the women's movement today would suggest that the Hindu code, and many Hindu social customs, are models of gender equality. Towards Equality points out the pervasive derogatory images of women in Hinduism. A woman "is called fickle-minded, sensual, seducer of men; given to falsehood, trickery, folly, greed, impurity and thoughtless action; root of all evil; inconsistent; and cruel." Her prescribed destiny is to be a faithful, subservient, and uncomplaining wife and mother: "In childhood a woman must be subject to her father, in youth to her husband, and when her lord is dead to her sons. A woman must never be independent". Hindu law forbids polygamy, but in part because economically dependent and uneducated women do not have the means to move the courts on their own behalf, "bigamous marriages are still prevalent among Hindus". Because marriage is woman's destiny, widowhood is considered deeply inauspicious, and widows, unlike widowers, by and large are forced to live a restricted life.

Islam, on the other hand, places women on an equal footing with men in the eyes of the Almighty, and the Quran is filled with injunctions aimed at bettering the lot of women. However, the codification of Muslim law (into the Shariat) has not been so kind to women. Over the centuries, the Qur'an has been interpreted in India so as to legitimize prevailing social norms that have placed women in an inferior legal, social, and religious position. For example, in law, whereas the testimony of a single male witness is respected, that of a single woman is not; her testimony must be corroborated by a second woman. Socially and economically, a Muslim woman is heavily dependent on men in part because of the insistence that her modesty and chastity be protected; her seclusion from men precludes her full participation in most educational and business fields.

With respect to the family, Muslim law allows women some important rights. Marriage is not religiously obligatory. It is a contract; thus divorce is allowed and there is no ban on a widow's remarriage. In social practice, however, both divorce and widows' remarriage is frowned upon. Furthermore, women's status within the family is gravely diminished by the legality and practice of polygamy, and by the fact that a husband can obtain a divorce simply by declaring it so. Of course, the husband's "absolute and unlimited right to repudiate the marriage at his will" (known as talaq) is uniquely his; the wife has no corresponding right.

In India, certain social customs that are not strictly speaking religious, and which may indeed cut across religions, are also extremely harmful to women. Towards Equality was particularly attentive to the impact of patriotically: throughout India, a girl upon marriage frequently goes to live in the home of her in-laws. At the very least, her family loyalties are expected to change upon marriage. Emotionally, as well as legally and economically, a girl is transferred upon marriage to another family. This one fact has a hugely negative impact on the wellbeing of girls and women. Within the natal family, boys are more valued than girls. A son will remain within the family; a son will care for parents in old age. Parents' investment of emotional and financial resources in their son is, therefore, a investment in their own future. Simply put, a son is an asset. A daughter is a liability. Thus, parents do not make an equal investment in their daughters; the poor literacy rate for women as well as the adverse sex ratio described above may well be a result of this distinction. When resources are scarce they are more likely to go to a permanent son rather than to a transient daughter.

The transfer of the daughter from one family to another is usually accompanied by an exchange of cash and/or goods; a marriage is most of ten arranged by the parents and is in part a commercial transaction. Westerners are sometimes surprised to hear that arranged marriages still predominate among all classes in India. Just as interesting is that neither towards Equality nor contemporary feminists cite arranged marriage per se as one cause of violence against women within the family or as a factor in sustaining women's inferior status. Indeed, according to Towards Equality the existence of caste in Hindu society, which traditionally limits one's choice of marriage partners to certain groups, as well as prescriptions within the Muslim community which may restrict marriage choice to certain socioeconomic categories or to particular categories of family relations "make arranged marriage the most desirable form of marriage.... Marriage cannot be left to the young if these restrictions and preferences are to work. The institution of arranged marriage thus fits well with the social structure".

Contemporary feminists say that even among educated, urban youths, there is a preference for parents to pick a future spouse from one's own religion, region, community, and caste. Girls and boys generally grow up separated from each other; friendships between boys and girls are typically frowned upon. Thus, young people have little opportunity to meet and select their own marriage partners. These social patterns are not seen as a problem by most contemporary feminists; that marriage typically occurs in the absence of love or even friendship is not a movement issue. Violence within marriage, including that which stems from exorbitant demands for dowry payments, is a movement issue. The commercial aspect of arranged marriage is condemned, but arranged marriage is not.

The transfer of payments upon marriage can work in one of two ways: when the payment is to the family of the bride, it is called brideprice; the money that is paid by the family of the bride is called dowry. The Dowry Prohibition Act of 1961 prohibits both types of transactions. In 1974 the CSWI declared that the Act had had no effect whatsoever; this remains true today, despite new legislation to strengthen it.

In the system of brideprice, one family pays the other for their right to have authority over the bride; the husband's family in effect buys him a wife. The status relationship is clear; only women are bought and sold. But at least there is an acknowledgement that the woman is worth something and that her parents should be compensated for losing her. The woman thus has some status. Furthermore, as she has economic value, parents do not so desperately dread the birth of a daughter since upon marriage she will bring them some material return. Under the system of brideprice, a husband is less likely to treat his wife too harshly since, if she leaves, it will cost him to replace her. The practice of brideprice has been giving way, however, to the practice of dowry. The shift is probably not in women's best interest. Traditionally the prerogative of higher castes, the taking of dowry is being emulated by those of lower castes and status as they aspire to higher status. Indeed, as a new middle class has developed in India the practice has spread. "Black money and unaccounted earnings have given impetus to dowry... A new class of nouveaux riches has emerged that buys a daughter's future with dowry, to raise its own social status by entering into marriage alliances with families of high status."

Some contemporary feminists are rethinking dowry and contend that it should be seen as a daughter's rightful inheritance from her father in an inheritance system in which women do not receive land. Others maintain, though, as did the CSWL that the practice of dowry sends horrific messages about it the worth of women. A woman is seen as parasitic, as a liability, thus a new family must be paid off to take her. In practice, the reality can be just as awful as the image. In paying dowry, the parents of the girl are trying to buy her a good life with another family; but the bride then becomes a hostage to her in-laws' desire for continued material wealth. Even after the marriage, the bride's family is "under compulsion and heavy pressure" to continue giving gifts to the husband's family. "In the first few years of marriage, the girl's treatment in her husband's house is linked to these gifts".

In present-day India, "dowry deaths"--in which young brides are murdered by their husbands and/or in-laws occur in the thousands each year. The murder is often preceded by demands for increased dowry payments; a dowry death may also result from the husband's desire to marry again and thus obtain a new dowry. Far from being an anachronistic holdover from a bygone age, dowry has contemporary meaning within an increasingly capitalist and money conscious society. The rise in education in India has led not to a decrease in dowry demands, but rather, to an increase. An educated man is worth more in the dowry market than an uneducated one.

There are more or less welldefined grades of dowry for men in different professions. For example men in the I.A.S. [Indian Administrative Service] and IFS. [Indian Foreign Service]... can easily expect to get in cash and kind at least a lakh [one hundred thousand] of rupees. Business executives rank next. Engineers and doctors stand lower than the business executives.

This class seems to expect that marriage would bring them not only a partner but also all the things needed to set up a modern household, such as a car, refrigerator, radiogram. These groups naturally influence those below. Thus a peon or a clerk would demand such things as a bicycle, a transistor, and a wrist watch. A scooter is a common... gift to the son-in-law in the groups at the middle level. In villages too there are similar demands. The education of women does help to limit dowry, but only if the husband's family has the expectation that the new bride will pursue a career, and thus bring money into the family in that way. They may prefer, however, that she not; a nonworking wife is a sign of her husband's wealth and contributes to his status.

The CSWI strongly criticized the ineffectual Dowry Prohibition Act of 1961 and made a number of suggestions for strengthening it. But the Committee spoke too of the need to arouse social consciousness "particularly amongst women, to enable them to understand that by encouraging dowry they are perpetuating the inequality of the sexes." It called for an improvement in women's self-image. Also critical to ending dowry, the CSWI argued, are increased opportunities for women's employment and a reassessment of the value of household work and homemaking. The Committee recognized that these are riot tasks only for government; the responsibility for change, the report argued, must be shared by the community. 'Towards Equality is thus in part a call for movement activity to mobilize public opinion, change oppressive social institutions and educate women as to their legal rights.

Nor can government alone bring about the changes required to bring women fully into the economic development process, since opposition to increased participation by women in the economic life of the country derives in part from social mores which deem women's "proper" economic role to be strictly separate from men's.

Nonetheless, Towards Equality strongly criticizes government's inattention to the particular and terrible problems that a "modernizing" economy has brought to women. With the shift from traditional forms of agriculture and production in household industry to an increasingly capitalist economy characterized by larger scale and organized economic activities, labour has ceased to be organized by family units and instead has become more competitive and individualized. As jobs became scarcer and more technical, women were handicapped by their lack of education and limited opportunity to acquire new skills; they were left behind in the labour market. The Committee found that women are the greatest victims of unemployment and underemployment, and that the proportion of women below the poverty line exceeds that of men. Governmental measures since independence to remove women's educational handicap, generate employment for women, provide equal remuneration, and end discrimination in hiring have been, according to the CSWI, "extremely inadequate".

The report painstakingly and clearly documents women's growing position of inferiority in the economy. Since the beginning of the twentieth century, the participation of women in the paid labour force declined in absolute numbers, in the percentage of female workers to the total female population, and as a percentage of the total labour force. The decline of women's participation in the industry and service fields means that women have become increasingly dependent on agriculture, which by and large pays lower wages than jobs in the other sectors. As significant to understanding women's economic status is the fact that only a very small percentage of women workers--approximately six percent--are in the organized sector. The other 94 percent work in what is called the unorganized sector, (81.4 percent are in agriculture; 12.6 percent in other occupations.) There, they are largely nonunionized, and are outside the reach of most laws that seek to protect labour from exploitation and unsafe working conditions.

The organized sector of the Indian economy consists of all public sector jobs and all jobs in the private sector that are nonagricultural and that employ ten or more persons. These include jobs in factories, mines and also, in the one exception to the "nonagricultural" category, on plantations, While women's employment by the organized sector has increased dramatically in numbers, moving from 1.37 million in 1962 to 2.14 million in 1973, the overall size of the organized sector has increased correspondingly, so that women in 1973 comprised 11 percent of all organized sector employees, just as they had in 1962. The stability of women in the organized sector is due to their increased employment by the public sector; the percentage of women in the organized sector employed privately declined from 65 percent in 1962 to 53 percent in 1973.

In the organized sector of the economy, a number of laws exist that are designed to protect workers in general and women in particular. Towards Equality argues that the burden imposed on industry by such laws cannot be held as the cause of the decline in the employment of women in private industry, since the laws are for the most part simply ignored. Payments of maternity benefits (guaranteed under the Maternity Benefits Act of 1961), for example, are "negligible."

Although required by law to erect separate sanitary facilities for women and men, and to supply creches in establishments employing fifty or more women, "many employers still do not provide separate toilets or rest rooms. Where they do exist, the arrangements are inadequate, without proper service and maintenance. Creches are very often only a room without proper arrangements". Nor can the requirement for equal pay for women and men workers be blamed for a cut back in women workers, since, it, too, is not honoured. Women's wages are held back by sex segregation in jobs: certain jobs are earmarked for women, and are paid low wages. But even within the same category of job, including those that are completely unskilled, Committee members found stark wage differentials that convinced them that "prejudices, rather than skill or productivity differentials determine wage differences between the sexes".

In any case, government standards are usually irrelevant, since the minimum wage law is usually, unimplemented. India's National Commission on Labour, cited in Towards Equality, put the blame for this not on government but on "the poverty and illiteracy of agricultural labour, the casual nature of their employment and their ignorance of the law," all of which conditions, the CSWI point out, apply particularly to women. Here, surely, is an implicit call for movement organizing. Towards Equality is even more explicit. No substantial improvement in the condition of female agricultural labour is possible, it argues, without "the organisation of labour... to improve the bargaining power of these workers, to prevent exploitation and low wages".

In closing its discussion of women's economic participation, the CSWI made a number of recommendations to the government. Most broadly, it urged the adoption of "a well defined policy to fulfil. The Constitutional directives and Government's long term objective of [the] total involvement of women in national development."It made specific recommendations with regard to laws regulating maternity benefits, provision of creches, working time and the equalization of wages. It recommended more vocational training for women.

But, recognizing the limits of government activity, and in light of its understanding that women were critically hampered by lack of organization, the Committee also called on labour leaders to organize agricultural workers and others in the unorganized sector of the economy, and recommended that existing labour unions form women's wings to empower them within the unions, and to look after their interests as workers.

The constitution of India provides for universal adult suffrage (Article 326) and Indian women have been active participants in every Indian election. Yet Towards Equality charges that women have had only limited impact on the political process. To be sure, women have been highly visible participants, they have served in both houses of Parliament and in the state legislatures, been governors and chief ministers of states, and served at the national level as ambassadors, cabinet members and, of course, in the case of Indira Gandhi, as prime minister.

However, despite the achievements of an elite few, women as a whole have been under represented throughout India in both appointed and elected positions; they have minimal power within the parties; and they participate in elections as candidates and as voters with less frequency than men.

None of these facts is unique to India. For example, the percentage of women in the Lok Sabha compares favourably with that in many western democracies. While in 1984, for example, the U.S. Congress and the British House of Commons each had fewer than five percent female members, female Membership in the Lok Sabha has ranged from a low of 2.8 percent in the first, 1952 election, to a high of 8.5 percent in the 1984 election. Still, Towards Equality criticized political parties for neglecting their duty to politically educate and mobilize women and for their failure to nominate more female candidates.

As important as the level of female participation is the degree to which the interests of women are represented by the political process. According to CSWI findings, women are most concerned with problems that affect their daily lives. These include rising prices, the scarcity of essential commodities, hoarding and blackmarketing, unemployment, and poverty. However studies cited by Towards Equality show that many women believe electoral politics are ineffective in solving precisely these problems; the Committee reported a growing disillusionment among women with the political process.

The presence of women in government had not alleviated this problem. The committee charged those women who had attained high positions in party hierarchies and political institutions with being unrepresentative of women and unresponsive to women's interests. Women's entry into the political process, particularly at the state level, "depends more on their support within the party" than on support within the electorate.

Female politicians acquire their positions "mainly through certain ascriptive channels"; they are most often women of considerable economic means and members of prominent political families. They have neither derived their strength from nor helped to develop a constituency concerned with problems that affect women specifically. As a result of this, and of their small numbers, the CSWI charged, they fail to voice the problems of women in the legislatures and in decision-making bodies within the parties.

Indeed, the authors of Towards Equality contended, the political elite as a whole had neglected the concerns of women, apparently believing them to have been solved by the constitutional and other protections adopted soon after independence. The report itself makes it clear that this is far from the case. Furthermore, "it is clear that despite certain legal and even institutional changes, the final legitimation for a successful reorganization of society lies in a revolution in norms and attitudes in the minds of the people". That change will occur, and the concern of political elites will be drawn to the problems of women, only when there is "an active women's movement". Again, here, the Committee explicitly called for movement activity to raise the consciousness, of women and men, and ultimately to move the political system to be responsive to Women's needs.

Early proponents of the family planning movement in India had presented birth control as a way to improve the health and status of women, and the CSWI agreed that women must be released "from the bondage of... frequent childbirth." However, the Committee disagreed with the notion that greater use of birth control methods will raise women's status; instead, Towards Equality argues, it is the improved status of women that will prompt more use of birth control. Only with a "rise in the age of marriage, education, employment, better living conditions and greater general awareness" will women adopt family planning methods.

Thus education is seen as a critical tool for the improved status of women. Article 45 of the constitution directs the State to "endeavour to provide... free and compulsory education for all children until they complete the age of 14 years. When Towards Equality was written, this goal was still far from being met, particularly for girls. In 1968-69, only 57% of all girls aged 6-11 and 18% of all girls aged 11-14 were enrolled in school (compared to 93% and 45% for boys of these age groups). These aggregate statistics are somewhat misleading, since rural girls are much less likely to have access to educational resources. Secondary education is largely limited to girls from the upper and middle classes, mostly from urban areas. This is even more true of higher education.

The Committee, in urging expanded literacy for women to achieve improvements in their health, greater employment opportunities, and the ability to exercise their legal rights, did not stop there. The CSWI urged too that the content of the curriculum be altered to challenge existing sex roles and cultural biases concerning women. Blasting the schools for reflecting and strengthening "the traditional prejudices of inequality," Towards Equality calls for a revolution in the values taught in schools.

"If education is to promote equality for women, it must make a deliberate, planned and sustained effort so that the new value of equality of the sexes can replace the traditional value system of inequality.

The Committee on the Status of Women in India raised expectations that government must act to improve women's lives, even as the perception grew that government's ability to do so was at best stagnant. The gap between the raised expectations and the capacity to meet them helped prompt the mobilization of concerned individuals to take up movement activity.

Towards Equality was itself to become a major text of the emerging transformation in consciousness among educated women. Its compelling descriptions of the vast and disabling range of problems facing Indian women heightened demands for their amelioration, while its compilation of facts has provided heavy statistical ammunition, particularly for those who have chosen to work in the "rights" segment of the movement. At the same time, Towards Equality marks a recognition that women's status cannot be improved through government action alone. The report consistently calls for changes in consciousness and in social structures beyond the reach of government. In doing so Towards Equality implicitly, and sometimes explicitly, recognizes that movement activity is essential, that the electoral process cannot perform the functions of personal and community empowerment and of ideological transformation as well as movement activity can.

It was the government's failure to protect women from violence that came to the forefront as the first target of the new post-emergency women's movement. Indira Gandhi's emergency seems, inadvertently, to have contributed to developing outrage about "dowry murder, in which a husband and/or his family threaten, beat, or even finally murder a (usually young) wife in the attempt to extort money from her parents in the years soon after marriage. During the emergency, Sanjay Gandhi issued his own five-point program designed to supplement his mother's twenty points. Among his dictums was "Never accept dowries as a condition for marriage." One prominent scholar and activist suggests that the attention thus focused on dowry may in part be responsible for the "completely unexpected and spontaneous explosion of women's anger against dowry murders" that occurred in the late seventies." Also contributing was the fact that, during the emergency, the press was stifled from writing about government abuses of civil liberties, even as the need to address human rights issues was never felt more keenly. As a result, dowry deaths became a topic of press coverage; human rights abuses could be covered if they were not explicitly concerned with government.

Finally, of course, the emergency brought forth a new militancy over human rights issues generally, coupled with a deep skepticism over how much the government and the police could be relied upon to protect rights. With the close of the emergency, a women's group closely associated with the new Janata government, Mahila Dakshata Samiti, began to systematically investigate cases of the "accidental" deaths often by burning in alleged kitchen accidents of young brides. Early in 1978, MDS published a report in which it alleged that many of these deaths, labelled suicide or accident by the police, were in fact murders; the report, in turn, was widely publicized in the national press." Protests began, and press coverage of these protests generated still more protests. In 1979, MDS demanded the strengthening of the 1961 Prohibition of Dowry Act.

In May of 1979, newspapers carried, not the usual short police blotter report of a woman's accidental death or suicide, but rather a full report of the burning of Tarvinder Kaur by her mother-in-law and sister-in-law. As she lay dying, Kaur made a statement to the police alleging that while she was watching television her in-laws doused her with kerosene and set her afire; the police nonetheless recorded the case as suicide. The papers interviewed her father, who said that she had been under constant pressure from her husband's family to get more dowry from her parents so that her husband could expand his business."

As a result of this case, individual women and some who belonged to civil liberties and political groups joined together briefly under the name Stri Sangharsh (women's struggle). Although this group quickly splintered, the meeting seemed to provide the catalyst for what became the first widely publicized demonstration against "dowry murder" on June 1, 1979. The demonstrators, armed with leaflets proclaiming "Women are not for Burning," marched through New Delhi neighbourhoods to the house where Kaur's murder took place, and there demanded the punishment of the murderers, and an end to dowry and to dowry deaths. Other demonstrations followed: outside the homes of other suspected murderers; outside the police stations whose officials consistently failed to act; in other cities and towns throughout India.

2

Higher Education of Women

Christian missionaries were the pioneers in starting colleges both for men and women. The method and syllable of the education curriculum were based on Christian religious practices. Besides the missionaries started building houses attached to the colleges for girls with big subsidy on the students bill from the money received from missionaries abroad in order to encourage the Christian education at all levels in the colonial India.

Of the five colleges four of them started by Christian missionaries and the government initiative came in very late by starting only one college in the later part of the 20th Century. As compared. 1946-47 to the years one can notice a continuous decline in terms of enrollment of students from the Anglo Indian and Christian communities. This might be due to the departure of many of the British officials from Indian to their native land as a consequence of freedom struggle to liberate India from British rule and Indianisation of all services.

As far as Scheduled Caste community is concerned, women students from such community accounted for 0.5% in 1921-22 as a proportion in total enrolment of girls students in the college. They constituted a very negligible proportion due to some socio-economic factors. Willingness on the part of the Adi-Dravida families to send their female children to schools and colleges was affected very much by the social degradation they were subjected to i.e... Untouchability, which kept them from the mainstream of national life. Moreover among depressed classes the education of girls did not seem to be a necessity for a long time.

University education being quite costlier and the scholarship given to them being meagre, these communities were prevented from enjoying the fruits of higher education. In 1946-47 the proportion moved up to 0.9% though a slight move but definitely a significant move. The teaching of mahatma Gandhi against the practice of untouchability in Indian's social life brought about a new thinking among people and the intensive efforts taken by the Congress in implementation of Gandhi's plans gave Adi Dravida community a moral courage to send their children to schools and colleges without any fear. Inspired by the teaching of Mahatma, educated women of the province condemned the practice of untouchability and worked wholeheartedly for the abolition of the evil through their organisation.

They carried vigorous propaganda in press and platforms to redress the handicaps experienced by Harijans. The principle of equality was implemented in the institutions started by the educated women of the province encouraged girls from socially depressed sections to come forward to avail the opportunities of higher learning. For instance 'Avvai' Home started by Dr. (Mrs.) Muthulakshmi Reddi promoted the ideals of unity among the various communities. The government gave full free remissions to students of this community. The Christian converts from the Scheduled Caste and their descendents were made eligible for all the fee concession for which the Scheduled Caste were eligible under the rules of educational institutions. Moreover the madras council passed the anti-Untouchability Bill and Civil Disability Bills during 1938-40 enabled Adi Dravida Community to be treated at par with the other communities.

In the year 1926-27 structural shift took place in favour of Brahmin and Non-Brahmin communities as the proportion of both communities accounted for 14.1% and 23.1%, respectively. Data presented shows that the years 1936-37 and 1941-42 though the years were interrupted by the World War II. Enrolment from the Brahmin Community increased from 18.2 per cent in 1936-37 as a proportion to total admission of girls to 23.5% to 23.8% in 1941-42 and that of Non-Brahmins from 25.21% to 23.5%. In 1946-47 though the percentage proportion of both communities increased to 26.9% and 32.5%, respectively, the increase was more for non-Brahmin communities. The main factors at work for this marked shift were the following:

(i) Social legislation increased the age of marriage of girls (Child marriage Restraint Act of 1930) indirectly enabled the parents to send their female children to schools and colleges especially in Brahmin and non-Brahmin communities.

(ii) During 1940-42 a new custom came into vogue among Brahmins namely that those young married girls after the birth of the first baby the 'Duty Child' took up their studies again and tried bravely and often successfully took their academic degree.

(iii) Moreover, the Bill on widow remarriage and the realisation by the parents the importance of school and collegiate education for their daughters which enhanced their social respectability for fixing marriage for their daughters, were responsible for the higher proportion of student population from Brahmin and non-Brahmin communities towards the close of the colonial period.

(iv) The Devadasi Abolition Act in the madras presidency released many girls from the shackles of temple services and they sought after education to lead a respectable life of their own.

(v) The social outlook of people towards the education of girls undergone a remarkable change due to the efforts of social reformers. For so many people education of girls did not seem to be a necessity for a long time. But slowly their opinion was changed and their outlook became brighter. For instance. Miss T.S. Kanthamma was the First Girl in the Vellala community to pass B.Sc. (Hons.) in 1937.

(vi) Many were kept out of university education because they had not got means to pay for a costly college course even though they were eminently fitted by nature to profit by it. The Government of Madras took some progressive steps towards the end of 1941. By awarding scholarships for intermediate and B.A. classes and fee concessions upto 20% to backward class candidates.

(vii) Members of depressed classes demanded more and more educational facilities for their communities in the legislative council and were able to get the same to a remarkable extent.

As far as Muslim community is concerned. Their percentage was nil in 1921-22. From 1926-22. From 1926-27 onwards percentage share showed an increasing trend. In 1946-47 they constituted 2.4%. Though their percentage proportion might be small even in 1946-47, the trend shown in Table 4.2 exhibits the increasing interest of the community to educate their female children beyond high school level. In the beginning discouraged by purdah system many were prevented from availing the higher educational facilities. Due to the efforts of the social reformers purdah was slowly given up by some enlightened Muslim families and they began to send their daughters for higher education. Again in 1946. The Government College for Muslim Women opened at Raya Pettah. Madras which was the first of its kind in the province enabled women of Muslim. Community to go for higher education. Moreover, a social awakening among the Muslim to their needs in the matter of education of girls was gaining ground towards forties and Miss Zamurth Begam of Government Hobberts Training School of Women. Madras was the first Mohammedan lady to take up the University Music course of Madras University.

Professional colleges

In this section it is proposed to discuss the changes in community composition in the selected years in respect of enrolment in the professional and oriental colleges in the State. The number increased to 175 in 1936-37. The years 1941-42 to 1946-47 experienced a spurt in the number of female students in professional colleges.

Communities considered are: European Anglo Indian. Indian Christian. Scheduled Caste. Brahmin. Non-Brahmin and Muslim.

Of the five communities, Brahmin and Non-Brahmin communities maintained an increasing proportion in the years prior to 1941-42. Enrolment from the Non-Brahmin community steeply increased as the proportions in 1921-22 was 5.3% whereas in 1941-42 it went up to 34.1% and declined to 32.0% in 1946-47, in the years 1926-27. 1931-32. 1936-37 and 1941-42 admission from the Non-Brahmin community had been stagnant without much improvement in their admission rates. The years 1941-42. 1946-47 witnessed that the proportion of Brahmin Community in the professional colleges in the presidency had increased claiming the share of 17.2% and 19.2%, respectively.

Admission into professional colleges from the Scheduled caste community began only in 1931-32 with one student on its rolls without consistent increase till 1946-47 witnessed that the proportion of Brahmin community in the professional colleges in the presidency had increased claiming the share of 17.2% and 19.2%, respectively. Enrolment of Muslim girl students started still later than the Scheduled caste in 1936-37 with five students on its rools. Their number increased to 25 is 1946-47.

Proportion of Indian Christian in the enrolment was accounted for 63.2% in 1921-22, it suffered a consistent decline till 1946-47 even though number of Indian Christian girls to the total student girls population in the professional colleges was increasing in the years. As compared, 1946-47 to the years one can notice a continuous decline in terms of enrolment of students from the Anglo Indian communities.

Oriental colleges

Oriental colleges in the State began to take girl students from the year 1926-27 on wards. In that year the strength of students, was 2, belonging to non-Brahmin community. In 1936-37, the total admission was 25 shared both Brahmin and non-Brahmin communities. The share of each was five and 18, respectively.

In 1941-42, though the admission from the non-Brahmin community increased to 35, its proportion fell to 57,3% from 72% in 1936-37, whereas the admission from the Brahmin community increased to 19 in 1941-42 from 5 in 1936-37 in terms of proportion, the percentage share of Brahmin in the total admission in oriental colleges increased from 20% in 1936-37 to 31.1% in 1941-42.

The impact of higher education among women made them to realise the importance of improving their rights. Privileges and status. Madras being once of the progressive Province was the home of great Reddi, a well-known and successful medical practitioner, a pioneer and fighter in the cause of women and children. She was widely respected as a devoted social worker.

Under her able leadership, the women of this province who were advanced in education took a very active part in the public life. Mrs. Margret Cousins at the All India Women's Conference. Bangalore confirmed it by saying that the desire for change so far had been confined to the educated sections of society had gone beyond them in affecting the backward class women also.

As early as 1903 women social reformers started their campaign against the child marriage and tried to fix the minimum age limit to 12 years for girls and 18 years for boys. In 1909 these were raised to 16 and 25, respectively. There was a vigorous agitation all over India to 16 and 25, respectively. There was a vigorous agitation all over India both by men and women in support enforcing it by legislation. But nothing was done by the British government for many years to pass. The evil was thriving all over the country which was responsible for a great extent for a very high rate of death among girl wives. For instance a cruel tragedy took place at Madras in 1926 due to child marriage. The age of girl was 13 years and that of the husband 25 years. Due to the misbehaviour of the husband the girl wife met a premature death.

Depressed very much over the sad occurrence Mahatma Gandhi observed that "the custom of child marriage undermined our moral and induced physical degeneration. A man who had no thought of tender age of a girl none of God. Such as undergrown man could not have capacity to fight for freedom and retaining of the same...Fighting for Swaraj meant not merely political awakening-social, educational, moral, economical and political.

He observed. "The Madras Tragedy would have been impossible if there had been a living opinion against child marriage since the young man involved in the incidence was not an illiterate labourer but marry or touch the girl it public opinion had been against the marriage ordinarily the girl under 13 years should have been in marriage.

Dr. Muthulakshmi Reddi in her thought provoking article on child marriage in "Stri Dharm" questioned the physical capacity of a child of 12 years to bear children. She remarked that not be respected in the world sap the very heart of the nation and India could not be respected in the world until she puts an end to this custom:. To give a final shape to these protests on February 1927. Rai Bahadur Hari Bilas Sarda, introduced his "Child Marriage Restraint Bill in the Central Legislature and the Bill was circulated for opinion. A large section of the public was against the proposal to invalidate marriage both on legal and religious grounds.

But the women's organisations took in as a challenge to support the Bill ad the All India Women's Conference at its first session passed resolution to give wholehearted support to Sarda's Bill. Meetings were held to mobilise public opinion in support of the Bill. Wires were sent to His Excellency the Viceroy, the Home Minister by the Women's Associations. But the Bill was sent to a Select Committee which made radical amendments and decided to republish the Bill.

In the mean while Dr. Reddi, Deputy President of Madras Legislative Council, wrote to the Central government for the sanction to introduce her Bill. "Age of Marriage Act 1928" in the madras Council for prevention of child marriage in the Presidency. But His Excellency the Viceroy's government sent it back with the remark that her Bill might wait till the fate of Rai Bahadur Hari Bilas Sarda's Bill was decided in the Assembly. But Mrs. Reddi, eager to achieve her object by some other means, drafted a resolution signed by a number of Brahmin and non-Brahmin members in support of Mr. Sarda's Bill moved in the Madras Council on 27 March 1928 which was duly seconded by Diwan Bahadur Kesava Pillai, Ex. Deputy President of the Council. Though supported by many, Government members opposed it.

In a thought provoking reply given to the opposition of Government could not but put it down with the firm hand. Child marriage is more dangerous and serious crime because the practice of sati involves only a two minutes suffering while by this custom of child marriage the girl child form the moment of her birth to her death undergoes the continuous life log suffering as a child wife, as a child mother and very often a child widow".

Dr. Reddi continued. As a medical woman it has been my ill fortune to witness with my eyes much sufferings and hardships and brothers who are here to cast their votes in favour of the resolution and thus save their daughters and sisters from the tragedy of child wifehood, child motherhood and enforced widowedhood.

The motion was put to the House and declared carried. As soon as the Bill for the prevention of child marriage was published in the local press, a few among the conservative section of the Hindu public began to attack Dr. Reddi both in open meetings and through the press. She had to face stiff opposition from the university graduates also. Orthodox sections challenged her articles and called her to open debates on the subject and they sent many memorials and petitions to government.

Dr. Reddi, not perturbed by the opposition, with firm determination organised large women meetings both in the city and outside and was continuously writing to the press in favour of Sarda Bill. Educated women of the province tried their best to bring out a wonderful awakening among their own women folk by explaining the merits of the Bill in several meetings held all over the Presidency. Smt. Indrani Balasubramaniam, under the auspices of Madras Presidency Reformist Association did active propaganda in support of the measure. All the women's associations of Madras set a Joint Memorial and appeal of His Excellency the Viceroy and the members of the Assembly to pass the Bill since the educated and enlightened women of all the communities were unanimously agreed on the urgent need for legislation to prevent child marriage. Again Dr. Mrs. Reddi wanted to make best use of Mahatma's visit to Madras in 1928 requested him to speak to the people during his South Indian tour about the social evils which were disgraceful to the society. Mahatma did accede to Dr. Reddi's request and freely and courageously expressed his views on those social evils, which were listened to with much respect by millions of people.

On 11 February 1928, All India Women's Conference sent a deputation led by the Rani of Mandi and 19 other members representing almost every province waited upon the Viceroy and leaders of political parties in the country to seek their cooperation in putting down the evil custom of early marriage. In her untiring efforts to pass legislation Dr. Reddi on 4 May 1929, wrote to Mahatma Gandhi requesting him as well as his congress leaders to advice the public about the importance of literacy among women which could be obtained only by liberation from the age long evil customs and wrongness of society. On 13 May she received a reply from Mahatma, assuring that he would make use of every opportunity of driving the truth home to men.

Women politicians like Smt. Ruckmani Lakshmi-pathi organised numerous meetings at Madras, vehemently attacked the attitude of orthodox people and their moves to prevent the passing of the Legislation

Ultimately the Government also supported the Bill and the Legislative Assembly passed it on 20 September 1929 by an overwhelming majority. It got the approval of the Council of States on 1 October 1929, applicable to all communities, penalising parties to a marriage in which the girl was below 14 and the boy was below 18 years of age. The Act came into force on 1 April 1930. Awbrey Albert Zellner rightly remarked, "it is striking that Sarda Act was passed Just One Hundred Years after the British declared that `Sattee' was illegal.

The passing of the Act was no doubt a crowning success of the time, yet the enforcement was not strict as expected; when cases came before the court, it took very lenient view, gave light punishments to the offenders or often acquitted the. Moreover the Government of India tried to amend the Sarda Act. Protest meetings were held almost at all the places. The Women Indian Association organised meetings, opposing amendment of the Act, which would limit its scope of operations. Under the auspices of Reformist Conference. Madras, leaders like Smt. Girija Devi attacked the Government for trying to amend the Act. The All India Women's Conference in its Sixth Session at Madras passed resolutions opposing the ensuing amendment, under the President ship of Smt. Rajkumari Amirth Kaur. The conference urged that steps would be taken for the strict enforcement and insisted that all the states should pass similar legislation.

To make the enforcement effective the All India Women's Conference appointed "Sarda Committee" in all the places and members were vigilante in securing punishment to the law breakers. Dr. Muthulakshmi continuously wrote about Sarda Act in the `Stri Dharm', Madras. According to `Stri Dharm' there were 14 cases of violation of the Act but only one got conviction. Dr. Reddi wrote, `The slightest extenuating circumstance which may be as frail as the proverbial straw a drowning man catches, is enough to rescue the offender. We feel that there is a desire to work more for the loopholes of escape than for the enforcement of this much needed law. Steps should be taken to create a healthy respect for the law in the minds of the people as they have for other laws.

The women's organisations and Sarda Vigilance Committee in different parts of the country defended the Act by all means.

The Act was successful to the extent that it gave an opportunity to girls for education in educational institutions for some more time and enabled them to enjoy the womanhood which was denied to them in the past. The prospect of employment and economic independence discouraged the practice of early marriage.

But there is a lot of resistance-and we attribute much of that resistance and the particular forms it takes of the fact that the new discipline centres around women. And that brings us back to where we first started-one of the reasons for the question 'Why women's studies? is that we live in a society where women are not taken into account and so the idea of an academic discipline about and for women is itself a contradiction.

A look at the socio-economic position of women conforms that our priorities are not men's priorities. Whether we live in western capitalist or socialist countries or elsewhere in the world it can be seen that women's status is not only not improving but in fact in many instances deteriorating. Gains that women have made are insignificant compared with gains some men have made during the same time: and losses are much greater. Why is it that the uncontested United Nations figures are not the basic for world-wide scandal and immediate action? They show that:

'Women constitute half the world's population, perform nearly two-thirds of its work hours, receive on-tenth of the world's income and own less than one-hundredth of the world's property.'

When women in Britain constitute forty per cent of the workforce yet, as Wendy Owen reports, earn only seventy-two per cent of men's wages, when since 1975 women's employment has increased by 207 per cent compared with sixty-one per cent for men, when women continue to perform vast amounts of unpaid emotional and material work- the labour of love at home- which is not just unpaid but is invisible in government statistics on employment-then my question is, *why* is Women's Studies not priority, a necessity?

Women's position in education mirrors precisely their socio-economic status at large: they are present in large numbers as primary and secondary school teachers and increasingly as university students and teachers in the lower echelons, but according to Eileen Byrne, men constitute ninety-seven per cent of the government of education. The British university statistics for 1980 state that women are 2.7 per cent of full professors and 6.4 per cent of senior lecturers and readers in Great Britain.

In some instances women's position is not improving but deteriorating. Despite the increase in numbers of women academics on lower echelons in the last decade, the percentage of women in influential positions in education has actually declined. In brief, women are absent from top positions of power in the policy and decision-making apparatus of the educational system. As Dorothy Smith has said 'power and authority in the educational process are the prerogatives of men'.

This information is incontestable- yet there is still a considerable segment of society asserting that women are better off now than they have ever been. Understandably for people who hold such beliefs, the issue of women's oppression is either solved or almost solved but in either case no longer relevant, and a field of study that concentrates on 'women only' is not only unnecessary but a luxury not to be afforded in these dire days of economic recession. There are, we are told, more important issues to be dealt with than whatever is left of 'the women question'. Important for whom?' is the question to be asked next. Who decides what a significant issue is? Who makes the rules and who profits? Who controls? Those who deny women's economic plight are also denying the systematic violence practised by one sex against the other and they accuse women of 'over-reacting' and 'generalizing' when we point to men's roles in incest, child abuse, prostitution, battering, clitoridectomy, sexual harassment, pornography and rape. Who are they and on what do they base then judgement? What are the assumptions, values, standards, ways of collating and interpreting evidence that enable them not only to oppress women but to remain oblivious to the very fact that they oppress us?

It might be argued that we all have our biases and assumptions and tend to think that we are 'right' and the others are 'wrong'. And there is no doubt that one of the unquestioned assumptions in our society is that the prevailing sexist ideology is not just a particular way of organizing the world but the *only* way. Looking at this issue in a detached manner one might come to the conclusion that 'truth' and 'objectivity' do not exist anyway and that it is all a matter of degree... However, 'detachment' leaves out the fact that it is live women of all ethnicities, ages and social groups who are beaten up and raped, that it is live women who lose their jobs and are humiliated and declared inferior, that it is live women who are portrayed as sex objects in the media. And it is these value judgements which lead me to think I am 'right' to want change: change in the theories that bolster such despicable treatment and in the praxis that effects it.

And here is the crux of Women's Studies: Women's Studies is not 'just' about facts and figures, it is not 'just' another academic discipline-it involves a different way of viewing the world. It is about change: in consciousness; in material and psychological circumstances; in the and control. It was developed in academia by feminists active in the Women's Liberation Movement and therefore has been called 'the education arm of the feminist movement. What Women's Studies grapples with is the premise that if women's oppression remains deniable and women's lives-work, art, culture-invisible, then there must be something in the values, standards, reason and logic of society which needs to be changed.

The absence of women from positions of power is reflected in the curriculum at all educational levels as well as sin the research that is being pursued and is thought important and worthwhile in all academic disciplines. As has been stated for psychology, for theology, for biology' education and for literature- to name only a few of the critiques of the present state of the academic disciplines it is *men*—in particular white, middle-class men-who continue to control the production, the assessment and the distribution of knowledge.

Consequently, females who have succeeded in getting access to education get a male-dominated, make-oriented and male-defined education: they are guests in Men's Studies. In this male-as-the-norm ideology there is more material about men and it is accorded more significance. It is knowledge produced, distributed and owned by men and because if focuses on men and their 'achievements' such as wars and revolutions, when women want to be successful in a man's world what else can they do but copy men's styles and become 'social males'? '...to assert that "it need not be" presumes both the ability to take the oppression of women as an object of understanding as well as to feel the oppression in a deeply personal way.

Moreover, this refusal to tolerate the conditions that we discover proceeds from the historical consciousness that the world could be different. *I*t assumes that alternatives are possible to the historically created male-dominated structures that presently oppose the freedom of women.

The women who are in Women's Studies-student and teachers both recognize and feel women's oppression from personal experience. By bringing these abilities to our attempts to understand it in an academic scholarly way not only do we 'deconstruct' and 'reconstruct' previous knowledge but we also construct new knowledge that includes women as self-determining human beings, that empowers women to explore ways to end their status as underpaid and overworked, abused and exploited second-class citizens. Women's studies is an intellectual necessity if we are to avail ourselves 'equal opportunities in education'. It provides us with a self - enhancing.

'Positive' education because it acknowledges as real and important not only the similar experiences, needs and interests of women as a group by equally their differences of ethnicity, cultural background, age sexual orientation, social status, religion. It parts women's perspectives at the centre of our intellectual quest for knowledge-a marked shift from perspective in Men's Studies that, as an example, asks the question 'Why Women's Studies.'

Women's studies

Defined by the founders of the US national Women's Studies Association as ''an educational strategy for change' owing its existence to the Women's Liberation Movement, it is important to stress that Women's Studies consists of both teaching and research. It is the interaction between feminist scholarship and learning that takes place in the classroom which respectively inspires, probes, reinforces, expands and develops them. Rather than transmitting knowledge as 'the truth from 'the expert' to 'the ignorant', students and teachers in women's Studies attempt the create knowledge in an environment in which all are learners. Some, usually the teachers, are more familiar with the existing scholarship on a topic and make this resource then contribution to the classroom.

Others bring their life experiences as a resource, and, as many of the students in Women's Studies are mature women, their contribution is just as pertinent in gaining and understanding of a phenomenon and developing and analysis. It is here that 'the personal becomes the intellectual and the intellectual the personal'. The enthusiasm that most students and teachers display in women's Studies courses stems from the attempt to blend theory and praxis, a rare happening in other disciplines. Whether the topic is work, health, politics or literature, discussing if from a perspective that puts women at its centre allows us to compare and contrast our own experiences with the give 'facts and figures".

Thus some of the dichotomies inherent in Men's Studies began to vanish: the division, for example, between 'public and private' 'intellect and passion'. 'Theory and praxis'. Women's learning experiences are no longer divorced from their lives. Instead, what emerges is an attempt to understand problems and to develop means of solving them. Piece come together in the process of discovery, and, for example, the use of language of information on women's job segregation might lead directly to action to change one's life.

As students and teachers working closely together we try to break down hierarchies, interact collectively rather than competitively, take each other seriously and respect each other's different perspectives, particularly relevant among women's from different ethnic/cultural backgrounds. In attempting to account for diversity, rather than dismiss it and seek for the one and only 'truth' we are trying out models for different forms of human relationships.

In women's Studies we are 'testing' the very same concept raised be feminists outside academia- to whom we must feed back our analyses and engage with in their actions- which is working towards a world free of power relationships. Trying to engage in such activities within and academic environment that is neither geared to nor inclined to welcome our presence and goals raises a number of serious questions, some of which we will discuss later. The 'subject matter' of Women's Studies is women, but women's lives do not exist in a vacuum: they are located in a social context which includes the study of men as well as the natural and the 'man-made' environment.

Women's Studies is not limited to specific 'women's issues' such as female biology, health care and reproduction, not to studies on the sexual division of labour or to women's participation in men's trade unions or men's wars.

In fact every human issue is a women's issue and at the core of women's Studies lies the demand to look critically at every facet of life from interpersonal relationships to politics from language to law, from the (ab)use of natural resources to the social construction of reality, and to look at it differently, from a woman-centered perspective.

Clearly such a definition shows that Women's Studies cannot remain within the compart-mentalization of knowledge as it is established in the present academic disciplines. While some call Women's Studies 'interdiscipli-nary', we prefer the term 'transdisciplinary', arguing that 'inter-disciplinary' still accepts as a give the only recently institutionalized academic disciplines.

Looking at the production of scholarship in Women's Studies—the body of knowledge classes in Women's Studies are based on- various types of research can be differentiated: however, they can all be done simultaneously. What has been called 'compensatory' by Learner and 'collecting' by Register is research that meticulously examines with a women-centred perspective where and how in what we currently call 'knowledge' women are 'omitted, distorted or trivialised'. Freud and Mard get re-visited; we ask 'where were all the women in history? 'and we find that they had a literature of their own'. Such work leads for example to a new periodization in history in which it emerges that the 'dark' middle-ages were much lighter for women that the allegedly 'enlightened renaissances. It also leads to a reconceptualization of the question of 'good' and 'bad' in literature, in art and in research itself.

Compensatory research and the collection of data cannot take place without 'criticizing' which eventually leads to the production of new theories and models which we find the most fascinating aspect of feminist research. *Men's Studies Modified The Impact of Feminism on the Academic Disciplines* is a collection of essays that looks closely at thirteen academic disciplines, criticizing and exposing their male bias and-after discussing the impact that feminist scholarship has or has not had on these fields- proceeding to discuss the new questions raised and the new theories that emerge.

The past decade has been seen a virtual explosion in feminist scholarship. There is hardly any field that has not been touched. However, much of it is still in line with traditional concepts, be it in asking the questions in using orthodox methodology.

While there is now a considerable amount of feminist theory written by marxist-feminists, radical-feminists, liberal feminists and 'other 'kinds' of feminists we need translators to make connections between them, intertwine them, point to similarities and differences and build new theories-women's studies Theories. We need to be what Liz Stanley and Sue Wise call 'breaking out' of our own disciplinary backgrounds, of our own upbringing. As Stanley and Wise say;

We're first, foremost, and last feminists; not feminists—phenomenologists, feminist-marxists of feminist hyphen anything else. Our interest and concern is with feminism, and feminist revolution.' We must 'withdraw consent from the patriarchal construction of reality'. We need more irreverence, more 'disobedience to partiarchy'. Adrienne rich herself if a good example for irreverence and her theories on compulsory heterosexuality and lesbian existence genuinely challenge previous notions of sexuality.

As we are pursuing our goal for a feminist future we become increasingly interested in 'Trying to find out *how* to find out what we know'.

At the heart of feminist research lies the imperative that it should be *for* women, in order to improve out lives inside and outside academia. As each of us has our own subjective experiences we must being ourselves and our 'conscious partiality' to our research and become and integral part of the research process. This is in marked contrast to the myth of value-free science' and 'objectivity' that still pervades much of traditional research. Being part of one's

Research demands acknowledging that we are both 'subjects' and 'objects': as women, we are members of an oppressed group, as empirical research, we try and replace research hierarchies by collaborative relationships with those we study. Put differently, we try to come to terms withe the dichotomy of 'researcher' and 'researched'.

These relationships not only influence the research process but the product itself: our own ideas and concepts changes through these interactions and we ourselves undergo changes in consciousness. The research process, which it is important to document carefully so that we can learn form one another, is not a linear progression from hypothesis formulation to experiment to verification/refutation. Rather, it is 'interactive, circular and reflexive', looking for synthesis rather than analysis, conceptualizing what we see as 'whole, entire, complex- and in context', cyclical, creating theory rather than testing it.

There are number of research methods that seem better suited than others to feminist research. But feminist researchers try to adapt and adjust their methods according to the varying circumstances in their work- to be creative and flexible rather than dogmatic and rigid.

As an example: for Stanley and Wise, research should not differ from what we do in everyday life, meaning that we should use the same approaches and procedures in each. The different strategies with which to survive in a sexist world are our methods and we use this 'documentary method' whether we are doing research, surviving in academia, or sitting in the London tube.

As to the priorities for feminist research: according to Stanley and Wise, 'what feminists spend our lives doing must obviously be the subject of feminist research' and 'We need to know how, in, minute detail, all facets of the oppression of all women occur, because if we are to resist oppression then we need to understand how it occurs.

Stanley and Wise's demand bring me back to 'What is feminist research?': whether we decide to research ourselves, other women, do a historical study or look at the influence of nuclear technology on our lives, it seems to me we have to start with connecting what we study with our experiences as women living in a patriarchal world. The discrepancy between 'what *we* see' and the responses we get will enable us to understand what exactly it is we oppose and what strategies we might devise to change it. As Maria Mies says:

> '.... we have to start fighting against women's exploitation and oppression in order to be able to understand the extent, the dimensions, the forms and the causes of this patriarchal system.'

Implicit in this statement are two messages. One is that it is imperative that in all we do we incorporate an historical perspective: partiarchy' was not invented yesterday and we had better learn about own sisters of the seventeenth, eighteenth and nineteenth centuries who had at least as radical ideas as we have and try to find out why and how they were prevented from having a largine impact on society. As Dale Spender puts it so pointedly: 'Men either use or lose women's ideas' and indeed, we have little reassurance that our new knowledge will meet with a different fate.

Re-discovered through 'feminist research emerge all those women who, even in spite of their ongoing oppression, have chosen not to be victims. They were strong, imaginative and for centuries have been developing an independent woman-centred understanding of the world. They asserted their power of choice and survived by creating what Lynn Herring has described as the force in Adrienne rich's poetry: 'the power of the ordinary-a universe of humble things'. Role models can be useful. The re-discovery of these women is reason for joy and it is in women's Studies that we can legitimately pursue the discovery and perpetration of our heritage: a validation both of the extraordinary resilience of women struggling in isolation and obscurity- "gaslighted" for centuries' - and of `the power of the ordinary'—of women's lives, past and present.

Women's Studies was a way of ending this domination, by shifting the male perspectives of Men's studies and putting women's perspectives at he centre of our inquiries. However, as the issue is about power, it remains to be seen whether we will succeed in making women's Studies strong enough to shift the power balance effectively. The external ones are clear:. there are men who do not understand, and/or are threatened and thus oppose us. Lack of money, menacing cuts, discussions about whether we are really legitimate and truly academic are one form or another of saying that *they* think *we* are not important.

Then there is the 'Men Problem' in Women's Studies: is there any room for men as teachers and students. However, although our present marginal status is clearly not a comfortable position to be in, why should it astonish us?

Sandra Goyner has said, with the real possibility of becoming a 'genuine Women's Studies, future Women's Studies scholars might be able to develop an 'autonomous identity' rather that the present schizoid state that often demands oscillation between two fields-Women's Studies and the 'ex'- pledging loyalties to both, feeling torn by the contradictions, being overworked by taking on this 'double burden'. As Marcia Westkott says about Women's Studies: To criticize the culture, history and procedures that undergird the institution through whose ranks we seek to advance, and to expect that our criticism will be accepted as a valid means to that advancement, is to face a ought problem indeed.'

And Elizabeth Moinnich highlights the revolutionary nature of Women's Studies:

> 'What we are doing, comparable to Copernicus shattering our geo-centricity, Darwin shattering our species-centricity. We are shattering *andro-centricity*, and the change is an fundamental, as dangerous, as exciting.'

Some of us will leave the institutions and give up hoping that the move towards a 'woman-centred university' can be achieved within the academic gatekeeping of the present institutions of higher education. Others will stay in the institution but will do 'projects of reform and repair' rather than work for fundamental shifts in consciousness and perspectives. This is Marilyn Frye's concern when she writes:

> 'We suffered a single flash of vision... and set about to institutionalize it; but the project has not liberated us or our students in a way which would make the unfurling of new vision a way of life.'

Hopefully there are enough of us who will insist on the intellectual necessity of Women's Studies in higher education and continue to struggle imaginatively, innovatively and with much physical stamina for a model of education that negates and transcends categories and concepts which do not hold for women.

And we believe strongly that Women's Studies does make a difference: just as we are inspired and get strength from the women of our past who were intellectual thinkers and survivors in the most difficult material and emotional circumstances, so students and teachers in women's Studies have a chance to get experiences validated and to participate in an alternative education to develop new theories on and for women's lives. Independent of which of the avenues we choose, we should not forget the purpose of our work. To quote Marcia Westkott again:

> '.. whether we leave the academy or attempt to survive within it, the goal of creating change for women guides us in our struggle.'

If higher education purports to be 'fair' then we cannot afford to ignore the feminist presence. Women's Studies exists and the proponents of Men's Studies should note that their work will not remain unchallenged.

To quote Mary Evans:

> 'Women's Studies has a most important part to play in ensuring that knowledge, itself a form of social power, is not produced solely in the interests of the powerful and the influential, to the determent of the powerless and weak.'

By changing the rules, we work towards changing power relationships and the exclusion of women from the production of knowledge. Maybe indeed change will occur!

Since the first individual courses in 1969 and two US Studies Programmes at Cornell University and San Diego State University, the Women's Studies movement in the US has grown considerably: the 1981 figures list over 20,000 individual courses, and over 350 Women's Studies Programmes, more that a hundred of which grant a BA, thirty-nine an MA, and eleven a Ph.D degree. In addition, twenty-two research centres for women exist. While the first programmes were established in less prestigious public and a few private colleges and universities, by 1981 even the prestigious 'top universities' such as Princton and Berkely and Stanford had programmes or at least a 'concentration' in Women's Studies.

The first clusters of courses were offered in the humanities, gradually spreading to the social sciences, while the number of Women's Studies courses in natural science continues to be low. Most of the programmes are interdisciplinary, i.e. the students choose and emphasis in social science, the humanities, and combine women's Studies, courses from various departments to meet their degree requirements.

The budgets of Women's Studies programmes range form a few dollars to approximately $ 150,000,00 and usually pay for a full-time- co-ordinator, the core courses and (a) lecturer(s) who may or may not have joint appointments in other departments.

Since 1977 women's Studies has had it own professional organization which serves as a network, has its own journal, organizes annual national and regional conferences and undertakes research projects in the field of Women's Studies. In 1981 the first National Institute in Women's Studies took place at the University of Michigan in Ann Arbor and brought together seventy scholars, teachers, and administrators in women's Studies to discuss developments in theory and praxis.

The current political climate in the US and the enormous budget cuts in higher education, are likely to influence the further growth of Women's Studies. However, as it continues to draw large numbers of students into its classrooms its existence is not jeopardized.

Two main developments are taking place in may institutions simultaneously; first, a trend towards more autonomy in terms of budget and faculty hiring procedures, the nature of course offerings, the position of women's Studies as a discipline of its own; and secondly, a trend towards the 'transformation of the curriculum of the traditional disciplines often promoted by offering so-called 'Faculty Development Seminars' that are organized by the Women's Studies Programme: seminars and workshops for interested faculty about feminist scholarship and teaching and, how to integrate these approaches into the various disciplines.

In Britain also, Women's Studies as a field of its own in institutions of higher education is growing. However, at the level of degree- granting courses it has taken a different path from US women's Studies: it is on the level of postgraduate education only that official degrees in Women's Studies are offered. These include an MA course in Women's Studies at the University of Kent at Canterbury an MA in Women's Studies at Brandford University and an MA in women's Studies at Sheffield Polytechnic. An increasing number of MA course offer an option in Women's Studies and so do many postgraduate courses in education. The polytechnic of Central London offers a Diploma in Women's Studies and a new diploma course is to start at Goldmiths' College London in Autumn 1983.

So far, there are no degree-granting undergraduate course, although since the early 1970s many courses have been offered, such as 'Women in Society' and 'Sexual Division in Society'. From 1983, the Open University is offering students in any faculty of the OU a 2nd year option called 'The Changing Experience of Women. The need for a national network in women's Studies is acknowledged and the first two national conferences in Women's Studies took place in London. Participating teachers and students from Women's Studies in higher, adult and further education discussed possibilities for a

Women's Studies organization to provide contacts and further co-operation between students and staff interested in doing feminist teaching and research in Women's Studies Association is underway.

In addition, it is possible to do research degrees, which although not officially conferring degrees in 'Women's Studies', provide, as the first national Conference in 1981 at Bradford University on 'Women Postgraduates Doing Feminist Research' revealed, the chance for feminists in Britain to do feminist research in institutions of higher education.

Should we be more concerned about the dilemmas women present for higher education or the difficulties higher education presents for women? There is a range of approaches to such questions in the literature and the purpose of this chapter is to make these approaches explicit and assess their contributions to the debate. The functional view stresses the production of appropriately qualified and motivated people to meet the needs of the economy. It is compatible either with a relatively conservative approach that advocates increased access for women tohgiher education and training in cases where society's 'manpower' needs are not otherwise met, or with a relatively radical one that points to higher education's pivotal role in the reproduction of the social and sexual division of labour. The cultural model emphasizes conservation and transmission of received wisdom and an approved culture. It can be usefully juxtaposed with the view that the problem for women in higher education is the exclusion of women's experiences and contributions from the defintion and production of knowledge.

The social service model sees higher education as aiming to serve equitably the interests of individuals. It has obvious conncetions with charges that higher education is in fact inequitable and participates in peerpetuating discrimination and injustice towards women. Finally there are the additional possibilities of seeing the problem as stemming from women's inadequate aspirations or simply denying that a nontrivial problem exists.

It might be said that, unlike Friedan's 'problem that has no name', our problem has too many names. Is women in higher education a problem of inadequate individual achievement, of social injustice, of under-investment in talent, of reproduction of the division of labour of bias in the production of knowledge-or no problem at all? Let us consider each possibility.

Women in higher education are sometimes thought tobe at a disadvantage so long as their aspirations and achievements differ from those of men. Although such statements refer to women as a group, the group in this view is a collection of individuals making choices; taking up or refusing options, seizing or missing chances, seeking or foregoing opportunities. Whilst a few commentators believe such choices are biologically based, most blame sex-specific socialization through family, school and media for producing women orientated to arts rather than science, altruism rather than acquisitiveness, co-operation rather than competition. When compared with men, women are said to 'under-achieve', to 'under-aspire', or even to 'under-apply'.

Many studies have sought the determinants of career commitment in the background and the social-psychological characteristics of student women. Sex-typed socialization experiences of women are thought to instil personality traits such as affiliative desires and dependency needs that hamper attainment of eeducational or career goals, especially when such achievements might cause loss of male approval. Beliefs that marriage will provide a prime source of identive push young women into keeping career plans vague and flexible. Student women find themselves in a double bind and feminie inferiority.

Married women students, especially those with children, are thought to suffer from impossible demands on their time and energy and from the expectation that the husband's career will have priority in case conflict. Those who have written about the university from such a viewpoint present an image of a fairly neutral institution, the source of the problem being located outside its compass. There is at least a hope that the university is fundamentally a meriocratic institution that will recognize and reward ambitions and talent in women once they can be persuaded to display it. This is not to say that feminists operating within this models have not criticized higher education for its complacency and its greater suitability, for the life cycle of the typical male rather than the typical female.

Nonetheless, for those feminists the major task is one of encourageing young women to make full use of their talents, not to settle for second best, to recognize that they will spend most of their adult life in the workforce. It becomes necessary to persuade girls and women that science isn't 'really' masculine, that men don't really dislike brainy women, that childcare isn't 'really' incompatible with career-in short that the barriers to public achievement are in the mind, not the marketplace. As Lady Platt, head of the Equal Opportunities Commission, says.

> If a girl is well qualified and prepared to do her homework, then the world is her oyster.

Reform is sought partly through education. Schools are charged with the task of reversing tradition through countering stereotypes, while university and college women are encouraged through exhortation, assertiveness training or consciouness-raising to oversome such handicaps as lack of self-confidence. 'Fear of success', need for approval and desire for dependency.

The problem of women in higher education can be conceptualized as a moral one. The very question of whether higher education is 'fair' or 'just' reflects this approach. Concepts such as 'fairness' 'justice', 'discrimination', 'equally' and 'opportunity' admit of a range of meanings. They are the subject of philosophical disputation and the stuff of political rhetoric. In the educational literature a phrase such as 'equality' of educational opportunity has been shown to have multiple meanings.

In America there are not only pitched legal battles but extended academic debates about the justice and morality of discrimination against women and minorities in higher education and about the appropriateness of affirmative action as an antidote. Relatively little of this debate has been rehearsed in Britian perhaps because our sex discrimination legislation only accords 'positive action' a minor role.

Those who stress discrimination and injustice have no difficulty in producing figures to show that women students and staff are not randomly distributed throughout the higher education system.

Women university students are likely to study French, English or sociology, but unlikely to do physics and engineering. Even today they are far more likely than men to study education, despite the massive cuts in recent years in teacher training places available. Of the 32,450 students in initial teacher training in England in 1981, 69.2% were female. Nearly a third of women university full-time postgraduates study education. Women were 35.8% of students in advanced further education in England in 1981.

Women constitue only a small minority of full-time university staff and are especially scarece at the higher levels. There are no women vice-chancellors. In 1980-81 there were 119 women professors. All but sixteen of these women were found in four of the nine subject areas used in the UGC statistics; forty-three were in administration/business/social studies, twenty-nine in medicine/dentistry/health., seventeen in language/literature/area studies, and fourteen in other arts subjects. Women are slightly better represented in non-university sectors of higher and further education-14.3% of full-time polytechnics. Here again, women are missing from senior ranks. In polytechnics, for example, there are 897 men and forty-nine women vice-principals or other halds of departments.

Women are better represented in the less secure posts in universities. Women are fully 41% of academic-related part-time staff, and 26% of non-clinical contract research staff. It is likely that some of these relatively marginal research and part-time positions will disappear with the contraction of the university sector standing in 1983.

Discrimination as defined by the Race Relations and Sex Discrimination Acts, basically consists of less favourable treatment for a member of one sex or ethnic grop whose relevant circumstance ae the same or not materially different. Built into the legislation in Britian is a concern with the fate of individuals rather than the welfare of groups, in most cases a complainant must calim discrimination in comparison with another individual. It is not sufficient to give evidence that a particular group in a firm or institution is under-represented in top positions but over-represented in bottom ones. Such a demonstration may be grounds for permission to provide special training to the disadvantaged group to improve their achievement potential.

Special training, however, is all that is permitted. Preferental hiring or promotion is not. So even if we can show that women students and academics are not distributed through the system in the same ways as men are, we have not legally establoished the presence of discrimination. Framework, however, are more likely to agree with Margherita Rendel in this volume when she argues that there is no reason to believe that women academics are less able than men, and therfore no reason, other than sex discrminiation, to account for their inferior status within the university.

There are tensions between the rights of the individual and the 'Reform' may merely involve giving further rewards to the most-advantaged individuals of a generally disadvantaged group. Moreover, attempts to equalize opportunities within education take on a paradoxical quality in light of the differentiation and difference at the very heart of an education system that participates in the sorting, selection and allocation of individuals to the various segments of the labour market.

Higher education serves only a fraction of the population, and in that sense discrimates against nearly everyone. Resources used to improve conditions for women in higher educatiion will not be available for the less able. Nagel usefully reminds us that a system which alocates rewards on the basic of intelligence can itself be labelled unjust even if we do not conventionally rgard it as such. The reply by defenders of higher education to charges of elitism will stress the benefits to the entire nation of educating the most-talented individuals and the crucial role of the university in conserving the culture and furthering scholarship.

Feminists whose main concern is the injustice suffered to women who occupied subordinate position within universities may not wholly accept the above detence, but they too generally write as if the university is-or with minor adjustments could be-a meriocracy. Thgey believe that within this system greater priority should be given to equalizing access, opportunities and outcomes between the sexes. They are critical of the age-graded acadmic career structure, which works to the disadvantage of women who take time out to have childrten. They have called for curricular reform, arguing that the neglect of women and distortion of their contributions to scholarship is unjust and discriminatiory.

Finally, they have argued in favour of a range of alterations to university practice such as improvements in maternity leave provision, children facilities, and grant allocation criteria, and they have asked for more support and less sexism from male staff and students.

These feminists put their faith variously in rational argument, economic and legal sanctions, and good will. Bringing to publc notice the fact that women receive unequal shares of academic rewards or the existence of sexism in the curriculum might result in those who control higher education taking steps to ensure that 'merit' becomes a sexneutral category and that the curriculum is reformed; but equally, it might not. Not everyone agrees that such discrimination exists or that it is inevitably unfair. Some commentators argue that the observed patterns are due to sex-differentiated personality characteristics or domestic responsiblities, rather than to bias in higher education.

One such perspective is the 'womanpower' approach. Here it is claimed that society cannot afford to ignore talent regardless of form whence it comes. It must invest in its brilliant women as well as its brilliant men. The 'womanpower' approach was especially popular in the 1950s and 1960s when it meshed well with functionalist and human capital theories dominant in social science at the time.

In Britian and in America, technological changes was thought to demand concomitant expansion of the education system, if the nation were to 'keep pace' and provide sufficient skilled 'manpower' to compete effectively with the Soviet Uniion. Through enlarging their lifetime options, individuals would also benfit from investing in their own education, provided society continued to reward materially those who engaged in extended study. These arguments could be used not only to support increased investment in education but also produce a rationale for efforts to reduce inequility of educational opportunity' and thereby avoid 'wastage of talent'. Studies in the British political arithmetic tradition did exactly this, though mainly confining their attention to the inefficiency of allowing social class beackground to override ability in determining educational outcomes. As is still the case today, arguments about sex inequality in the 1950s and 1960s were found mostly in books about women rather than books about economics or the labour forvce or social class and education. But in spirit the discussions of equality for women were much the same as those concerned with 'manpower' more generally. The womanpower approach requires a fairly uncritical view of institutin of higher education. It education is a good thing for men, then too must it be a good thing for women.

Such arguments were found in both Britain and America. In Britain, Arregger, writing of graduate women claimed that the country needs them, Their knowledge, their experience, their skills. Manpower shortages, especially in the professions, are one of the most intractable problems. There is no untapped reserve of men, but what of the women?" And Fogarty *et al* state. It is clear there are good economic grounds—apart from any question of personal interest and satisfaction or of civil right—for enlarging the field so as to give women too their chance of selction for the top. Top jobs need the best available talent. it is in employers' and the economy's interest that women with great ability should have the chance to replace men of less ability *et al.*

In the United States, the Carnegie report on women in higher education adds this.

This supply of superior intelligence is limited, and the demand for it in society is ever greater. The largest unused supply is found among women. Since women in the United States with higher degrees have very high rates of labour force participation. Carnegie Commission and are thought to give better care to children and greater service to the community, social gains could be expected from investing in higher educaion for women.

Most succinctly, the author of a 1967 book on American women pleads. America needs its womanpower, and the American women need to be needed. Harbeson goes to urge American women to provide a good example for women in 'underdeveloped' countires.

Today human capital and functionalist arguments have lost much of their appeal. For feminists, who probably used womanpower arguments as much as a tactic as anything else, given the difficulty the oposition had in rejecting offers of talent, the argument has proved to be uncomfortably double-edged. Because it was essentially an elitist argument, it could not be used to help the great mass of women with 'average' talent or less; indeed the consequiences would be that some of these 'average' women would be required as domestic servants and childcarers to release the talented ones for their career pursuits.

Even the point made by Fogarty et al, about the importance of highly placed women as role models for the others does not completely deal with the problem. Even more damming was the way in which the womanpower argument could be turned on its head; if women were needed to alleviate labour shortages in professional fields, then persumably when there were no labour shortages then services could be dispensed with. No occupation illustrates this as well as teaching. In the 1960s pleas abounded for married women teachers to return to work and some incentives were provided toward this end.

Currently many owmen in Britain who left teaching to raise a family find it difficult otr impossible to re-enter the profession through the traditional part-time route', while others still in service are returning shortly after childbirth and maternity leave despite their personal preferences otherwise. In Canada, Watson and Quazi advise authorities to reeduce numbers of re-entrants in order to achieve a better age distribution across the profession. In Britain ACSET, the committee set up to advise the Secretary of State for Education and Science in England and Wales, has recently set the maximum percentage of entrants to teaching who are returnees at 40% for primary and 20% for secondary education, and has strongly urged that prefenrence be given to new entrants, who have better qualifications and more up-to-date-knowledge.

It is arguable that human capital theory has been used more effectively against the interests of women than for them.

It has been extended, for example, to provide a rationale for women's subordinate labour market position in terms of their expected time out for child-rearing, which is thought to lead to ytheir lesser investment in education and greater choice of occupations that permit interruption and do not require more than initial training.

Fitzpatrick shows how a high-prestige university using rational economic criteria alone would necessarily seek to minimize female enrolment. And finally there is cross-cultural evidence that the expansion of education per se does not necessrialy increase and may decrease opportunities for women and girls. Nor does educational expansion always reduce occupational sex segregation.

In many countires parents who act as human capitalists have good reasons for not investing in the education ogf their daughters, especially when school places are limited and those for girls are more abundant in the private sector.

The 'opportunity costs' are simply too great. It may be true that our rate of return measures do not accurately measure returns on women's education, especially as they leave out indirect benfits, discount the value of unpaid work in the home and use the individual rather than the married couple as the unit of analysist-but persumably most of the 'investors' go by cruder criteria.

Higher education as playing an integral part in schooling's complicity in the reproduction over the generations of an unequal and hierachical social and sexual division of labour. Women in higher education are found in restricted numbers and in limited subject fields because this is what capitalist society expects,. even 'needs'.

In recent years sociologists of education have concentrated on developing their understanding of social and cultural reproduction and the role of scholing in such processes There are numerous debates among advocates of alternative positions that I cannot deal with here. But all these approaches suggest that schools play some part in perpetuating the role of scholling in such processes economies. For Bowles and to take one example, workers must be equipped with character traits that will encourage their allegience to an economic system that operates fundamentally to their disadvantages.

Largely through its characteristics rules and relationships, the school, in concert with the family, encourages differntial personality dispositions for students ar various levels of the structure, and from various social groupings, in line with their probable level of entry to the labour market. The popular American view of education as a strictly meritocratic sorting ground is an illusion, they argue schools perpetuate, not mitigate, inequality and stratification. According to Bourdieu what schools applaud and reward as 'talent' may be mostly the possession of 'cultural capital' derived from the family. Families with economic capital are more likely to have cultural capital as well.

What role has higher education in all this. Relatively little attention has been paid in these works to higher education as a separate sector. We can make some extensions, for example, the role of Oxbridge in Britain in confirming elite status is almost self-evident even to those not sharing these radical views. It is well known that students in the university sector as a whole are disproportinately drawn from upper social groups. Compared to Britain, Americans seem to cling rtencaciously to the image of higher education as a meritocracy, even today. Perhaps this relfects the greater actual availability of higher education to a large proportion of the population.

However, the higher education system in the United States is actually highly stratified and the most prestigeful institutions, with fees out of-reach of most of the population, can be seen as catering for a socially as well as an academically select clientele.

Some writers in the United States argue that expansion in higher education, especially at the Communities for 'new students' operates mainly as a mechanism of social control and social selction. There remains only the wistful hope that the massess of students in higher education will be in a better position than most to analyse and expose their own situation. Judging from the conservative attitudes that university students are reported to hold this does not seem likely in the near future.

Most of the 'reproduction theories' pay no more than passing attention to gender. In recent years feminist theorists have tried to rework and reshape these approaches to permit their extension to the analysis of schooling's role in the reproduction of gender relations as well as class relations.

They point, for example, to the inability of most reproduction theories to account for the sexual division of labour and the reluctance to expand their concern to include the reproduction of women's responsiblity for household and children in the domestic division of labour.

Such arguments arise from a broadly socialist-feminist standpoint. Relatively few empirical studies of girls and women inschools and colleges have emerged from a socialist-feminist approach, which tends to be theoretical and macrocosiological. With a few exceptions empirical material within this tradition relies on historical and/or documentary analysis.

Studies of access, achievements and experiences of girls in school such as those found in Spender and Sarah and Stacey et al, more often drw upon feminist p;erspectives which emphasize socialization, descrimination, inequiality, and sometimes male dominance, rather than the relations of production under capitalism.

Historians writing of women's struggle for access to university arte frequantly aware of the middle-class bias in the arguments of the pioneers and the elite-reinforcing nature of their appeal to bourgeois self-interests. But when we turn to questions of contemporary higher education, we find a virtual silence about its role in reproduction of sexual inequality. The absence of papers in the present collection that tackle contemporary higher education from an explicit 'reproduction' perspective reflects the gaps in the field. Nor can we develop a suitable account of higher education from this perspective in this chapter. However, we can make a few suggestions about the direction in which such an analysis might proceed.

The conventional profile of 'where women are' within higher education might be a starting point for discussion of why they are there. Women are less frequently represented than men among the higher degree students, in the senior and influential levels of the university hierachy in the research realm and in the scinetific and technological spheres. Women are visible in certain arts-based subjects and in the subjects linked with the 'helping professions'. A follow-up study of 1960 women graduates found that most ended up as teachers, if not straight away, after a period of time in another occupation.

A few writers have suggested that the disproportionate recruitment of women into school teaching plays an important part in perpetuating the sexual division of labour, for examples by reducing competition for other occupations, by institutionalizing a pattern whereby women adjust their labour force participation to school hours and child care, and by providing an unspoken message for the younger generation about appropriate feminine pursuits. Another promising approach would draw upon the Weberian concept of social closure, of increaqsing interest to writers on the professions Closure.

Boradly refers to the process by which given social collectivities seek to regulate market conditions in their favoour, in face of actual or potential competition from outsiders, by restricting access to specific opportunities to a limited group of eligibles.

Such monopolization can rest on 'virtually any group attribute'. Parkin extends the concepts to include both strategories of exclusion used by insiders and strategies of usurpation used by outsiders. An example of an exlcusionary strategy is the requirement for formal credentials for entry into privileged occupations, since economiccally well-endowed families can ensure their children are in line for these vredeintials. Usurpationary forms of social closure include mobilization of trade union power against management or, outside the class context, movements such as Women's Liberation. One of the ways in which this approach differs from traditional Marxist analysis is in its greater attention to intraclass divisions along lines such as race or sex and its acknowledgement of the use of exclusionary strategies by more powerful segments of the working class against less powerful ones. Parkin uses the term 'dual closur' to refer to the simultaneous employment of usurpationary and exclusionary strategies, for example the use by male workers of usurpationary strategies against management and exclusionary ones against all women and against ethnic minority males. Another examples of dual closure comes from the further education sector, where the complex system linking promotion chances to grading of courses has been said to favour men, who tend to teach those course with higher grades. In such a system male lectures may fight as usurpationary unionists for more privileges while guarding those they already have against would-be intruders.

Professional occupations are frequently thought to practise exclusionary closure; this includes closure against women, most complete in the case of the clergy but remarkably successful in the case of university teachers also, it is sparse representation of women in British universities can be taken as evidence. It was only in the 1970s that the quota restricting the proportion of medical school entrants who are female—a blatant example of exclusionary closure—was removed. Occupations such as teaching and nursing have been far less successful than medicine in gaining full acceptance as professions. These are occupations which are bureaucratically organized and closely supervised by the state; they also have high proportions of women workers. Parkin suggests we might see these as occupations which have not been especially appealing to men and therefore which have not been able successfully to operate exclusionary devices against women. At least in the case of teaching there are numerous historical examples of attempts by men to restrict women's participation, including unequal pay and marriage bars.

We might usefully look at aspects of higher education in much the same light. Those segments with lower prestige within the system have in each case been less able to restrict women's entry. Future researchers might advances our analysis by identifying the strategies of exclusion and usurpation used by groups in different structural positions within higher education. Saks criticizes closure theories for advancing exaggerated claims with insufficient empirical support; to my knowledge no empirical work on contemporary women and higher education has yet been conducted using this promising framework.

Correspondences between sex-differentiated subjects and the sexual division of labour in the labour force are not difficult to find, but the links with domestic labour also need elucidating. There is an apparent contradiction between the concept of higher education as a venue for reproduction of an elite and any representation of women. Why should anyone encourage women to aspire to occupational areas where thy are hardly welcome? The answer may lie in the class origins and destinations of these women. Especially among the professional middle classes, their future role is likely to be as 'domestic pedagogues', ensuring their children have a good stock of cultural capital with which to face their school years. So too will they be companions to their husbands, whose professional or business careers frequently depend absolutely on 'domestic capital'-the altruistic service of a wife.

Hochschild shows that the clockwork of university careers is built on the life cycle of a traditional married man. She turns our attention, though not in an explicitly socialist-feminist way, to 'the system' rather than the individuals within it. Perhaps in time others will build on her insights. Clearly the image of the university from this standpoint will not be one of meritocracy, or as a collection of individuals acting for good or for evil.

The segregation of women within and among institutions of higher education will be seen as an integral not an accidental lecture of their societal role. It is not surprising if women 'under-aspire' and the university does little to counter it, if such under-aspirations mean that the university is producing well-educated wives and mothers for the bourgeoisie. The direction for feminist reform within education is, however, cloudy-if capitalism is at the root of things there are limits on what one can accomplish by challenging the education system. perhaps a little learning will deepen discontent-and ultimately be 'a dangerous thing'.

The question whether higher education serves capitalism logically leads to the question whether it also serves patriarchy. Men not only dominate women, they preside over the creation and distribution of knowledge. It is often accepted that women and men in effect inhabit two different cultures. It is argued that knowledge generated by the women's culture has been 'muted' while that produced by the men's culture is universalized and recognized.

Interest in the possibility of 'two cultures' stems from empirical studies that produce differing 'his' and 'her' versions of 'reality' from anthropological observations of 'dominant' and 'muted' groups and the socially-determined 'inarticulateness' of the latter, from extensions of the Marxist concept of 'hegemony' used to describe the ways in which ideas derived from the ruling class and serving their interests are accepted as commonsense knowledge by society in general; and finally. from attempts by feminist sociologists to understand and conceptualize the gap between their own experiences and what they have learned about society through their studies.

The notion of separate cultures remains problematic, for several reasons. It is unclear whether women share a culture on the basis of common biology, common social experience, or both. If it is the former, arguments sail close to those historically used to condemn all women to inferior status and opportunities. To argue that, say, women are more co-operative or sensitive or peace-loving than men-whilst it may be empirically true-may be to give ammunition to those who will wish to restrict women to sphere where co-operation, sensitivity and peace are the only options. If the argument is based on sex-differentiated social experiences, in a given case the divisions among women often appear to outweigh the similarities.

Ivan Illich, using both the biological and social approaches has recently argued that the pre-industrial practice of organizing society around separate gender groups, with a clear demarcation of labour between them, has now given way to a 'genderless individualism' where female individuals compete with male individuals for scarce rewards-and almost inevitably lose the competition. Whilst there are provocative, illuminating facets to his argument, it nevertheless seems to leave only a depressing choice between accepting subordination as a group or subordination as individuals.

Even if we cannot resolve the difficulties of defending the concept of women's culture, we can turn to one outcome of such conceptualizations, the assault on what is seen as men's knowledge, in its masquerade as human knowledge. Much of the effort that has gone into 'Women's Studies' in recent years is an attempt to transcend what is argued to be arbitrary disciplinary boundaries and to create new forms of knowledge free from the distortions introduced by men's power to create knowledge in their own image.

Critiques of numerous disciplines have appeared in recent years. To some extent Women's Studies can be produced within the 'Discrimination' framework, for there is a central concern with fairness. Some feminists in this volume criticize for retaining conventional academic approaches, attempts to contribute to fairness by remedial work in their disciplines; adding studies of women, filling gaps within the existing literature. Others insist that the disciplines are so distorted that we cannot trust what we know. that if sexism were removed from the curriculum little would remain. Socialist feminists tend to be somewhat suspicious of the more sweeping statements. Barrett, for examples, criticizes relativist arguments, which she sees reflected in some forms of Women's Studies, ie those that deny all claims to objective knowledge and locate truth in the pens of its producers and the eyes of its consumers. There are dangers attached to such a wholesale rejection of the possibility of objectives knowledge, it is a high price to pay for the demystification of existing bodies of knowledge. Defenders might reply that the aim is not to relatives knowledge but ultimately to replace pseudo-objective knowledge with a more truthful version that reflects human experience.

The claim that women and men occupy cultures is easier to conceptualize within a specific setting such as an institution of higher education. As we have seen, women tend to be clustered in certain departments and relatively junior positions, which might well contribute to a sense of common consciousness among them, especially when this is seen as a consequence of common experiences of marginally within the institution. Those who are promoted to senior positions, or who study atypical subjects to doctoral level, are isolated from a 'women's culture' and instead exist on sufferance as individual anomalies in man's daily world. Carol Dyhouse tells of the horror in the Senior Common Room in the 1920s when the Egyptologist Margaret Murray dared to intrude-and one suspects that the few professional women in Margherita Rendel's statistics, and the 25 per cent of Daphne Taylor-son's doctoral student sample who were the only women in their departments would recognize the continuities between their experiences and Margaret Murray's.

The difficulty of negotiating between a gender identity and an academic identity, to use Daphne Taylorson's terms, though no doubt experienced largely as an individual problem, may be the defining characteristic of much of women's experience in higher education. Higher education in this view is the quintessential male preserve, where decision-making power is concentrated almost exclusively in the hands of men. Women will inevitably be the aliens in this scenario-either uncomfortable as individual representatives of womanhood or ghettoized in departments accorded low status and little influence because they are 'dominated' by women.

One feminist solution to this situation is to build upon separateness and make of it a virtue. An approach to the concentration of power is to encourage women-controlled institutions, where women can determine priorities. Where this is not realistic, the emphasis is on the production of ideas, namely the elaboration of Women's Studies within established institutions. This strategy has been most successful in the United States, as the appendix to Renate Duelli Klein's chapter in this volume shows, where programmers are welcomed provided they attract students and thus money. It is more difficult to initiate Women's Studies in the framework of British higher education where innovativeness is controlled not so much by the market as by the vetting by the CNAA and by Faculty Boards, often traditional in their view of higher education and its functions.

In both countries the possibilities remain that 'ghettoization' of Women's Studies will simply remove the responsibility of the traditional disciplines to tackle reform and that whenever economies are demanded, the institutional tolerance for Women's Studies will diminish.

Finally, we must consider the view that the problem of women in higher education is no problem. In this perspective we may include arguments that the battles lot access to higher education are safely in the past and that opportunities are now there for those who want them. It has been suggested that this popular view among academic has been responsible for the AUT placing little emphasis on women's rights until very recently. Others arrive at the 'no problem' perspective from the difficulty of making decisions about where one's perspective from the difficulty of making decisions about where one's priorities for reform are most urgently required. It is not uncommon for left wing ideologies to argue that the women's movement divides the working class, diverts the energies of women, and sets back the struggle for socialism.

Socialist feminists might reply that socialism cannot be attained without justice for women while radial feminists point out that violence practised systematically against women worldwide is hardly an insignificant instance of oppression.

Even within feminist ranks, many believe that the position of women in higher education is relatively unproblematic. In the British context, Eileen Byrne argues that feminist concern is more properly turned toward girls who are multiply disadvantaged by factors such as class, region, and level of ability, rather than academic women who are an elite among women.

In a worldwide context, it is clear that higher education is unavailable to the masses of the world's population; even universal literacy is beyond the reach of many countries. In many developing countries, the extent of education provided is not great for either sex. However, the disadvantages to girls is often more pronounced. Unesco figures for the educational enrolment of the population aged sex to twenty-nine in thirty-nine countries show a higher enrolment rate for girls than boys in only five countries. In the developed world and most of Latin America, there is partly of enrolment at primary level.

But 1977 World Bank figures for thirty-eight low income countries reported 90 per cent of males but only 64 per cent of females were receiving primary education. When children move from primary to secondary level in the developing world, boys almost always receive preferential treatment according to Deble. It is difficult to find clear country-based factors that systematically account for variations in provision for womens' education. For example it is not simply the extent of expansion of the education system overall that makes a difference-sometimes this works for, sometimes against, opportunities for women. In a study of five development countries, Smock find that structural considerations appear more significance than cultural ones.

Half of the world's population today is less than 25 years old. One adult in three is illiterate and the other two need continually to bring their knowledge up to date. Education has tremendous task to cope with, yet it is still treated like a poor relation: every year mankind spends of an average $7,800 for each soldier, but devotes on an average only $100 to each pupil. Fully but, also very ancient folly. Four centuries ago Martin Luther protested. 'If, every year, so much money is spent on buying machines of war, making roads and building bridged and a thousand and one other objects of public utility, why should not much more, or at any rate as much, be used to provide for schoolmasters, active and intelligent men capable of bringing up and teaching our young people? Yet considerable efforts are being made.

Many developing countries are allocating a quarter of their national budget to education, and some of them even more. But, despite the immense sacrifice that are being made, these efforts must be kept up unceasingly and it should never be thought that the goal has been reached. In those parts of the world where there is a fairly old tradition of school education there are difficulties in plenty at every level of the education system: primary and secondary school syllabuses and teaching methods which are frequently ill-adapted; shortage of teachers; inadequate technical schools; out-of-date universities; and lack of occupational openings for student-every-thing seems to need overhauling and working out afresh.

In those parts of the world where school education has existed for only a few decades the difficulties are multiplied. The developing countries have often inherited their school syllabuses and teaching methods from the former colonial powers; they have to create a type of education that will suit their particular culture and meet their needs, and often they have to reach the painful decision as to what language is to be the medium of instruction. They also have to build schools and print textbooks, as well as manufacture or buy educational equipment. They have to train teachers.

And yet, when they have successfully completed such cast undertakings, they have to recognize the obvious fact that although education is gaining ground, the ground to be conquered is widening even faster- in other words, the number of children entering school is increasing less rapidly than the number of births. And, despite the enormous cost of each pupil- a cost which is proportionally twice or there times what it is in the industrialized countries because of the higher stay-down-rate-the proportion of drop- outs is sometimes so high that the money seems to have been spent to no purpose at all.

Having received inadequate schooling, the children are all the more certain to revert to state of semi-illiteracy because their family environment remains one of illiteracy. The developing countries thus find themselves faced with a crucial choice. Is it better to educate the maximum number of children-and, with that object, to opt for a short course of primary education-or is it better to institute a selective educational system, whereby a minority of the population of school age would receive a complete education?

Inequality of opportunity for Higher Education

With 'education at the crossroads' throughout the world, how can we ignore the problems concerning the access of girls and women to education? Of a total of 428 million pupils in institutions of primary, secondary and higher education throughout the world in 1967/68, North Korea, 1886 million were girls; of every 100 pupils fifty-seven were male and forty-three female. These figures are sufficient to show that girls do not have the same opportunities for access to education as their brothers. Even so, this a world average for the three levels of education combined, while in Asia and in Africa girls receiving an education is schools account for no more than 38 per cent of the total. However, primary education is being given to 73 per cent of the total pupil population, and it is at this level that the proportion of girls is the highest.

There has, moreover, been no improvement in the situation in recent years. Despite the extraordinary increases in the world school-going population between 1960/61 and 1966/67- an increase of 32 per cent in six years- the disproportion between the number of girls and the number of boys remained more or less unchanged instead of lessening, for the increase in the number of girl pupils was comparable to the over-all increase, and not higher. The educational opportunities for girls and women therefore remain distinctly below those open to boys and men. And this is true only in quantitative terms, but also in qualitative terms.

Equality of rights

On 7 November 1967 the United Nations adopted the 'Declaration of the Elimination of discrimination against Women'. Article 3 stipulates: 'All appropriate measures shall be taken to educate public opinion and to direct national aspirations towards the eradication of prejudice and the abolition of customary and all other practices which are based on the idea of the inferiority of women.'

Yet this idea still has currency. Women do not enjoy all the educational opportunities they should have, and often do not have any at all. Nearly everywhere in the world they are given less education than men, and, over vast areas of the globe, the majority of illiterates are women. The continuation of this state of affairs lends support to the traditional view which, in turn, contributes to the perpetuation of the *status quo*.

Education contributes in large measure not only to the elimination of the idea that women are inferior but also to the elimination of the inferiority of their actual status. Over the past centuries this fact has been realized by a great many women, in Europe and in the United States. To give but one example among many: about a hundred years ago, an American woman journalist, Mrs. Hale, writing in the magazine *Jodey's Lady's Book*, pointed out that little had been said about the rights of women, the first of which was the right to education in its widest sense, an education that would enable women to develop fully their individual, intellectual and moral qualities. One women had access to education there would be no problems in regard to their rights, and those same rights could become harmful if women were incapable of exercising them.

'Outside' and "inside'

The inferior status of women is linked to their traditional role. This is an 'inside' role, within the limits of the family home. Evelyne Sullerot quotes a remark made by Xenophon twenty-four centuries ago: 'The gods created women for the discharge of duties inside the home, and men for all the others. If behaves women to remain within the home and it ill becomes them to "hang about" outside'. And the French sociologist shows that this 'outside-inside' contrast is in fact equivalent to a 'superior-inferior' distinction.

It is fact that all over the world for thousands of years women have remained confined within more or less narrow limits. The women's role was dictated by the prime necessity: survival. Mothers did not have enough time to cope with all their 'inside' duties: agricultural work; tending animals; pounding millet; making candles, soap, preserves and clothing; carrying water and wood; and washing-all of which were exhausting tasks. Until quire recently the performance of these duties called for no skills other than those that were handed down from generation to generation within the home, the concession or the tribe.

Being confined 'inside', women were subject to men-not so much because they were more ignorant than men but because they were their chattels, body and soul. In many civilizations only one thing counted, namely the honour of the daughter or of the wife. Even today there are many countries where the laws grant almost all rights to the husband over the wife and to the father over the children. And even in many of the countries where the law confers practically equal rights on both husband and wife, women do not feel really free. This can be shown by one example.

In 1956, Japanese sociologists conducted a survey among the population of Nagoya and the surrounding districts, asking them the following two questions: 'Are you glad to be a man/ a woman? If so, why?' Six out of ten men said they were glad 'because men are free'. Not one woman gave this as a reason. On the contrary, one out of every three bemoaned her lot 'because women are not free'.

The dead band of the past

This dependent status in the past, this traditional subservience still weighs heavily on woman's mentality everywhere. Indeed, whereas the number of girls and women who want to improve not only their won lot but also that of others and of society is constantly increasing, the number of those who fear change is still distinctly greater.

Such intertia is a matter requiring the greatest attention, for it constitutes a force of resistance to progress-and not only directly through the attitude of women, but also indirectly through the attitude of men, to whom it offers a most convenient excuse for neglecting the fate of women. In this respect, too, education is indispensable. Through education, men as well as women must be convinced of the need for change. However, though education is necessary, it alone is not enough to change people's attitudes and to shake off the dead hand of the past. The future prospects of women depend also on far-reaching economic, social and legal changes being made that will promote the access of women to education.

Economic and social consequences

If reference has been made to the past in speaking of the inferior status of women, although that status has often continued to be a reality, it is merely to show that the roots lie in a social system that us doomed to disappear. Wherever it still survives as a coherent whole, its foundations are already cracking.

Everywhere indeed women have the right to education. But to what kind of an education? Just as education was originally often the preserve of boys, so modern technological and scientific know-how remains in many cases the privilege of men. The force of habit and prejudice, the lack of information, the innumerable difficulties that women encounter in the exercise of some occupations and in the discharge of their domestic duties-all these things tend to limit the opportunities of girls and women. In so socially advanced a country as Sweden it has been observed that if the whole working potential of the female population were exploited there would be a 25 per cent increase in the national income, and if discrimination against women and all other barriers were completely eliminated there would be an increase of approximately 50 per cent in the national income.

In the industrialized countries a great many women give up work in order to look after their young children. However, by the time they are about 35, their youngest children are going to school and their domestic tasks are considerably eased by the aids and appliances they have in the home. Before reaching middle age they find themselves with time on their hands, and if they had the possibility of re-training in their former occupation, or of learning a new one, they could still play their part in the life of their country for another thirty years or so.

In theory, a political life is open to women since, with the exception of a few countries, all women have the right to vote and to stand for election. But how many actually occupy a position of responsibility?

Instead of taking the path followed by the industrialized countries, the developing countries have fortunately taken a short cut. On gaining independence many of them rejected at the very outset any form of legal discrimination against women-at all events in regard to education and participation in the political life of the country. Yet, in these parts of the world, the number of girls attending schools is nearly everywhere below that boys.

One is bound to feel concerned at the consequences of this disparity. If care is not taken they will lead to a many-sided social disequilibrium. It is not unusual, for example, for educated men to refuse to marry uneducated women, and it is this reluctance that has often been conducive to a movement in favour of education for girls. On the other hand, men are sometimes afraid of marrying women who are too well educated, and it is this fear that often impedes the access of girls to higher education and scientific studies. According to an American survey, the more educated the mother the easier it will be for her children to win higher the easier it will be for her children to win higher education diplomas. Conversely, if left in ignorance, women will hamper the progress that needs to be made in hygiene, dietary habits, child care, health and so on.

In addition to social imbalance there is an immediate economic loss. Agriculture is the loser since women play a decisive part in the agriculture of their country, and if they have received neither education nor occupational training, how is agriculture to progress? There is also an industry and commercial loss, since the development of industry and commerce requires the mobilization of all available labour resources. How can an enormous enterprise succeed of from the very start it deprives itself of the contribution of a qualified pool of female labour?

This labour is so necessary to most of the industrialized countries that, if it were lacking, their economies would collapse. Lastly, there is an intellectual loss. In ten years' time the developing areas of the world as a whole will urgently heed one and a half million engineers and technicians, not to mention countless doctors, teachers, architects, accountants, administrators, and so on, who are in such sadly short supply. Faced with these needs, which are so imperative, the countries of those regions cannot afford to neglect the training of half their population.

It is because progress-which is the urgent need-simultaneously creates and requires a new type of women that the education of women has become a world-wide necessity. It is not a question of providing the rudiments of an education on humanitarian grounds; women must be given all the means of participating in the building of the world.

The urgency of the need is thus linked with the desire for justice and with respect for the individual-which make the idea of the inferiority of women intolerable. Woman is as much human being as man; she is equally entitled to develop her abilities, all her abilities, to choose the sort of life she wishes to lead and carry on all the activities and assume all the responsibilities that go to make up human dignity.

Like work or scientific and economic progress, education is a matter for the whole of mankind, for men and women alike and not for one of the two sexes only. This is a truth worth remembering when, as so often happens, the human personality of the individual is crushed by the economic machine. Instead of this machine being harnessed to serve the development of humanity, it is man who serves it. And woman, too.

For, after all, the history of the past and of recent times, offers examples of how the mass of women have been 'manipulated'. According to economic needs the needs of the moment, or what was in the interest of men, conflicting images of woman have been created. French women know this well for, during the First World War, they 'worked like men', but then, once the warriors had been demobilized, had to return to their domestic duties or to their so-called women's occupations.

American women know this, too, for they were encouraged to obtain university degrees and then to revert to the traditional role of the woman in the home, but a woman who had become a consumer.The list of examples could and most areas-occupational life, fashion, household duties, social activities, not forgetting motherhood. In such cases women are more or less aware of being manipulated without any regard for their individual being or for their deepest aspirations. And this is perhaps why they are often afraid of losing their ancestral role.

For women, progress means a fundamental challenge to their very being; it deprives them of their role. It changes their manner of being wives and mothers-and cuts the umbilical cord linking them to the world. Once the traditional image has been thrown of the flames, what other image will arise had been thrown to the flames, what other image will arise to replace it?

Faced with this uncertainty, how could women not feel-doubtless more than their mates-the need for an education that will enable them to reflect and to order for themselves their new mode of existence as women? And how could they not feel, as do men, the need for an education that will enable them to master the economic and technological machine?

Because they want to participate in the life of a world that has been organized independently of them, women are questioning the whole of society. But the facts are there: how is the world to be recast in such a way that women can find a new place in it when those in control are chiefly-and sometimes solely-men? What can men accomplish if women are not working beside them? And how can they co-operate with men when they are illiterate and overwhelmed with duties in the home, or cannot accede to positions of responsibility because of male and female prejudices, or refuse such responsibility for fear of being incompetent? A vicious circle, to the breaking of which education must contribute.

Since ages, Indian women were educated and cultured. They also enjoyed the status of equality with men, a place of honour and were equal partner in war and peace. No work was considered complete partner unless wife joined the husband yojna. Whenever the education of women was neglected they lost their economic independence and consequently their status also.

There can be no uplift of women without the spread of women's education. The University Education Commission observed that there can't be educated people without educated women. "If general education had to be limited, that opportunity should be given to women, for then, it would most surely be passed on to the next generation. If women is educated the whole family is educated. The mother is the first teacher and the teacher the second parent, for, the education starts first at home and then at school. Man may educate the world, but the woman educates the man himself. Bearing children, bringing them up, educating them to live as citizens are undoubtedly the handwork of women. The woman is, therefore, harmonius combination of teacher, wife, mother, homemaker and now-a-days co-bread winner and administrator. No wonder the saying goes that the hand that rocks the cradle rules the world. The ancient culture and education of Indian women was lost in the centuries that followed due to political unheavels and social changes that took place in the country due to foreign invasions, war and feuds. Women were denied the rights and freedom enjoyed by them. The education and status of woman declined miserably by the end of the 18th century. Though lot of efforts were made to improve the educational, economic and social status of woman but the result have been far from satisfactory. In new education policy also emphasis has been given to remove the such imbalances through education, the only alternative. The new policy will lay special emphasis on the removal of disparties and to equalise educational opportunities by attending to the specific needs of those who have been denied equality so far.

Besides, education will be used as an agent of basic change in the status of woman. In order to neutralise the accumulated distortions of the past, there will be well-conceived edge in favour of women. The National Education System will play a positive, interventionist role in the empowerment of women. It will foster the development of new values through redesigned curricula, textbooks, the training and orientation of teachers, decision-makers and administrators, and the active involvement of educational institutions. This will be an act of faith and social engineering. Women's studies will be promoted as a part of various courses and educational institutions encouraged to take up active programmes to further women's development.

In addition to this, emphasis has been placed on elementary education in policy and recommended that the removal of women's illiteracy and obstacles inhibiting their access to, and retention in, elementary education will receive overriding priority, through provision of special support services, setting of time targets, and effective monitoring. Major emphasis will be laid on women's participation in vocational, technical and professional education at different levels. The policy of non-discrimination will be pursued vigorously to eliminate sex stereotying in vocational and professional courses and to promote women's participation in non-traditional occupations, as well as in existing and emergent technologies.

After independence, lot of efforts have been made to improve the conditions of girls education. Special schemes have been formulated for the welfare of women education. More funds were allocated in National Five Year Plans. With these efforts undoubtedly there has been improvement in the education of girls. During 1900-21 the literacy rate was only 1.8% which was increased to 7.93% in 1951. In 1961 the literacy rose upto 12.95% and in 1971 the literacy percentage was 18.69% which rose to 24.88% per cent in 1981. The average rate of literacy during 1971 was 1.8% which has increased to 2.4% during 1981. But the progress of woman education is far from satisfactory despite such efforts. The literacy rate is very low and there is glaring disparity between male and female literacy. During 1951 the literacy of male was 24.95% and the female was 7.93%. The male literacy was more than three times in comparison to female literacy. This trend followed in coming decades also. During 1961 and 1971 the literacy rates between male and female were 34.44% and 12.95%, and 39.95% and 18.69%. In 1981 Census also, the gap between male and female literacy was too much and the literacy of male was just double in comparison to female literacy. This is more accentuated in rural areas than in urban areas. The female literacy in rural areas of Kerala and

Rajasthan state varies from 64.7 per cent to 5.4 per cent. Bihar, Madhya Pradesh and Uttar Pradesh, which accounts for 38 per cent of rural families in the country female literacy percentage range between 8.99 per cent and 10.17 per cent. If we see the female literacy of backward section including scheduled castes and scheduled tribes, the situation is quite worst.

In the case of enrolment at elementary stage also there is lot of disparity between boys and girls. The enrolment ratio in age-group 6 to 11 years in classes from I to V between boys and girls was 110.3 and 75.5 during 1983-84. The enrolment ratio at this stage in boys was more than one and half times than that of girls. In the case of middle stage in the age group 11 to 14 years, the enrolment ratio of boys was about double than the that of girls.

The drop-out rate is quite high among the girls as compared to boys. There are various reasons responsible for the drop-out and non-attending the school. Parents don't realise the importance of girl's education and consider it as luxury. The consider that she has to depend on man for her subsistence. They also utilise the services of their daughters either looking after the young child or helping the family in their household work. They are also prejudice and believe in superstitions particularly rural parents are deadly against girls' education. Some girls are used for labour and supplement income of the family. Early marriages are also hindrance in the education of girls. Sometimes girls are removed from the school because suitable bridegrooms are not found for educated girls. Absence of suitable co-curricular activities and distance of school from home are also the reasons for drop-out. Such a huge wastage and stagnation among the girls education created a big hindrance in achieving the target of universalisation of elementary education. So the educationists, thinkers, administrators and planners though non-formal education as a strategy for the universalisation of education. Non-formal education means to provide learning opportunities in organised provision outside the formal system in a flexible manner suited to the local specific needs and situation. In new policy also it has been recommended that a large and systematic programme of non-formal education will be launched for school drop-out, working children and girls who can't attend whole day schools.

The non-formal education serves the four priority tasks:

(a) Provide out-of-school education and training for the school drop-outs in the age of 9-14 and so ensure that all girls acquire the minimum learning skills.

(b) Provide functional literacy, learning for the illiterate adults, beginning with rural women doing field work, so that working women acquire uniform learning skills.

(c) Provide farm education and training to filed and landless working women enabling them to raise their income and agriculture production.

(d) Provide industrial health and family planning, social welfare, arts and crafts and even teacher and management training to all girls and women of different age.

There are five salient features of non-formal education programme.

(i) The first feature common to all the programme is that they provide opportunities for learning to women of all age groups, literacy skill, farming, industrial, trade, management skill, commercial skill, health service, social welfare, teaching skill or sports etc.

(ii) Each programme will be organised by some agency, governmental or non-governmental, with learning programme in the form of curriculum.

(iii) All such programme take place outside the formal educational system. That is outside the school time table, discipline outside of curriculum, examinations certificates, diploma or degrees associated with the present formal education, in school, college and university, etc.

(iv) Every programme is motivated by the desire on the part of the participation to improve one's general or technical knowledge or qualification in order to augment or increase one's earning or employment prospectus.

(v) Programmes may cover the entire life-span of the individual covering all age groups including child and adolecent drop-outs and those of elder age.

This scheme has been implemented largely in the country as a parallel system of formal education. Various programmes and innovative schemes have been implemented in various part of the country according to their own situations.

Special scheme for girl's education

There is a special centrally sponsored scheme of non-formal education in nine educationally backward states for girls. The states were being assisted on a 50:50 sharing basis since 1979-80. It was established that girls constituted 70% of the non-enrolled children in these states. Various measures were undertaken, but not much could be achieved through the formal schools due to socio-economic conditions. The government planned provision of non-formal part-time education centres exclusively for girls which are staffed preferably by woman teachers. The scheme was revised in 1982.83 and prepared on liberalized basis. It was proposed that 90% assistance will be given by the Centre and 10% will be borne by the state. It is hoped that the states will accelerate the programme of UEE through liberalised scheme of financial help for NFE for girls. During 1983-84 a sum of Rs.59.12 lakhs has been released to seven educationally backward states for opening 1000 non-formal education centres exclusively for girls. Under this programme girls who wish to pursue the normal curriculum, will avail themselves of the formal schooling or non-formal schooling under the M.P. Model.

Integrated child development programme

The programme of ICDS was started during the Fifth Five Year Plan. The main objectives of the ICDS are to improve the nutritional and health status of children in the age-group 0-6 years, to lay the foundation for proper psychological, physical and social development of the child; to reduce the incidence of mortality, morbidity, malnutrition and school drop-out, and toenhance the capability of the mother to look after the normal health and nutritional needs of the child through proper nutrition and health education.

The six package of service namely supplementary nutrition, immunisation, health check up, referral services, nutrition and health education and non-formal education have been provided under this programme which are mutually re-inforcing to provide optimum impact. One of the packages provides services of health check up, immunisation against tetanus, supplementary nutrition, nutrition health education to expectant and nursing mothers. The services like supplementary nutrition, immunisation, health check up and referral services are delivered to children less than three years. Non-formal pre-school-education is delivered to children between three to six years. It will enables themto develop desirable attitudes, values and bahaviour patterns and aim at providing environmental stimulation.

Functional literacy programme

Functional literacy programme has emerged from the dire need of imparting the skills of literacy to more than 80% of illiterate females in the country so that they fruitfully participate in the development efforts in the community. The main objective of the scheme are to enable illiterate women to acquire the skills of literacy through functional literacy classes and to participate in the development efforts of the community; to promote better awareness among women of modern methods of health and hygiene; to impart training in home management and child care, to bring about attitudinal changes among women so as to enable them to play their role as good citizens and to adopt follow up measures to sustain the interest created among the beneficiaries.

This programme renders the services including non-formal education using functional literacy as the means covering the following subjects;

1. Elements of health and hygiene including environment sanitation, personal hygiene, pollution and contamination of drinking water, use of laterines and smokeless choolas etc.

2. Food and nutrition education with special emphasis on malnutrition, preparation of balanced diet and low cost meals, preservation food etc.

3. Home management and child care which would include cookery, fruit and pickles preservation, needle craft, pre and anti-natural care, family planning, home nursing, and baby feeding etc.

4. Civic education, in which knowledge of national flag, national anthem, duties and responsibilities of citizens, observance of national festivals etc, will be imparted.

5. Vocational and occupational skills including kitchen gardening, poultry farming etc. The scheme of functional literacy is implemented in the areas where Integrated Child

Development Services projects are located. However, if any other scheme of non-formal education is already operating in a particular area, efforts will not be duplicated. Infrastructure available for ICDS scheme are being utilised for running the scheme of functional literacy.

Curriculum does not fulfil requirement of girls and is not relevant to their needs. So the curriculum for out-of-girls should be varied according to environment including practical utility for the day to day life and to suit the particular society so that it may attract more and more girls within the fold of education.

It should be according to the needs of the locality. It has also been emphasised in new education policy to redesign the curriculum and text book according to the local specific needs and areas. The time and place of the centre should also be adjusted according to convenience to the locality.

The facilitators particularly the women are not appointed in these NFE centres. The woman even less qualified if available in the same locality or village should be given preference in appointing as facilitator of the NFE centre. The New policy also recommends that talented and dedicated young man and woman from the local community will be chosen to serve as instructors and particular attention paid to their training.

The NFE programmes are lacking in vocational input. It should be provided alongwitheducation so that women can become economically dependent and co-bread winner. They also contribute to the economy of the family not by domestic alone but by creative productivity. The policy also emphasises that appropriate formal and non-formal programmes of technical education relevant to their skill will be devised for the benefit of women, the economically and socially weaker sections, and the physically handicapped.

The NFE should be switched over to secondary, senior secondary and university level also. This will provide further chances for those who were unable to prosecute their studies beyond the secondary and senior secondary stage and also give them the option to continue their education till they are qualified for a degree. They can choose subjects from a wide variety of subjects.

The parents particularly from the backward sections believe in superstitions, old belief and are not aware about the importance of education. They don't send their daughter to the NFE centres. A wide publicity should be made for the NFE programme to persuade and motivate both parents and wards. Mass-Media should be utilised for creating awareness among parents through various programmes and activities and also for creating a favourable and attracting atmosphere towards non-formal education. New education policy also recommends that modern technological aids will be used to improve the learning environment of NFE centres.

Administration and management of NFE system differs from state to state and there is adhoc arrangement which does not facilitate the system. So there should be separate administration for NFE system like formal set up. Woman should also be associated in planning and management of the NFE scheme. New education policy recommends that an overhaul of the system of planning and the management of education will receive high priority. More woman should be inducting in planning and management of education.

Only few children join the formal stream from these centres because there is a lot of gap between formal and non-formal syllabus. The bridge course should be prepared for those who wish to join the formal stream after completing two years in NFE centre in class sixth or after three years in middles level centres in class VIIIth. All the agencies are not working together to fulfil the target of universalisation of elementary education.

So there should be proper coordination among various agencies viz, village level worker, gramsavika, panchayat, teacher, political leaders, health visitors, field publicity unit for running the NFE programmes. Voluntary organisation should also be encouraged to run the NFE centres. Training should be provided to all the workers to work in coordinated way, regarding home, health, hygiene and nutrition, etc.

Early marriages are still in vogue and female children are either withdrawn from the NFE centre or don't send to the centres in fear of not getting bride after their education or due to other social evils. The parents should be made aware about the population education through curriculum and new techniques etc. They should be educated about the bad effect or early marriage.

Training for non-formal education is not being provided in effective manner. The same teacher who are teaching in formal schools have been running the NFE centres. Training should be provided to teachers at least twice in a year with short period of ten fifteen days. They should be oriented about all the functioning of NFE centres with modern techniques and methods.

3

Women Empowerment in Islam

The advent of Islam brought about significant social changes among the Arabs converted to Islam by introducing new mental attitudes. Efforts were now made to remove old oppressive social practices. An important element introduced was the honour and status bestowed on women as human beings and the regard as the members of the social community They were also protected from the severities of the customary laws through Koranic directives. Female infanticide was strictly prohibited. It was inevitable that once purdah became a symbol of respectability, it should be adopted by even poor families where it assumed it worst features.

In fact, Purdha a proved an added factor in depriving women of any participation in public affairs, any activity in political or social fields. Men while confining their women folk to cloak seclusion and depriving them of cultural or recreational pursuits, created a professional playground for themselves. Thus the double moral standards took place-man was free to extra-marital liaison as a result of which a class of women lived only to toil for family while the other lived only to provide pleasures and relaxation to men. Incidentally, women were inflicted with the acceptance of the double standard as an instable phase of their society.

Islam had is non-social pattern and laws especially on marriage, divorce, inheritance, etc. Marriage under Islam is a simple civil contract struck by formal proposal on one part and formal acceptance by the others. Duties of a wife are more circumspect than categorical, like obedience to reasonable demands, even marital submission must be in keeping with health and property.

The wife is protected from physical violence of the husband, and is entitled to outside visits to parents and relations. Shias can marry for a stipulated period with an automatic end, but it is hardly availed of. But with the others divorce seems simple for the men, for marriage, as it is normally understood, can be terminated by the men's merely uttering the word 'Talak This is a weapon of repression. However, the marriage can be terminated by mutual consent.

The custom of dowry, which, as it is called is there under which the bride gets an amount from the groom. Part of this payment can be deposed, and is supposed to act as a deterrent. The Muslim law gives half share of the same to the daughters, and the husband exercises no rights over his wife's property. What is more, she can alleviate it, if she so, wishes. Where a woman inherited a house, she exercised absolute rights. However notwithstanding these Muslim customs, the women's oppression began as the Muslims expanded their domains and ruling powers. For this historians hold the fanatical theologicians responsible.

Islam came to India in its bigoted from specially with purdah which became the provisional prominent hallmarks of feudalism, synonymous with high status respectability. It enforcement became so pervasive that any woman found without a veil was dubbed as shameless and outside of decent society. Soon even non-Muslims felt compelled to wear the veil to prove their status. According to Syed Amir Ali, an eminent scholar of Islamic religion and history, explains that it is not the sayings of the prophet but this bigotery of early ulemas that tried to help down the women. The ruling interpreters of those early times legends hushed from the feudal societies of Persia and Turkey. According to Syed Ali's interpretation, what Islam recommended was observance of privacy and not seclusion and confinement of women. To prove this point, he points out that women members of the prophet's family enjoyed remarkable freedom from such restraints which were enjoined on women, that Fatima, the prophet's daughter, took part in religious and legal discourses and Ayesha, his wife commanded her own troop at the Battle of the Camel.

Islamic women broke the barriers of veil number off times and distinguished themselves in various fields, including administration as queens who not only ruled but personally led victorious armies into battle like Razia Sultana, Chand Bibi and Noor Jehan, who practically ran the empire. There were quite often literary talents like Jahan Ara, Shahjahan's daughters. Jamila Brijbhushan, a noted writer in her recent book on Muslim women, reveals names that go back to even prophets time like Shiwa, the foster sister, a noted poet, layla-bint-e-Abdullah, who ran the market in medina.

Fatima bibi was actively involved in politico-religious activities during thee regime of Third Caliph Usman. initially noted Muslim reformers like Sir Sayed Ahmed Khan were against Muslims education but later Muslim rulers like Sir sayed were enthusiastic promoters of omen's education and promoted his movement around 1986 by setting up a member of girls, schools. One of the earliest was the Muslim Girls High School in Lucknow, which drew students from all over India. To attract with greater care they were all conducted in strict purdah.

Condition of Muslim Women in India

Koran lays "Men have authority over women because Allah has made thee one superior to the other, and because they spend their wealth to maintain them. Good women are obedient. They guard their unseen parts because Allah has guarded them. As per those whom you fear disobedient, admonish them and send them to beds and beat them if they d not obey you. Take no further action against them if they obey you, Allah is high supreme".

Shah Bano Begum field her case under Sec. 125 of the Criminal procedure Code for maintenance in April 1978 in the local court of Indore. Shah Bano's husband, an advocate, said there was no obligation under this personal law to maintain his wife, once they are divorced.

Shah bano did not give up, she argued that she had the right to maintenance under the Common Criminal Code, Section 128 of the Code of criminal procedure. In 1973 the Cr. P.C. laid that husband has one obligation to maintain his wife which includes a divorced wife, children and parents. Shah Bano fought her case for more than seven years and she finally won. Her contention was upheld by the Supreme Court in 1985. The court held that " It is a matter of regret that Article 44 of our Constitution has remained a dead letter". A common civil code will help the women of habitual integration by removing desperate loyalties to laws which have conflicting loyalties".

Shah Bano won the case not only for herself but for thousands of other- ill-fated Muslim women like her. The Supreme Court decision grating alimony to a divorced Muslim woman, celebrates the growing consciousness of women towards their rights. In fact, the degradations of Muslim women and their plights is worst than their Hindu counterparts

According to Dr. C.N. Ahmed Moulvi Quoran has been grossly misinterpreted to suit the whims of unscrupulous and that in fact the Shariat endows women with status as men.

The Women's plight is worse in securing alimony from the moment she filed a petition before the judicial magistrate. The woman faces the prospect of envy. Her quest for justice scuttled at various stages by the husband. Apart from this delays that cripple, delayed dispension of justice, the award of maintenance by the first Class Judicial magistrate can be challenged by the husband at the Sessions Court. Strangely enough, after running the legal marathon from the first Class magistrate's Court to the Supreme court, which takes several years, the women armed with a favourable verdict has to approach the magistrates court again for execution off the order. A notice is issued to the husband, if he refuses to pay despite the notice, his immovable and movable property is seized. If he has no such property, the court issues an a rest warrant against him. if the husband persists in his refusal to pay after being arrested and produced in court, the Magistrate can send him to jail for a period not exceeding one month for every breach of the monthly payment. The maximum amount as maintenance can be awarded by the First Class Judicial Magistrate is Rs. 500/- per month for an individual. But if the husband chooses to go to jail, the divorced wife ends up getting nothing.

The Kerala High Court ruled that a divorced Muslim woman is not entitled to invoke Section 127 of the Code of Criminal Procedure, which deals with maintenance to divorced wives, after the coming into existence of the Muslim Women Act, 1986. This ruling of Justice Chettur Sankaran Nair came in a case filed by a PWD engineer, Mr. Gafoor Kunju, challenging an order of the Additional sessions Court, Trivandrum, enhancing maintenance awarded to his divorced wife, Ayya Ummal Pathumma Beevi. Maintenance was awarded to the wife and daughter earlier. A Chief judicial magistrate dismissed her Plea to enhance the amount. She approached the Additional Sessions Court which revised the order of the CJM and enhanced the amount, Abdul Gafoor Kunju challenged only the enhancement in favour of his former wife.

The Sessions judges held that a divorced Muslim wife is entitled to invoke section 127 of the CRPC even after May 1, 1986, the date on which the Muslim Women Act came into force. He said the Act supplemented the right ensuring to a divorced Muslim wife under sections 125 to 128 of the CRPC. The reason was that there was no repeal of sections 125 to 128, express or implied, in the Act. According to him the Act supplemented, widened or enriched the contents of the rights ensuring to the divorced wife.

The High Court said that the Sessions Judge was Right in his view that sections 125 to 128 of the Cr PC did not stand repealed the act contains no provision to repeal the sections. Besides, those sections are not confined, in their operation, to Muslim wives alone. They apply to a host of others, such as divorced wives in other communities, neglected parents and children without sufficient means.

Relying on a Supreme Court ruling relating to special laws, the High Court Ruled that when a special law, namely the Muslim women Act, was enacted to govern maintenance payable to Muslim wives, the application of general law under the code, is excluded or restricted.

The contention of the counsel for Avvi Beevi was that the Act dealt with only the personal law and that it augmented the provision in sections 125 to 128 of the Cr PC. The law relating to the prevention of vagrancy in the code remains intact. The right the code is independent of the personal law and is unaffected. The context in which the act came into existence or objects leads to the conclusion that it was intended to provide additional rights the counsel held.

The judge said it was difficult to accept this view. The Act was to specify the rights to which the divorced wife is entitled to and not to add to those rights in sections 125 to 128. The preamble to the Act also indicates that is was intended to provide maintenance or provision payable to Muslim wives on divorce. That apart, the language of the Act and the indications in sections 5 and 7 of the Act clearly show that, except in cause provided under Section 5 the provisions under CrPC are inapplicable for divorced Muslim wives.

Under section 5 both parties by consent may elect to be governed by the sections of the code. That clearly suggests that in such cases only, the provisions of the CrPC can be invoked. Section 7 of the Muslim women act also suggests that the CrPC provisions are not available even to pending applications originally instituted under the Code, the Court said.

Consideration based on repeal is thus alien to the context. Neither is it possible to subscribe to the view that the Act applied to the rights under the code. The Act was enacted in the post "Shah Bano" case was intended to restrict the Code. The Court set aside that part of order of the Session Court enhancing maintenance to the wife, but the enhancement in respect of the daughter is confirmed.

The poets address odes to it. Films depict it flowing serenely into a never-never land of romance, a woman's sigh interwoven in its ripples. The Kallai river, south of the booming trade centre of Calicut, is resplendent with romantic folklore. Much of this folklore has been perpetuated by men immune to the ironies of place and time, and most of all, to the life context of the women who inhabit the area.

For where the waters of the kallai invade the thresholds of broken-down dwellings, women of varying ages sit huddled, staring into a void. They are united by a common agony; each is an abandoned wife, callously cast away by a Muslim male exercising his "religious" privilege to divorce. each of these women has known the sudden pang of punctured dignity. And each of these women, cocooned by poverty, is a trenchant critic of those aspects of the shariat or Muslim personal Law that lend themselves to abuse in the hands of men and which discriminate against women.

The Supreme Court decision granting alimony to a divorced Muslim woman, Shah Bano Begum, celebrates the growing consciousness of womens rights. Yet there are dark pockets where the landmark judgement cannot beam its message of hope, where the much proclaimed free legal services have yet to penetrate. Muslim women in certain localities of Malabar, for instance, have no access to justice in the matter of alimony. Women in the kallai river area are either too poor to afford legal means of redress or simply have no knowledge or access to legal aid services. Perhaps more insidious than the rigours of poverty is the lure of obscurantism among the hungry and desolate. Here the Shariat becomes an instrument of whim in the hands of callous men; here the shariat is invoked to bolster false motivations, to buttress the greed for quick money.

Here Mohammedan law turns into a legitimate means of female oppression. Legal redress is fantasy. House after house harbours broken women peer out like creatures of the dark, figures of male brutalisation leaning back on ugly memories. Women compelled into marriage at adolescence, discarded soon after or after years of menial domestic subjugation, stranded penniless. Ever so often the man scamps off with his wife jewels after setting up a small business with the dowry money she has paid him. These are men who turn the shariat into an adventure in exploitation, going from one marriage to another or luring adolescent girls with the Gulf dream. Zainaba was 11 years old when she married Moihuddin, a saw mill worker. Her age was no inhibition; mother Aisha knew only too well the perils of turning down an offer of marriage for her daughter. even as she dreamed of her first baby, pregnant Zainaba heard of her husband's marriage to someone else. " My daughter had not yet been born, but her father had already darkened her furture 'Zainaba says, looking down at the rough floor plastered with cow dung for lack of cement. Her daughter Fatima grew up with glimpses of her father who came whenever he was in a benevolent mood, but continues to contribute towards the upkeep of his family.

With each step Fatima look into adolescence her mother and grandmother panicked. How would they marry her off? They had no jewels, no, wealth, except the leaking roof over their heads and Aish's monthly window's pension of Rs.55 Then, like a boon, a proposal came on day. Zainaba informed her husband. but Moihuddin disapproved of the match and refused to meet the expenses. Zainaba went ahead with the marriage anyway. They collected Rs 1,200 from neighbours and friends and conducted the wedding. Moihuddin was outraged. His pride was hurt. He left, never to return and cut his wife off without a penny. That was two years age.

Zainaba contemplated legal redress on the advice of asocial worker. Weeks ago Moihuddin paid her a visit, brandishing his hurt pride, threatening her with the wrath of the Shariat if she went to court. " Where was his pride when he had to marry off his daughter? Aisha asks" Our curses are on him" Aisha looks at the lined face of her daughter. Zainaba has begun to look far older than her 356 years. But there is one solace. Her daughter Fatima has escaped her mother's hell. " For how long? Aisha wonders aloud.

The case of 35 year old Zaina, living a few houses away, is a variation of the same theme: the Shariat laws exploited by an errant husband for martial duplicity. After nine years of wedded life with Zaina TV Salim disappeared from their home. He left with three gold sovereigns which belonged to his wife. He did not send her any maintenance money. In the ensuing years news trickled down to Zaina about her husband's marriage to a woman from Pandalur in Travancore.

Then, one day, out of the blue, Salim sent her a letter from one of the gulf states. The contents were replete with endearment and then the revelation that his second wife had become an invalid. He also informed her of his imminent re turn. The condition of extreme poverty does not preclude the quest for dignity Zaina spurned her husband's offer and plants instead to claim maintenance for the period of desertion. For a woman like Zaina a court battle is vague prospects. She has no means to pay the legal fees. And the local legal air services probably don't know she exists.

The human dilemma that springs from the distortion of religious sanction has a diabolical dimension. Teenaged girls from poor Muslim families and young abandoned wives are particularly vulnerable to predators of the flesh who disguise their intentions under the provisions of Muslim personal Law.

Foremost in this class of mean are itinerant Arabs sporting fat purses and false promises of marital bliss. They hire the services of touts who scout poor homesteads for eligible Muslim brides Arabi Kalyanam is fast becoming a widespread social evil in the Malabar region. Arresting the Arabs has served to highlight their misdemeanours but the malaise persists in pockets of poverty maiming the psyche of young Muslim girls.

Twenty two year old T. Safia of Palliparai married an Arab when she was 15 years old. At the outset he gave her Rs.

1,000 and moved into her home. The domestic force deepened for the Arab didn't know a word of Malayalam and Safia a word of Arabic. A local interpreter eased matters for them. When Safia was two months pregnant, the grab left but returned in her eighth month. He stayed on till the child was born. And abruptly left when the baby girl was three months old. This time he never came back.

Safia married a local Muslim. Another baby, and the husband dropped out of sight. To support her children and elderly mother Safia went to the gulf accepting an offer to work as a maid servant with a Malayali family. The Gulf sojourn is a lucky break for a Muslim girl in the through of society. Safia returned with the inevitable two in one tape recorder and other symbols of post-Gulf prosperity. One night there was a knock on her door. Her second husband arrived to stake his claim to Safia's new found gadgets and assaulted her when she refused. Throughout he referred to the authority of the Shariat to buttress his demand. Neighbours intervened. Safia had enough She approached a social worker for guidance to go to court and decided to fight for alimony from the Arab and the local Muslim.

If there are discarded wives who have no access to justice for one reason or other, the picture is not as rosy one either for scores of women with the will and the means to fight court battles for alimony. The first Class magistrate's court in Calicut is littered with Maintenance cases and on most days of the week women crowd the corridors of the courtroom where their petitions for maintenance are heard., Most of the women are Muslims dressed in their distinct rural attire and almost all of them belong to the poorer sections of society. Many hold wailing babies in their arms. The scene is at once tragic and hopeful. Tragic because many of these women have been divorced by their husbands purely on a whim, sometimes for reasons so trivial and absurd that the very facility of divorce mocks the law that permits it. Hopeful because the crowded corridors of the court bear testimony to the burgeoning spirit of emancipation among oppressed Muslim women, their will to rectify the wrong done to them.

Protest against Shariat Laws

Indeed, awareness has grown to military. From the bowels of the city, its slum expanse, scores of Muslim women paraded the streets off Calicut in protest against the Shariat. Further up the social scale Muslim women in secure or affluent circumstances marched with placards in Calicut denouncing the marriage and divorce laws that discriminated against women. Status constraints compelled the demonstrators to don black robes and veils. but their message wads driven home.

It was a gesture that challenged the hardcore conservatives of the Muslim league leadership in the state, the self-styled champions of the Shariat. In the wake of the momentous Supreme Court verdict granting alimony to Shah Bano Begum, Indian Union Muslim League leaders like Deputy Chief Minister Avukader Kutty Naha railed against the Judges. IUML National President Sulaiman Sat expressed moral outrage and described the court's ruling as a sacrilege. Through it all, Chief Minister Karunakaran upheld the medieval attitudes of his ruling front colleagues. All three men emerged as moral parodies before an overwhelming question that involved the status and dignity of Muslim women very where, a question that loomed over petty political motivations and called for a redefinition of male attitudes to women. To compound the parody, certain Muslim women parliamentarian spoke in support of the shariat in effect endorsing female oppression.

Clearly politicians who wield the mike such panache have not seen the degradation of Muslim women in parts of

Malabar, where a man can divorce his wife because he is not served chicken on a particular day because the woman wears a sari that the mother in law disapproves of. Instances of this nature from the substance of many a lawyer's record.

In the upper social strata, a critical attitude to Islamic tenets invites censures and social ostracism, a prospect held in terror even by affluent and educated Muslims. the fear of censure haunts most liberal Muslims who criticise shariat in private but hold their tongues in public. A classic example of the coercion implicit among Muslims is the volte-face enacted by prabodhanam, the official organ of the Jsmmaat-e-Ialam which is an editorial hailed the Supreme Court decision to grant alimony to Shah bano Begum. The moment the Muslim League leaders lampooned the court's decision the magazine turned coat.

On rare exception to this trends is Dr. C.N. Ahmed Moulvi, credited with being the first man to translate the Quran into Malayalam. A religious scholar of wide repute, Dr. Ahmed Moulavi is an outspoken critic of discriminatory practices against Muslim women. I his view, the Quran has been grossly misinterpreted to suit the whims of unscrupulous men and that in fact the Shariat endows women with equal status as men. He efforts the interesting insight that most Muslims abide buy the sayings of holy men rather than the Quaran itself and that religious scholar and holy men have consistently championed the interests of women down the ages.

P.P. Ummer Koya, ex-education Minister and a liberal Muslim argues for a modification of shariat laws to sit the times However, he adds the lack of a consensus of opinion among the various Muslims sects does not allow for a Uniform Civil Code. But the philosophic distinctions cannot quell the fall-out of the Muslim system of marriage and divorce. Orphanages and children's homes in the state are crammed with inmates fathered by Muslim men who divorced their wives and whose children are not welcome in the new homes. And because their own mothers are not able to maintain them many of the children go vagrant. The juvenile wing of the police department picks up truant children at railway stations and bus stops and whisks them off to children's courts.

Expansion of Judicial System

The procedural hurdles of securing alimony is in itself a harrowing experience for an impoverished Muslim divorces.

From the moment she files a petition before the First Class Judicial Magistrate, the women faces the prospect of having her quest for justice scuttled at various stages by thee husband. Apart from the delays that cripples swift dispensation of justice, the award of maintenance by the first Class judicial magistrate can be challenged by the husband at the sessions court. The sessions court is empowered to stay in the earlier verdict. The case languishes longer in this court because the sessions judges have to try sessions offenses, hear criminal appeals and maintenance revisions arising from the judgement of several First Class Magistrates in the district.

Even after the case is disposed of by the sessions courts a husband has a right of appeal at the high court. An adamant husband can then push the case even to the Supreme Court.

After runnings this legal marathon from the first Class magistrate's court to the supreme Court, which takes several years, the woman armed with a favourable verdict has to approach the magistrate's court again for execution of the order. A notice is issued to the husband. if the refuses to pay the amount despite the notice, a distress warrant is issued against him whereby his movable property is seized. if he was no such property the court issues an arrest warrant against him.

If the husband persists in his refusal to pay even after being arrested and product in court, the magistrate can send him to jail for period not exceeding one month for every breach of the monthly payment. the maximum amount as maintenance that can awarded by the First Class judicial magistrate is Rs. 500 per month for an individual. but if the husband chooses to go to jail, divorced wife ends up getting nothing.

If religion is the balm of hurt soul, then an impoverished Muslim woman has been forsaken by her God. Or is man masquerading as God, taking upon himself the divine right over a woman's life? There is a breed of men who like Sulaiman Sait see not babarity but only justice is stoning a woman to death who deem it unnatural for women to aspire for equal rights with men. But the day those Muslim women poured into the streets of calicut protesting against unjust marriage and divorce laws they opened for Muslims woman everywhere, the doors of a new option.

The human toll of the indiscriminate use of the divorce provision is rarely noticed by society. th scars are never worn publicly but remain emblems of a deeply private anguish. Twenty year old Suharabi's fingers are seen to keep time with her grief as she warps sweets one by one amidst the crackle of paper. Wrapping 1,200 sweets in two kilo packets fetches 50 paise. this has been her livelihood since the time her husband invoked the magic word talaq four years ago. Enlisting the effort of her four-year old daughter Kunjumol, Suharabi earned upto Rs 3 a day by wrapping sweets for a local confectioner.

Suharabi narrates the collapse of Muslims girl's dreams with a deepen face uncharaterstic of her age. The gleam of youth has gone out of her eyes. Staring down at the sweets poised between her toiling fingers, she speaks in a voice that moves with monotony of a coveyor belt. Nothing seems to alter its cadence, no sudden excitement or remembrance or anything at all. The child stated on the table surrounded by every child's dream item, is strangely unmoved by the lure of candy.

Suharbi speaks of her marriage to Mustaffa as a sort of crescendo, the peak point of germinating dreams of marriage, a family, moments of laughter. it is as if, when dreams shatter they have behind an aura, something that lingers in the aftermath. Suharabi and her child wrapping sweets for a living are fragile as a dream in their loneliness.

Her mother in law had been ill-tempered and spiteful. She fouled her son's mind with strange occult practices. In fact, Mustaffa worked as an exorcist, ridding local Muslims supposedly possessed by demons. But he himself was possessed by his mother's spite for Suharabi. One night his mother had a dream. She dreamt that Suharabi was sleeping wit another man She told her son of his wife's adultery.

They cross-checked with the spirits by spreading ink on a glass pane and reading the signs. There was no doubt about it. Suharbi to go. She Picked up her infant girl and left her husband's home bewildered bereaved and hardly checking her cascading tears. Mustaffa divorced her and went on to marry three more women, one of whom died when he kicked and punched her pregnant body. Suharabi recalls the news without a flutter.

She had asked Mustaffa to return her dowry of Rs. 1,000. He retorted with a threat to destroy her with black magic but returned a part of money. Suharabi's uncle filed a case for alimony on behalf of his niece. The court's verdict went in her favour. It is a year and a half since the verdict. mustaffa has to pay rs 3,5000 for that period. So far they have received only rs 750 from him. His whereabouts are a mystery, say the police. 'Then how did he marry three more times 'Suharabi wants to know. But the question dies in her throat.

After 1947, westernmost and easternmost sectors became the Islamic states of Pakistan and, later, Bangladesh, there was a considerable movement of non-Muslims out of them, and of Muslims from India into them. Muslims are now about 97 per cent of the Pakistani population of 83.8 million, and about 90 per cent of Bangladesh's 87 million. In India Muslims were about 11 per cent of the total Indian population of 684 million in 1981. In Uttar Pradesh their proportion was about 16 per cent of the total state population, 111 million in 1981.

Muslims and Hindus have lived side by side for centuries through most of the purdah zone. Since the great majority of Muslims on the subcontinent are descended from converts to Islam, there are many cultural affinities in each region between the two groupings whose formal religions are so disparate. A useful source for comparisons of Hindu and Muslim patterns is provided by the volumes on Indian Muslims edited by Imtiaz Ahmad. In his overview of the volume on family, Ahmad writes that "Muslim family norms in India correspond closely to those held among Hindus". In his introduction to the volume on caste and stratification he notes that the contributors (with one exception) "...are of the view that social stratification among the Muslim communities studied by them is certainly comparable to the Hindu caste system though an exact parallel cannot be said to exist". In the volume on ritual and religion he concludes, "It is clear that as a practiced faith Islam is far more pluralistic in character than the extreme degree of reification attributed to it by Islamicists and Muslim theologians would admit".

That is, the actual religious beliefs and acts of Indian Muslims include a good deal that is of the country as well as much that is of the Koran and its commentaries. Ahmad emphasizes the importance of the Koran and of the distinctive Islamic plant for the day, the year, the life. But he also notes that Muslims of the subcontinent "participate simultaneously in both a local and an Islamic culture". The local components are considerable and vary considerably from region to region. The ways in which Muslims of one region differ from Muslims of another region, as in subsistence patterns and daily life, usually correspond to the ways in which the Hindus of the same regions differ from each other.

Similar though the Muslims and Hindus of a locality may be culturally, in many respects they remain separate socially. There is typically little interchange between them in domestic matters; there are few of the solidary bonds that connect kinsmen. Religious observances are carried on separately, in different ways, at different places. Each side attributes the social separation to their differences in religious ideology.

Yet cooperative engagement is also maintained. Muslims and Hindus within a locality commonly exchange goods and services, there may be some mutual participation in village ceremonies; and all in a village or town neighbourhood generally unite against outside encroachment, whether by government officials, natural calamities, or intrusive exploiters. And in India there is now a record of the decades since independence of mutual participation by Muslims, Hindus and other religious-ethnic groups in common national pursuits—administrative, political, commercial, industrial, and educational.

The extent of local social separation has varied from time to time and from region to region. From his studies of Kashmir villagers, T.N. Madan concluded that Kashmiri society consists of dual social orders that are accommodated within an overarching framework of common language, customs, and state government. In villagers' perceptions, the duality is far more important than the common frame. By contrast, L.M. Bookman's account of communal relations in a village of Saharanpur district in Uttar Pradesh tells of much cooperation in economic and political affairs as well as of the sharing of some basic values.

When violence broke out in the district during the partition riots of 1947, the Hindu elders called the village Muslims back from the place to which they had fled and successfully protected them when they returned to their homes. In such matters, the Muslims and Hindus of the village act "as members of a common society and culture." But, Bookman adds, in those social situations that touch on the nature of self and society, there is divergence.

Muslims identify themselves as Muslims and with Muslims, Hindus with Hindus. There are, to be sure, social cleavages among the village Hindus of different factions and castes, and marked social separations among the four Muslim groups of the village. But on the whole these villagers, as do most others in the land, tend to see Hindus and Muslims are more radically distinct than they appear to be on an inventory of culture traits. Each person considers himself, if it comes to a test, as being either Hindu or Muslim.

It was this perception of difference that underlay the partition of Pakistan from India at the moment of independence. The everyday practice of purdah in a Muslim household follows the general pattern we have sketched, but with some notable differences in emphasis and scope. A Muslim bride also comes to live with her husband's family. There she may cover her head and face before her husband's father and elder brothers, and avoid direct gaze at or speech with them. But she less often comes as the complete stranger that a Hindu bride of the north usually is.

Muslims have a general preference for arranging marriages between two who are already related, as the son and daughter of two brothers, real or classificatory, or as the children of friendly families. A girl who becomes engaged to be married to a kinsman must then veil before the young man, who up to then she has known as a familiar relative. Perhaps it is because some Muslim brides come into familiar families that young Muslim wives usually to not have to keep quite a rigorous avoidance within the household as is required of comparable Hindu wives.

Because some of a person's relatives through marriage may also be related through descent, there is not the sharp demarcation between affinal and consanguinal kin that prevails among northern Hindus. Thus, a Hindu matron in a Madhya Pradesh village must veil before her children's senior affines, as, for example, to her daughter's mother-in-law, and that woman must veil before her. Muslim women need not keep themselves so meticulously distanced from their affines or their children.

Veiling by Muslim women emphasizes a different dichotomy. It is between those kin and close friends who come within the trusted circle of the family and all others who are considered outsiders. Some of these outsiders may be well known to the family as neighbours or as remoter kin, but they do not come into the inner parts of the home.

Doranne Jacobson's account is particularly illuminating on this score. She tells that among the Pathan Muslims she studied, "the element of trust is central" to purdah observance. Should a woman come to mistrust a close kinsman, she may begin to seclude herself from him. Kinsmen who quarrel may order their wives to veil before their opponents and to avoid the now distanced relatives.

Muslim women tend to keep even more strictly to their own quarters of the house, the zenana, than do their Hindu counterparts. Larger houses usually have a room at the front entrance beyond which strangers may not go unless invited. Adjoining it is a room in which the men of the family entertain visitors. The women do not enter these outer rooms. Behind them is the courtyard where the family women stay; there they may meet female visitors and trusted men. In the rear of house is the space where women and small children pass much of the day and where they sleep at night. Even the family men do not usually linger there. Where the houses are built with flat-topped roofs and adjoin each other, women visit across the rooftops. They entertain women guests there unless the men want to come up, perhaps to enjoy the cool of the evening. Warned, the women then go back to their courtyard and inner domain.

Within the household, a Muslim woman covers her head or veils her face not only before her husband's father and elder brothers, but also does so before any man among the family intimates who is namaharam, "not forbidden" to her, that is, not forbidden as a possible husband. They are the men whom she could have married and who, should she become a widow or divorcee, might be eligible spouses. An educated Muslim woman from Lucknow told Reshma Yunus: "My mother to this day speaks to non-maharam men from behind a partition."

A woman does not similarly avoid those men who come into the household and who are not possible husbands, such as her father, brother and sons. Just who among kinsmen and friends should be included within a Muslim family's circle of trust is a matter of choice by the family elders. A Hindu woman's father and brother rarely if ever enter her married home, but such affines may be family intimates in a Muslim household.

Thus, on Panjgur oasis in westernmost Pakistan, decisions as to which among related men are allowed to come into the home are "left up to individual households." In villages of Comilla district in Bangladesh, "each family has made its own list, of family insiders".

Muslim women do not veil before certain classes of men whose roles of life-styles exempt them from the *prima facie* distrust of strangers. When a common consults a religious specialist or a holy man about her personal problems, she sits before him with head covered but with face unveiled. Veiling before male servants varies by region and class. Pukhtun women in Swat do not keep purdah before house servants or house slaves because such a man "was often considered a sort of junior family member". Perhaps also among these fierce people, a servant whose eyes were too closely fastened on a young woman of the family might soon feel a terrible swift dagger across his throat. In Panjgur also, women do not veil before house servants and men of the lowest rank, sweepers and water-carriers, who are defined as not posing any peril to family. Some shopping may be done by older Muslim women. If the family is wealthy enough, merchants bring their wares to the house for examination.

More commonly, women may visit shops for special purchases, as for a daughter's trousseau. They discuss the goods and prices with the shopkeepers. If he is a long-time purveyor to the family, they may engage in conversation with him. In general, Muslim women must be vigilant about observing purdah for reasons that are similar to those given by Hindus but with different emphasis. Hindu elders are more concerned with the danger to family unity and honor from within, from the younger wives who comes as aliens to the family and who may alienate their husbands from it.

Muslim family elders are not insensible of such dangers, but are much less perturbed by them. Their affines are, often enough, also consanguines: a new bride is not necessarily perceived as a potential disrupter. Muslims concerns are much more fixed on the danger to family honor from without, from the encircling world of mistrustable strangers. If a Muslim woman can be more relaxed than her Hindu neighbour about avoidances within the household, she must be more strictly careful about maintaining social invisibility outside.

Almost all Muslim men, Zaidi says Bangladeshis, strongly prefer that the women of their families keep strict purdah "against strangers and distant relatives". The preposition indicates the sentiment, a woman should be perpetually defensive against all those outside the family circle of trust. A Muslim woman from Abbotabad in northwest Pakistan told Reshma Yunus that if a woman is forced by necessity to speak to a man who is a stranger, she should speak to him as if they were enemies. She should use a harsh voice and even be rude, because if you speak nicely, then he would be attracted to you and this could lead to evil.

In the Muslim view, girls are invested with this electric attraction when they reach puberty. At that time of their lives they take on the full panoply of purdah. In some families, a girl's puberty is anticipated and she begins her social seclusion between ages nine and twelve. And Shibani Roy notes that among the Muslim families she studied in Delhi and Lucknow, girls in the age range of five to nine are discouraged from playing with boys and from visiting in neighbouring household. In Hindu families, however, a girl does not have to assume purdah observance until she is married. It is her acquisition of a husband and in-laws rather than her sexual maturation that impels her into purdah.

Sexual attraction is differently phrased, Hanna Papanek notes, by Hindus than it is by the Pakistani Muslim men she has interviewed. Papanek has the impression that Hindu men and family elders tend to see a young woman as the temptress, while Muslims tend rather to believe that both men and women have strong sexual desires which they can control only with difficulty. Zarina Bhatty similarly remarks that Indian Muslim men deem strict seclusion to be necessary because a woman inevitably arouses, by mere appearance, sensual desires in men over which they are not expected to have any self-control.

In all, a Muslim woman of "respectable" family should venture out very little, and then only in the portable seclusion of a burka, an all-enveloping garment, and be accompanied, preferably, by a trustworthy companion. When she travels by vehicle, her passenger space should be completely curtained from prying eyes whether the vehicle be an ox-cart, a horse-drawn two-wheeler, a railway compartment, or a Mercedes-Benz.

A Hindu woman of similar status usually takes care to cover her head and possibly veil her face when she is within view of strangers, especially when traveling. But Hindu families do not usually insist on the sight-proof outer foil required en route for many Muslim women. Curtains are not usually practical on a bus or airplane; a Muslim woman bus rider has to make do with the shield of her burka and her aloof demeanor. And occasionally, on a city street, one may see a figure in a burka on a scooter, riding side-saddle behind the driver. Among a few Hindu groups, as those who were close to the former courts of Rajput rulers, the zeal of stringent observance of purdah resembled that of Muslims of similar rank. Rama Mehta has described the high degree of seclusion observed by the women of the Oswals, a jati that traditionally provided administrators for the Maharana of Udaipur and other princes of Rajasthan. An Oswal woman veiled even to the maidservants of her household. When she went outdoors, she wore a thick sari over her indoor dress.

As the powers of the princess and their courts were abolished after independence, the Oswals and similar communities abandoned such rigorous standards of purdah. Hindu women of the higher jatis wore a blanket-like shawl on occasion, especially when traveling. It was about as all-covering as the Muslim woman's burka. But while the burka is still much in use, this shawl is now rarely seen. In the Bhopal region, such wrapping is worn by young Hindu women at certain joyous ritual events, perhaps as much for protection from the evil eye as from lascivious male stares.

The traditional burka is made of cotton, all white or all black, and envelops the wearer cap-a-pie. In recent decades, a new style has become popular among the more affluent and less stringent families. It is the two-piece burka, consisting of a long, sleeveless coat over which a cape, nearly waist-length, is worn.

The cape covers the head and has an attached veil which falls over the face and can also be thrown back. This burka style is made of silk or rayon, comes in various solid colours; some are even shaped a bit to suggest a waistline and may be in pastel hues. This newer style is more comfortable to wear and, at least to the casual observer, just as concealing. While some Muslim women, mainly those of high education and wealth, now find the burka an intolerable impediment, many more say that it is really a liberating garment which permits a certain freedom of movement not possible without it, allowing them to go out of the house or travel to visit their natal home.

Moreover, for poor people it is a hallmark of status. Muslim women who must work in the fields, usually aspire to slip into a burka and be rid of filed labour.

Muslim women of the Delhi Pizadas, like the Hindu women of Meerut, must be particularly circumspect in their own mohalla, the neighbourhood where they and their families are known. When a woman gets on a bus with her husband to ride to another part of Delhi, she usually throws back her veil to see better. "When returning, she lowers the veil again as they approach their mohalla".

There is one kind of public place into which a Hindu woman may enter and a Muslim woman does not. It is the place of worship. Hindu women come to pray and make offerings at the temples where their men go and they may go with them. While they may not be allowed into the inner sanctum, they are not barred, as women, from sacred precincts.

A muslim woman does not usually enter a mosque. While she may, if suitably accompanied and attired, attend fairs and festivals, participate in the women's parts of religious ceremonies, visit local shrines, and make long pilgrimages, she does not participate in the daily congregational worship that is mandatory for Muslim men. Hindus approach the congregation of their Gods singly or as a family. Muslims pray publicly to their single God in congregations of males only. Since the mosque is the central public gathering place for a community's men, it is not a suitable place for women.

This is not to say that these Muslim women are cut off from religious participation. They are typically engrossed with domestic devotions, with performing the women's portions of rituals, with worship at shrines. In her study of a Muslim village in Pakistani Punjab, Zekiye Eglar tells of the women's involvement in and direction of gift exchanges between families, especially at weddings. These exchanges, in Eglar's account, are of great importance for family prestige and for village economy. And these transactions are essentially under the control of the women.

Muslim women of rural West Bengal, Lina Fruzzetti tells, carry on parts of the life-cycle rituals and conduct all the rites and worship of the local saints, pir. That worship is an important part of their lives. Men share in the beliefs about the powers of the pir but do not participate in the worship. These Muslims separate the functions of their supreme deity from those of the saints in a way that parallels the distinction made by Hindus between their transcendental and pragmatic deities. Among Hindus, women generally have more to do with the pragmatic supernaturals than do men, but there is not the sharp differentiation in worship by gender that is made by these Muslims of West Bengal.

In their rationale for purdah, Muslims invoke religious reasons much more than do Hindus. The close seclusion of women, in the popular Muslim belief, is a fundamental precept of Islam, ordained in the Koran, and is a universal hallmark of he true Muslim way of life. Muslim teachers and preachers, Maulvi, regularly exhort the faithful to safeguard that precious quality of Islam and often admonish their audiences, whether male or female, about derelictions from this essential rule. In Bangladesh villages, purdah "commands respect in a way that money alone does not, because of its religious connotations, since it is considered good behaviour from a religious point of view".

For Hindus, purdah is not so integral a part of religion. It is more a matter of social concern for family and caste-group, rather than a principle of religious sanction. Mandates for purdah in Hindu holy writ are not commonly invoked. Hindu religious teachers tend rather to emphasize, especially when addressing women, the scriptual ideal of patrivrata, the complete devotion of a wife to her husband.

There are some Muslim scholars who challenge the popular, orthodox view about the Koranic foundations for purdah. Thus, Fazlur Rahman, an Islamic modernist, states. "The Quran advocates neither veil nor segregation of sexes but insists on sexual modesty." He cites evidence to show that in Arabia, before Islam, women were a central focus of a man's honor and were subjected to close restraints. Paradoxically, according to Rahman, the Koran aimed to remove certain abuses to which women had been subjected because of excessive preoccupation by men with their honor. Rahman reviews the relevant verses of the Koran and concludes, "there is nothing in these verses that calls for purdah as such". These views may eventually be accepted as valid interpretations and may provide scriptual justification for reforms to come. But they are far from the currently prevailing belief among Muslims.

In the nineteenth century and later, a number of social reformers—Hindu, Muslim, and British—advo-cated changes in women's status. Their efforts did influence the program of the Indian National Congress and ultimately the Constitution of India. But they had little direct effect on the lives of South Asian women in general.

A Muslim reform movement that did have influence on women's activities was that centered in Deoband, northeast of Delhi. Like reformist drives in other world religions, its proponents preached a return to the true meaning of Islamic scripture, as they interpreted the sacred text.

A principal publication of that movement is a 1905 book about women, Jewelry in Paradise, by Maulana Thanawi. The title conveys the author's message to women, that they be less concerned with their actual jewels and more with their real jewels, their good deeds and conduct.

In her lucid study of this book, Barbara Metcalf tells that it has been enormously successful. It is still widely available and has been translated from the original Urdu into many other Indian languages. This book, like the Deobandi movement itself, received greatest acceptance among upwardly mobile Muslims who were attracted to assertively scriptual religion as a mark of respectability. Through his teaching and writings for this class, Thanawi became "one of the most influential Muslims of twentieth-century India".

A central element of Deoband teaching was the restoration of women's rights which, these reformers argued, are inherent in Islamic scripture but which have been eroded over time. They preached that women are not outside of, or irrelevant to, true religion, as was then a popular belief, but are capable of religious fulfillment. Thanawi expounds this thesis, consistently writing that women do have capacity for moral behaviour. He argues that this is so despite their inherent shortcomings for right conduct, such as excessive emotionalism, flightiness, loud talk, and lack of due care in protecting their valuables and their honor.

The book urges women to develop their moral capacities by engaging fully and conscientiously in the rituals prescribed for them. Thanawi advocates that women be literate and educated in Islamic law. A woman so schooled can better perform her wifely duties, improve herself, and, importantly, advance the status of her family. A literate women can enhance her own and her family's respectability. She will not violate seclusion through clandestine correspondence. "Rather than compromise seclusion she can preserve it, for she can communicate with her distant relatives without going to any outsider". Thanawi's recommendations for some education for girls and for greater involvement in religious pursuits by women struck a responsive chord among those Muslim men who aspired to better economic and social status under twentieth century conditions. He pointed them in directions in which they wanted to go, provided scriptual reasons they could readily accept.

Purday-Izzat and Variations

Izzat (an Arabic and Persian word) is the term for which "honor" is the usual translation. It is a word often heard in men's talk, particularly when the talk is about conflict, rivalry and struggle. It crops up as a kind of final explanation for motivation, whether for acts of aggression or beneficence. It expresses a salient theme and includes some of the most highly valued purposes of a person's life. For the Pukhtun of Swat in northern Pakistan, their code of honor "is everything." For the Pirzada of Delhi, it is described as being their central concern. Like any term of strong emotional resonance, it is used in various overlapping meanings and with many nuances. But it always refers to how a person carries out the group's values, how he or she realizes them in actual behaviour. For Jat Sikhs in the Punjab, Joyce Pettigrew writes that their concept of izzat is a complex of values, it is a philosophy of life that includes their paramount concerns with power, with reciprocity in giving, equality in vengeance, and nonsubmission to threat. A family's izzat must be preserved at all costs and increased whenever possible. And "if the honor of a family's women is lost, so also is the family's entire public position".

Public positions are the province of men, and so the primary referents of izzat are men. While a man's izzat is assessed by his kith and kin on several scores, the conduct of a family's women is always a cardinal consideration. Women are said to bear izzat also, as when it was remarked in a Himachal Pradesh village that it is bad for a woman's izzat if she does ploughing. But two women of that village were in an "uncertain moral position" because each had become economically independent of her husband. "The honour of her family depends on her behaviour; but if she cuts herself off from them she has no honour of her own".

Izzat can be a corporate or a personal attribute or both. Since a person's behaviour in the community is commonly seen as a reflection of group traits rather than the isolable acts of an autonomous individual, izzat looms as a group and especially a family quality. Hence each woman's observance or nonobservance of her group's standards of purdah affects the izzat of all in her martial family, and not of them only. Should she grossly violate those standards, the izzat of her natal family will be hurt as well. A bride may be reminded by her parents that if she does not behave properly in her new home, her notoriety will damage the marriage chances of her still unmarried sisters and so may diminish their whole lives. Conversely, the reputation of both families will be enhanced if her conduct is devoted, dutiful and irreproachable.

Izzat, then, takes in the zealously sought qualities of prestige and status, rank and esteem, respect and self-respect. Shame (sharm) is the antithesis of izzat, to be avoided as diligently as izzat is sought. The term is also used often with positive connotation, as when a little boy is praised for having enough sensibility of shame to avoid the women's quarters.

The kind of izzat open to a person and family depends on their social position. A family of a generally poor, low-ranking group can scarcely aspire to the izzat attainable by a family rich in land and proud of inherited status. But there are families of greater and lesser izzat within each set; a family of a lowly group may gain high regard both among its peers and more widely in its locality; one of high caste rank may come to be disdained by all.

Izzat and the dangers to it are judged in relative perspective. Zarina Bhatty tells of a Muslim family in a village of the Lucknow area. Its elders had long debated whether an unmarried daughter should be allowed to take a post as teacher in the village school. At the same time, they were proud that a woman of the family had been elected to the U.P. Legislative Assembly and had become a Minister in the State cabinet. Her political activities required her to mingle with many kinds of people and to be exposed to public gaze. "Such exposure was tolerated because to be a member of the State Assembly carries high prestige, but similar exposure in the midst of the village folk at the relatively low prestige level of a school teacher was clearly undesirable".

Izzar is best promoted by broadly based, desirable achievements, such as tangible wealth, unimpeachable piety, success in competition, the besting of one's enemies, the retention of followers and dependents, the skillful managing of allies, the tactful distribution of gifts and, critically the conduct of the women of the family. Local public opinion is the gauge of family's izzat. It is the general perception of a family's worth held by kinsmen, neighbours, and others in its social networks. That opinion is rarely unanimous in judgment, is often volatile in ratings, usually varies among local groups but it is nonetheless a force that affects much of a person's and family's striving.

A person and a family who gain high izzat in their community thereby command influence there. Thus, izzat is a symbolic summary of past achievements and a main element in present power. Power, properly deployed, enhances izzat: izzat legitimates power. While the family is the primary vessel of izzat, broader groups are also involved. An individual's serious failing may tarnish, or a notable achievement burnish, the izzat of all in the lineage, jati or village. These are the wider circles with which a person identifies or is identified, in which he or she actually participates or may potentially participate. A person's grand achievements are likely to be paraded by members of his or her wider groups to enhance their own izzat.

Another dimension of izzat is more internal to the individual Clues to it emerge when a man talks about how he has made (or will make) a good name for himself that will be long remembered. And a villager's typical desire to have several sons who are strong, good and grown, stems not only from the material and political benefits they bring to him but also from the satisfaction of knowing that his name and the memory of him will last for at least another generation after his demise. So a man's drive to achieve a good name and a high degree of izzat is also a means of coping with the thoughts of one's passing. Together with religious acts, it is a way of overcoming oblivion, of defeating death.

The achievements open to a women are mainly in raising a large set of vigorous, united, dutiful, children. In earlier times, a Hindu widow of some castes who committed sati, self-immolation on the funeral pyre of her husband, elevated the izzat of her family and lineage. A Muslim woman who, in the company of husband or son, completed the then perilous pilgrimage to Mecca, accrued a woman who, say, ears a medical degree or wins a post in the higher echelons of government service.

Izzat also devolves from distinguished ancestry. But if those who claim ancestral glories are to benefit, they must live up to them. If a group's inherited izzat is to count for much on the ground, its members must strive to uphold it. Izzat does not keep well; it has to be continually reaffirmed in practice, reinforced in action, defended against challenge, and rewon and advanced in competition. Ancestral memories are predominantly about males, and genealogy is usually reckoned through males only. Yet family izzat is not only pivotally dependent on the conduct of the wives, but also that izzat is inevitably tested when the marriage of a daughter is arranged.

In negotiating a marriage, each side carefully considers the izzat of the other family, the amount of the dowry and other material transactions, as well as the personal qualities of the prospective spouse. Each family ponders on how these ratings will affect their own standing and so influence the prospects of any unmarried daughters and sons. Among Hindus, the family that gives the bride is the defined inferior in the transaction; a bridegroom can be married to a spouse of somewhat lower standing than his without loss of family face. Not so for the bride and her family. They must, to preserve or increase family izzat, secure a bridegroom of as high a personal and family position, within the caste span of possible spouses, as their own resources and reputation can provide.

Each of the families linked by the transfer of a daughter and the acquisition of a bride expects to gain from the affiliation and usually does. Each tends to support the other in political and material ways unless contrary circumstances arise. Thus, if a Bangladesh villager is to enhance his ijjat (the Bengali word for izzat), "it is required for him to have a network of ... powerful affinal relatives". Among Jat Sikh families on the other side of the subcontinent, the ties formed through a marriage "connected families otherwise isolated and placed a whole network of links at the disposal of each of the members".

A brother who gives freely and lavishly to a married sister and her children gains in local esteem. Gift-giving is, in general, an important means of accruing izzat, especially when the gifts are made generously, judiciously and publicly. Those to a married sister and her children are among the more meritious of presentations.Izzat is mainly positive in connotation; it embraces what a man should do if he can. Purdah is more negative, it covers what a woman might do but should not. There is some feedback between a family's izzat and its purdah practices. The practices, properly done, enhance the izzat. The izzat, to be property maintained, requires unfailing purdah observance. So purdah strengthens izzat as izzat strengthens purdah.

Within these broad patterns of purdah there are regular variations. One variation is by age, another by linguistic-cultural region, a third by economic class and educational level.

Age is always a factor because purdah is a cultural attribute of women rather than of females. Before her puberty, a girl does not have to guard her movements and signal her deference as she does after puberty. True, she is taught from early childhood that she must sit differently, behave differently, carry different responsibilities than do the boys, but a Muslim girl does not assume the full mangle of purdah until she is nubile, and a Hindu girl not until she is married.

Later in her life and particularly as she becomes busy with caring for her growing children, she can gradually ease the stringency of some of the purdah practices she should follow as a young wife. She begins to move about outside more, perhaps to do a bit of shopping or expand her visits to women of other households. As an elder matron, she can have still more leeway. But, as we have noted, some proprieties are not abandoned. Even an elderly matron will cover her face and fall silent before her husband's father so long as they both shall live. Nor does passing through her menopause permit a women to pass insouciantly through town and village streets.

Purdah practices also vary by linguistic-cultural region. Ahmad points out how Muslim as well as Hindu family and kinship relations differ in different "regional cultural environments". For the Punjab, Joyce Pettigrew notes that Punjabi-speaking Sikhs, Hindus and Muslims have quite similar cultures in fundamental respects, including relations between the sexes. The Punjab and the other regions of the subcontinent are better defined in terms of core social-cultural and linguistic characteristics than by neatly drawn map perimeters that demarcate what are usually mixed, transitional border territories.

There are gradients by region in the strength of the purdah-izzat complex. It is upheld most stringently and zealously among the peoples of the northwestern sector of the subcontinent, through the middle Ganges basin and Bangladesh. The purdah zone thus comprises all of Pakistan and Bangladesh, plus the Indian states (each roughly a linguistic-cultural region) of Punjab, Rajasthan, Haryana, Uttar Pradesh, together with adjoining parts of Madhya Pradesh, Kashmir and Himachal Pradesh. Purdah is much less compelling among Hindus of Bihar and West Bengal but is strongly sustained among Bangladeshis. It is given greatest weight among those Hindus who are most dedicated to the Rajput-Kshatriya model. By contrast, those Hindus who follow the Brahmanic model of eternal vigilance about ritual purity and pollution are generally less worried about the danger to men's honor and the disruption of men's polity by women. There is much less veiling and less rigid seclusion among the Dravidian-speaking peoples of the south. Not that the relations between men and women in South India are utterly different from those in the north, rather that the emphases are differently placed, fears and rectitude differently arranged.

This is well shown in Pauline Kolenda's comparison of wedding rites that she has observed among Hindu villagers of the north and of the south of India. In the northern village of Khalapur, north of Delhi in Uttar Pradesh, she studied the Rajputs, the dominant caste in the village. The other village group is that of the Nattati of Kanyakumari District in southernmost Tamil Nadu.

Weddings present particularly good avenues for the study of gender relations, all the more so in South Asia where weddings are of great social and personal concern. Kolenda finds structural similarity in both sets of rites and suggests that the similarity stems from a common base in Sanskritic rites prescribed in Hindu scriptures.

There are also fundamental differences between the two which reflect divergent images of man, woman and family.

While the analysis is focused on the comparison between the Rajputs and Nadars of the respective localities, Kolenda indicates that the differences between them represent, at many points, the general differences in gender relations as between the Dravidian south and north of India. Among the Rajputs, a bride is given as tribute by a subordinate family to a superior one. The act of being bride-givers makes the one family *ipso facto* the inferior of the family that receives the bride. That formal inferiority is made manifest through the wedding ritual and long after, when the women's family is obliged to make periodic gifts to the husband and his family. The bride-receivers are under no obligation to reciprocate.

The Rajpur wedding ceremony includes several dramatizations of antagonism between the two families and the trauma of separation felt by the bride and her family. The Nadar rites invoke no such antagonism or trauma, their emphasis is instead on easing the new union and fostering the fertility, the "blossoming" of the woman. Thus, at one juncture in the ceremony, the Rajput bridegroom is "teased unmercifully" by the bride's female relatives but a Nadar groom at a similar juncture is "treated respectfully and affectionately" by female kin of the bride.

When a Rajput bride leaves the house to be taken to her new household, she weeps copiously, with both ritual and real sorrow. The women of her natal family weep and wail with her. Such weeping is repeated whenever her brother or father comes to escort her back to her childhood home. Arriving there, "she weeps ritually on her mother's shoulder, chanting the misery of her separation and recalling their mutual sorrows". No such display of sorrow is required of a Nadar woman.

When the Rajput bride arrives at her husband's home, the sisters of the bridegroom bar her entrance. The groom then presents each of them with a gift, buying off their opposition as it were, and the bride is then permitted to enter. Among the Nadar, the sisters of the groom, far from opposing the bride's coming play an important part in the formal welcoming and preparation of the bride. They help place the tali around the bride's neck, it is the prime material symbol of the union.

In both communities, a girl is given a series of pre-nuptial baths. The Nadar explain this as a special cleansing of her menstrual pollution. The Rajputs say that these baths symbolically terminate the bride's virginity as necessary preparation for the physical termination to follow. Pollution and purity are subsidiary matters in the Rajput rites, cardinal considerations for the Nadar. Jawaharlal Nehru once told how surprised he had been by the response of Indian women in 1930 to Gandhi's call for the Civil Disobedience Movement. "I think that the most important and significant feature of that movement was the tremendous part that the women of India took in it. It was astounding".

He succinctly stated his views on the status of Indian women in a speech he gave in 1949. "I am quite convinced that in India today progress can be and should be measured by the progress of the women of India". In ascribing such importance to women's status and conduct, Nehru was in agreement with traditionalist Indian Muslims and Hindus. Though they might disagree with every other aspect of Nehru's ideas about women, most of them would concur that the status women is of great concern to each man and to all of society.

Nehru's astonishment at the staunch uprising of many women at Gandhi's call is more akin to the surprise expressed by Western observers when they find that demure and self-effacing Indian women may, in certain life situations and at certain historical junctures, take decisive action with spirit and determination. Indian men are usually not quite so surprised on such occasions. Nehru was speaking of all of India. Our inquiry here is primarily concerned with the people of the north of the subcontinent among whom the separation between women and men tends to be more marked than it is along those in other parts of South Asia.

Women veil and seclude themselves before men through the large part of South Asia that includes Pakistan, northern India through Uttar Pradesh and Bangladesh. They do so before certain kinds of men and not before others, in given social situations and not in others, and as one expression of a more general mode of conduct in which a women's behaviour directly affects the personal and family honor of the men closest to her. These men believe their honor and the linked demeanor of the women to be of central importance in their lives.

The most common term for these practices is purdah ("curtain," purda in Hindi and urdu). The term has been used narrowly, for specific traits of physical covering and spatng enclosure, but we here take the broader usage, which also includes the beliefs and values about the behaviour of women, the restrictions on their movements outside the household and the requirements for their respectful and deferential demeanor within the home. Purdah is maintained by most peoples in regions of the northern tier of the subcontinent, the basins of the Indus and Ganges rivers.

Among them, purdah is a constant element of everyday life; it symbolizes some fundamental values, it influences other parts of their cultures, it has important consequences for personality, economy and society. A sketch of so important a feature in the lives of so large a part of the world's population must necessarily be done in broad strokes, emphasizing the general similarities rather than the myriad differences in detail.

These regions are here called the purdah regions. While there is much social and cultural differences between, say, Hindu or Sikh Punjabis and Muslims Bangladeshis, and the staple crop is wheat for the former and rice for the latter, it is useful to refer to both as being among the peoples of the purdah regions. The term purdah zone is similarly used here to include those regions of the northern parts of the subcontinent (except for Bihar and West Bengal) where purdah practices are taken to be central elements of social life. There is no abrupt shift from a purdah to a non-purdah region, but rather a gradual transition through the intervening regions to the quite different gender relations of South India.

A family can properly practice purdah, as propriety is defined in its locality, only if its members can afford to do so. Those who must worry about their daily food (a large part of the population of the purdah zone) cannot support the full seclusion of women. But those of the poor who prosper commonly adopt more stringent seclusion. In addition to this basic difference by economic class, purdah is carried on in two principal versions, one Hindu (and Sikh), the other Muslim. We first examine the elements common to both, then consider the differences between them.

The common features, including factors of personality and socialization, are then reviewed in the broadest perspectives of time and space, in terms of cultural evolution and would area comparisons. The area of particular relevance, the Middle East (including North Africa), is given separate review. Traditional purdah concepts and customs are still maintained among most peoples of the northern subcontinent. But these ideas and practices are everywhere being challenged by people's experiencing of modern influences. We will make some assessment of the contested and evolving responses, especially in urban and educated families, where the changes are most pronounced.

Veiling by women is so frequent, common place, and reflexive an action that it is scarcely noticed among these peoples unless it is not promptly and properly forthcoming. But when an English anthropologist, Ursula M. Sharma, came to study the people of a village in Himachal Pradesh, the practice struck her as "most alien and curious." She writes, "I found it disturbing when an informal conversation with a group of women was interrupted and my companions would veil themselves and become silent and restrained as an older man passed by the courtyard where we were sitting".

These were Hindu women; Muslim women also veil before senior men of the family. A woman quickly covers her head at the approach of an older man of her husband's family, using either the end of her sari or the separate head scarf, dupata in Hindi, to do so. She draws the edge of the cloth across her face so that only her eyes are uncovered, or pulls the headcloth forward in a cowl from which she can peer out. The gesture is but one feature of the mandatory code for a woman's conduct which requires that she behave modestly, restrained in speech, restricted in movement. She must observe, as Sylvia Vatuk puts it, "shyness of demeanor, avoidance of eye-contact with males, avoidance of loud speech and laughter (particularly in the presence of or within earshot of males), and the limitation of conversation with non-family males to necessary work-connected topics."

A woman rises or shows other signs of respect within her home before male visitors as well as to older men of the family. If she is unavoidably in the presence of a conversation among men, she should not actively participate, and if she does speak she should cover her mouth with hand or cloth. Far more than for a man, a woman's conduct, especially in traditional and rural settings, is expected to be constrained and, with relatively few exceptions, to be so in practice both inside the home and out.

Within the household, men and women often live, for the greater part, in separate places. They sleep in separate rooms or on separate sides of a hut; they relieve themselves in separate fields or locations; they sit apart at all social or religious occasions. Men spend most of their time in their own quarters, which may be a separate structure or platform, an outer room, a veranda, or, among the poor, just a cot set outside the house. There the men talk, smoke, work, lounge, entertain and sleep; there a woman rarely sets foot.

The women of the household remain apart in a courtyard or inner room where they carry on domestic and child-rearing tasks and in general spend most of their lives. Into these precincts a man of the family comes to take his meals, to do necessary chores, to exchange communications, and to share a bed briefly and quietly in the still of the night.

Overt time, a woman modifies some of her behaviour showing respect. When she comes into her husband's parental family as a bride, she must be most diffident, shy, and self-effacing, quite un-like her far freer demeanor as daughter in her own parents' house. She keeps her gaze lowered, her voice still, her features covered and her whole presence unobtrusive. She may even veil herself before her mother-in-law and perhaps her husband's brother's wives. After a period of days or months, she begins to emerge from the bridal shell. After she has borne a child, she is likely to reduce some of her veiling, such as veiling before her mother-in-law.

A young wife must appear completely uninterested toward her husband when they are in the presence of others. She must veil before him, and must not speak to him directly or even look steadily at him. A young couple must remain aloof from one another in public, and avoid direct communication until they can manage to be alone. Only when couples become more senior in the family do they relax restraint between themselves in public.

One relationship is relatively easy from the start—that between a wife and her husband's younger brothers. There is usually a casual joking relationship between them, and even newlywed wives can appear barefaced before these younger brothers.

In sharp contrast, a woman should never stop sending signals of deference and respect before her father-in-law and her husband's elder brothers. Neither the passage of time nor the patina of familiarity should be allowed to blur these symbolic statements. A woman makes these gestures not only before the senior males of her married home, but also typically before the senior males of that whole village. Kinship terms are commonly used among fellow villagers of all groups. Even a man of lower caste-rank than hers may be called, through fictive extension, by the term for a husband's older brother. And a woman will veil before him as she does before the actual kinsman. Since there are many such elders, a daughter-in-law usually veils whenever she goes out of her house.

Senior men, in turn, bear responsibility to keep their distance. If they have to enter the women's place, they usually announce themselves with a warning cough or some other signal. Messages to women are commonly carried in by children so that the courtyard need not be immobilized by the entrance of an elder male. About Muslim men in Delhi, Cora Vreede-de Stuers noted, "Curiously enough, I had more the impression that the men were excluded than that the women were secluded".

Women do not encourage the men of the family to linker in their space. It conveniences them and discomforts any women who may come to visit. Outside her household, a woman's movements are restricted in distance, duration and purpose. She should not venture out alone beyond the immediate vicinity of her home. She should not go beyond the village or town limits except for purposes approved by family elders and then preferably accompanied by a male kinsman. Woman who must go out to work in the fields cannot be as closely circumscribed as those who do not. Work groups can include both men and women, but a woman labourer will be reprimanded if she strays out of the circuit of work and home neighbourhood. In the fields she is likely to pull a cloth across her face in the event she might see an elder male approaching. Some household tasks, such as shopping, are often done by the men (or by servants in wealthier families), but may also be done by the women of a household. Such tasks should be carried out expeditiously, with as little tarrying as possible.

Sometimes a young wife is not allowed by her mother-in-law or husband to visit other homes. In his autobiography, Gandhi tells how as a young husband he insisted that his wife should not go out anywhere without his permission. Doranne Jacobson gives an extreme example of a Muslim woman in a Madhya Pradesh village whose sister lived close by in a neighbouring house, but the two women were never allowed to visit one another, because their husbands insisted that they remain strictly secluded within their own homes. Some women take pride in their close confines. Ursula Sharma mentions a Hindu woman of a village in Himachal Pradesh who told her that she hardly ever stirred beyond her four walls. "Later I realized that it had been said in a spirit of pride. She did not need to stir beyond her four walls".

In religion, women have small part to play in events that are societal, transcendental, or public. They do perform major roles in domestic rites and conduct those ceremonies that are only for women. In some regions, certain women, usually from the lower-ranking groups, can become possessed and may act as shamans, but there is no claim that these performances have much to do with supernal forces of the high religion.

Women not only should avoid places where men congregate, they should also shun spaces where few or no people are. When a group of women cross wastelands or woods, they tend to quicken their pace lest they attract the attention of male strangers in places where, in case of attack, their cries might go unheard. Women's participation in secular public affairs is minimal. Many women now vote, exceedingly few, except for highly educated women, ever speak to public occasions. There are exceptions, and even in villages, voices in a higher register are beginning to be heard at local meetings, especially from women who hold official seats. Women's absence from or silence at such meetings is still the rule, however

There are marked differences, as we shall discuss later, between a young woman's tightly controlled conduct as a daughter-in-law in the village into which she has married, and her easier, unveiled behaviour in the village where she was raised and where she is always considered one of the daughters of the village. A Hindu bride in these regions must be married out of her childhood village. This is not necessarily so among Muslims; a Muslim bride who is married within the village does not undergo quite so dramatic a shift in her conduct.

In settings where a woman's conjugal family is not known and so its reputation is not so directly at stake, a woman can afford to be somewhat freer in her conduct. "When one is not in one's own place (apni jageh) one's neighbours do not have the same power to sanction." In towns, Ursula Sharma adds, there is enough anonymity about public places to make women more willing to venture into them if they have some business or purpose there. But in all outside places a woman must take care to keep herself guardedly aloof from contacts with men.

Sanctions on wayward behaviour, real or alleged, can be severe. Neighbours' gossip about an unmarried girl may undermine her chances for a worthy marriage. A husband who suspects that his wife's conduct has damaged his and his family's honour may beat her. He may also refuse to allow her to visit her parents' home, a considerable penalty on a young wife. Perhaps worse, he may send her there and refuse to take her back. There she will languish, neither maid nor wife, until her natal kin can negotiate a resolution.

Muslim husbands can divorce a wife in the simple way prescribed by Muslim law, although the incidence is not as common as the case of securing it might suggest. A disgruntled Hindu husband generally accomplishes the same purpose without any legal ado.

A woman's daily guidance and reproofs come from the senior women of her family, particularly from her mother-in-law. When, in her turn, she becomes a mother in lay, it is her obligation to see to it that her daughter-in-law maintains the rules and niceties of the kind of purdah that is proper to the family's status, wealth and aspirations. Why then must a woman send forth, within her own household, an unremitting stream of signals, day-long, life-long, affirming her subordination, restating her modesty? Why must she curtail her movements beyond her threshold, take care not to be alone abroad, avoid direct eye contact with men or any implication of inviting cordial personal relations?

The answers come readily from the women and men even though this behaviour is for the vast majority of women, part of the given circumstances of their lives. Given, but not unchallenged. They are aware of challenges from various sources, from youngsters who must be properly socialized, from the example of the occasional village woman who, because of personality or circumstance, flouts some of the purdah rules, and from the implicity defy posed by those women, usually well-educated and Western-influenced, who talk freely about the streets with no more shield than a confident air and a pair of sunglasses.

Two kinds of answers are forthcoming, one about the dangers to a women outside her home, another about the dangers from women inside their households. The contrast between outside and inside is a basic one. The title of a novel by Tagore (made into a film directed by Satyajit Ray), Ghare Baire, "in the house and outside" (The Home and the World is the English title), is a common and key Bengali phrase. Within her home, as Mary Beech notes for Bengal, a woman enjoys shelter, while "outside there is a lack of protection, a sense of potential danger, an insecurity. One takes risks in going outside".

Women are not expected to be able to cope with the exigencies of the outside world. The prime danger is from male strangers who are seen as liable to take advantage of an unescorted woman. Such strangers, as a category, are presumed to be sexually predatory and always ready to pounce. Some young men (and some not so young) reinforce that notion in town streets and in buses through the common practice known in Indian English as "eve-teasing."

In the anonymity of the streets, some men who would spring fiercely to the defense of the women of their own families, leer, hoot, pinch and make sexually pointed remarks at passing women whom they do not know and who do not know them. However, they rarely act that way in their own mohalla, neighbourhood. Assaults on women and rapes do indeed occur, perhaps as often in some places as in some Western societies.

But in these lands, the dangers to women have heightened consequences. Women are viewed by men and view themselves as physically weak, perhaps sensually willing, certainly exceedingly vulnerable. A woman alone is unable, so it is thought, to withstand a stranger's sexual demand not only because he is generally bigger and stronger but also because her stringent training to be submissive makes her submit in these straits. Moreover, both women and men, especially when young, are considered to have uncertain control of their sex drives; people tend to suspect that assaulted women may, wittingly or unwittingly, have led a man on.

If a woman does have an illicit sex encounter, whether by force or consent, and it becomes known, the shame may well blight the rest of her life. Village gossip frequently buzzes with rumors of illicit liaisons. But when clear evidence becomes public knowledge, hard sanctions often ensue. In extreme cases, an unmarried, pregnant girl may be killed by her own father or brothers. An errant wife may be driven out of her husband's family, forever separated from her children. Others also incur grievous hurt by her default, be it voluntary or involuntary. The shame falls not only on the hapless woman. Her husband and all in his family suffer grave dishonor.

To fend off such consequences women are kept and keep themselves guarded in movement and manner when they venture outdoors. As for the display of deference and avoidance inside the household, the reasons given are phrased as the need to show respect within the family, and as the need to preserve the solidarity of the family. Both explanations simply a certain danger from the women, both have to do with domestic power and politics perhaps more than with concern about extramarital sex within the joint family.

The myriad face-veilings and head-coverings before affinal kinsmen are made and received as signs of respect. They are acknowledgements of the right of the receiver to superior status and to priority of consideration. They connote acceptance by the sender of her subordinate role. In the instant of response a woman does not ponder the meanings of her reflexive reaction when, say, her father-in-law comes into the room. But loud the lengthy excoriations about any lack of proper response will be directed by a mother-in-law to a negligent young daughter-in-law. Signals of respect are common in most face-to-face encounters. Thus, a grown man may snuff out his cigarette in the presence of his father lest such self-indulgence be taken as lack of proper consideration of the father's status. A younger brother usually defers to his older brother in public even though the show may be quite cosmetic. It is as though people need to elicit the endless streams of respect signals because they see their societies as being innately and rightly hierarchical but with every particular hierarchy in need of active reaffirmation.

Muslim scripture decrees equality within the brotherhood of Islam. While Muslim women have important scriptural rights and equal opportunity for salvation, there is no more idea in Islam of complete social equality between the sexes than there has been in other world religions. Muslims, in these regions, like others of the Indian cultural sphere, share the assumption that hierarchy pervades gender as well as most social relations. So among all religious groupings, in all sectors and levels, most social encounters are presumed to be between a superior and a subordinate.

Yet the balance of hierarchy is felt to be precarious, especially between those who are close in rank. It is so within a family as among the groups of a locality, because people believe that those who are inferior in a given exchange will press to alter their lower positions if and when they can. Hence expressions of general respect and specific deference are required at every sensitive point and moment.

So respect displays are flashed in many social contexts. They take on particular importance within a joint family because family elders tend to view an incoming bride as a potential threat to family solidarity. A bride comes to live with her husband in his parental household together with his brothers, their wives and children, and the unmarried daughters. Almost all village and many town couples live with the husband's parents, at least for a time. In some groups it is for only a few months, in other classes and castes for the lifetime of the husband's father and sometimes beyond.

In the everyday interactions of family life, a women defers to the en in many formal ways. At meals, a woman eats only after the men have been served. When a wife walks with her husband she follows a few steps behind him. Nazmul Karim writes of his Bengali Muslim community in his parent's generation that "in order to inculcate the habit of obedience a female newcomer (a new bride) was taught to salute her husband by touching his feet every morning before he went to work". Karim implies that this is no longer done in his community. It is not obsolete in other communities across these regions. Those wives who still make this ritual gesture would scarcely agree that it is enforced upon them but rather that they do it as an affirmation of respect, devotion, family harmony.

Panctilious deference by junior wives is considered to be essential in a joint family where several couples must live close together with enough accord to function as a family. Hindu brides of these regions come in as strangers from another village. Each has her own interests and loyalties, so to her own natal kin, that are not those of her conjugal family. Muslim brides are not necessarily strangers, but both Muslim and Hindu family elders tend to be skittish about signs of rift among the sons. They are likely to attribute family discord and difficulties to disruptive pressures from the wives. To avert such separatist tendencies, a wife is required to keep at some social distance from her husband and children in the presence of others. Among Rajputs of a village in western Uttar Pradesh, "covering the face in the presence of one's husband is also a sign of respect for his mother, another of the customs designed to protect the mother-son relationship from being threatened by a son's attachment to his wife".

In the Madhya Pradesh village studied by Doranne Jacobson, a man should avoid fondling or carrying his own child in the presence of his elders. A woman also feels embarrassed to give obvious affection to her own children in full family view, although both men and women feel no shyness about playing with the children of others in the family. "Thus, the special kind of interest and affection which might otherwise grow between a man, his wife and children are subordinated in order to permit close ties to develop between members of different nuclear units within the larger family".

Respect-avoidance is also supposed to avert improper sexual attraction. "Presumably brothers are less likely to lust after each other's wives if the latter's charms are concealed from them". This explanation does not tell why a woman may appear unveiled before her husband's younger brothers. One reason may lie in the greater power and authority attributed to an elder brother. Should an elder brother make sexual advances to a younger brother's wife, it might put the younger brother in so intractable a bind between his differing obligations as husband and as junior brother that he would separate from the joint family. But if an elder brother objects to an overly warm relationship between his wife and his younger brother, he can, presumably, scotch it promptly.

In some caste groups of North India, sexual liaison between a woman and her husband's younger brother are considered to be good for the family and to provide no cause for objection by the husband. If the husband should die, the explanation runs, the younger brother will already have emotional links to the widow and so will readily take responsibility for her and her children.

The ideal of a large, harmonious, cooperative joint family is much cherished, but such families are known to be difficult to maintain and destined eventually to disintegrate. People prize the ideal for solid practical reasons. The most prosperous, socially successful, secure, admired families are apt to be joint. Jazmul Karim recalls that his father often held up to his children the example of a large Hindu joint family in a neighbouring locality in Bengal. As many as forty took their meals together, it had more than a dozen university graduates, and its children excelled in curricular and extra-curricular activities. "My father used to say that the progress of that family had been assured by cooperation and joint action. ...If the members of his family worked on the same principle, his family also would be as renowned as the Dattapata family". These were "progressive" townspeople, landowners and civil servants, Muslims and Hindus. The same esteem for the joint family still prevails among many villagers and some urban families. For them, jointness is the precursor of prosperity and power.

Close cooperation among grown brothers living in one household is, to begin with, economically rewarding. Cultivators in a joint family can divide tasks more efficiently, mobilize hands when needed, manage household costs more cheaply, negotiate better with local authorities, take over for a sick or disabled member and work the unfragmented family lands as a team. With the gains of their joint efforts, they are better able to acquire improved implements and, possibly, more land, to boost their wealth and status. Moreover, village society is commonly highly competitive, violence not for offstage. A man's strength is enhanced if he is one of a band of brothers in a joint family.

That concerted strength can be projected politically, or physically if need be, in the common struggles among village factions. With augmented wealth and power, a family can raise its social rank, particularly through arranging prestigious marriages for its daughters.

But people also know well how difficult it is to attain and to maintain the advantages that come from living in a strong joint family. When brothers threaten to part, they are typically beseeched by their best-loved kin, by caste and village elders, to remain as one household. Yet centrifugal forces eventually prevail; the family separates; the possessions are divided. This occurs either during the waning of the father's command or not many years after his death. Blame for the separation is usually put on the wives of the brothers. Commonly enough, relations among the brothers have also become quite brittle, but the male bond seems to be too precious and too tenuous to be so impugned. The inclination to separate is usually pushed along by the changing relations between husband and wife. Despite the culturally constructed barricades between them, despite the lack of pillow talk, and the dearth of opportunities for confidences, the two characteristically grow together in affection and personal intimacy as the years pass. One need only see a wife bringing the mid-day meal to her husband working in the fields, watch them sitting together, or overhear them talking cozily about the day's events to know that they have surmounted the barricades and have created their private togetherness apart from the commonality of the joint family. As the bonds between husband and wife strengthen, those between brother and brother tend to weaken. It is not so much that one causes the other as that there is a sharpening of a built-in contradiction. Brothers are both equal and unequal. They are unequal as elder and younger, but are equal in that each gets his equal share by Hindu law and South Asian Muslim tradition when they divide the joint family property.

Further, many men are restive as subordinates in fraternal relationship. Though all share the belief that most human relations are hierarchical, each wants to take the dominant part in his own close encounters when he senses that he can do so. As a younger brother gains some social standing on his own, he tends to feel himself to be more of an equal partner in the family enterprise. So an elder brother typically comes to find the younger increasingly willful and the younger finds the elder overbearingly domineering.

At this juncture each brother is likely also to take his wife's complains more seriously than before. Many men feel caught in an uncomfortable bind, entangled in the tension between mother and wife. Subordinate though she is formally, his wife usually manages to let him now that she is being treated unfairly. She does not challenge the requirements for her role. What a daughter-in-law commonly does challenge are the unjust burdens and slights that she feels others in the joint family are placed on her.

So eventually the husband decides to split; about the time he does, his brothers may well be of a similar mind. In poor, landless families, this entails only the simple division of family effects and moving out. It is likely to occur not long after a bride has been brought in, perhaps while other brothers are still unmarried.

But in families with land and valuables, the brothers must take the necessary legal steps to divide their common property. House, land, implements, and utensils, down to the last bag of salt, are apportioned. Each brother then lives separately with his wife and children; the cycle of family development begins a new. A nuclear family becomes joint when a son marries and brings his bride into the household. With her coming, the choreography of distancing by a daughter-in-law begins again, part etiquette, part ritual, and part defense and self-defense.

Wives are thus seen as both guarantors and disrupters of family and patrilineage. Their fertility produces the blessings of children and the blessed continuity of patriline. But fertility has to be decoupled from sex. A women's sexuality is suspect because, for one reason, it may be a means by which she can entice her husband away from unswerving allegiance to parents and brothers. The potential of sex to impart shame is abated by such devices as the separateness of wife and husband in public and by the hurried, almost clandestine visitations for intercourse. Female sexuality also involves menstruation, a pollutant state (as childbirth is also) during which a woman must observe an intensified degree of seclusion so as to shelf others from the ritual dangers of contact with her. Older women may wield much influence, as mothers and mothers-in-law, in their family's business affairs and sometimes even in their community's decisions. But they rarely exert that influence openly, publicly, or directly. Occasionally, men do acknowledge the realities of a senior woman's political capacity, as is testified by the examples of eminent women leaders from the Rani of Jhansi to Indira Gandhi.

While people readily tell that restraints on women serve to protect the women outside the home and to protect family cohesion within it, both functions also protect the men. A man, too, is socially vulnerable. Should a woman of his family be degraded by outsiders, he feels himself disgraced, his honor defiled. Should his joint family come under scorn as an arena of female discord and discredit, he and his close kinsmen feel under contempt and honour diminished. An ambitious man strives to build his honour through industry, loyalty, duty, judgment and craft. However successful he may be in this, a critical cachet of his achievement is won through the marriage of his daughters into suitably high-ranking families.

Marriage System for the Muslims

Temporary marriage follows a practice said to have been common in Arabia ever before Islam, when a special class of women was kept from this purpose. It received the name Mutaa, meaning 'Pittance', because the man gave the woman a gift "either in cash or kind." Before the Hijart (migration of the Holy Prophet from Mecca to Medina to Medina) it was not countenanced by the Holy Prophet or his companions. But conditions changed with life at Medina, where there were frequent military expeditions when men left their wives at home, writes Abdulla Ibn Masud. "We respected (to the Holy Prophet) whether we should emasculate ourselves. He prevented us from this (course) and then permitted us to resort to Mutaa...Some of us used to marry a woman for a specified time by giving her a piece of cloth."

Mutaa marriage is sanctioned by the Quran in verse 24, Surah IV, Para V reading "...and all (women) besides these are made lawful for you, provided that you seek (them) with your property, marrying (them) without committing fornication there as to thereby (marrying) whom you profit, give them their statutory gifts, and their is no blame on you about what you mutually agree after that which is stipulated."

Thus Mutaa is as temporary form of marriage in which the man stipulates that he would keep the woman as his wife or a stated period only, after which the marriage is dissolved *ipso facto*. The parties do not inherit anything from each other. This is in force among the Shias. The Sunnis hold it to be unlawful, largely on account of Caliph Umar's prohibition, excepting the small sect called Malkis. Mutaa is not compulsory; it is only a provision in case of necessity.

"In the technical language of Islamic Law, Mutaa is a contract of Nikah for an agreed period in consideration of an agreed dower (Maher) payable by the husband to the wife. It is not Safah (the mere satisfaction of the sex urge) but a form of Ihsan which literally means fortification in the sense that the women thus married to a particular man cannot legally (for the time) enter into sexual relationship with any other man; the children are entitled to the same rights of inheritance and social status as the children of a Nikah."

Hence it may be affirmed that Mutaa resembles Nikah in all the essential features except that it is of a temporary nature.

The Shia law recognizes two kinds of marriage namely (1) Nikah (Permanent) and (2) Mutaa (temporary).

A Shia male may contract a Mutaa marriage with a woman professing the Mohammadan, Christian, or Jewish religion, or ever with a woman who is a fire-worshipper, but not with a woman following any other religion. A Shia woman cannot contract a Mutaa marriage with a non-Shias. It is essential for the validity of a Mutaa marriage that (1) the period of cohabitation be fixed and this may be a day, a month, a year or a term of years, and (2) that some dower has been fixed, the contract is valid. If the term is fixed but the dower is not specified the contract is void. But if the dower is signified the contract is void. But if the dower is signified and the term is not fixes the contract, though void, may even operate as a permanent marriage.

The Mutaa marriage is subject to four essential conditions which are:

(a) The oral offer and acceptance.

(b) The eligibility of the partners to marry one another.

(c) The fixation of a definite period for conjugal relationship.

(d) The specification and payment of the Mahar (i.e. dower, payable from the man to the woman for such a union).

Its was prevalent during the time of the Holy Prophet and was declared lawful on the occasion of the temporary needs during wars. But it continued even during peace times as stated on the basis of its practical application by the prominent companions of the Holy Prophet. It has even today continued to be a legally accepted from in the Shia community.

So long as the economic condition of Muslims in general, and Shias in particular, was prosperous, those who could afford it used to keep families by Mutaa marriage, but as general economic conditions have changed, people can hardly afford to continue this practice. Respondent's qaum, occupation and age regarding the Mutaa marriages contracted by them have been examined in this connection.

Lastly, why Mutaa is not so common now as before has to be pointed out. Society is a dynamic force and social conditions do not remain the same in all ages. They change from generation to generation under changing conditions of society. Mutaa is not only an enjoyment but also brings certain responsibilities. The greatest responsibility is to maintain the mutaai woman and in these hard days even well-to-do classes sometimes find themselves unable to do so.

On the other hand, the Mutaai woman herself feels that her social status is lower, than that of a Nikahi wife, and this feeling of inferiority generally deters a woman from contracting a Mutaa. Another restraint is the impact of Hindu culture on Muslim culture in India, which prevents a Shia woman from contracting Mutaa marriage.The main justification for the institution of Mutaa rests mainly on religious grounds. The Holy Prophet had declared it and it has continued since then. The main reasons, however, advocated by respondents are that it checks corruption, increases the population, satisfies the excessive sexual urge in a legalised manner and sets are rest the problem of illegitimate children.

Thus, the main aim of a Mutaa marriage is to avoid corruption in society and fulfillment of sexual urges in keeping with law and religion.

So far as the legal aspect is concerned Mutaa seems to be a unique institution, suggested and ratified only by the Holy Prophet of Islam. It is unique in the sense that it allows a contract for a period and for automatic dissolution which is found in no other religion. Although it is not different from permanent marriage in any other sense, the precautions about lineage and sexual fidelity are the same in Mutaa as in Nikah. In Nikah, separation requires divorce but in Mutaa the termination of the stipulated span of time or gifting of the period are sufficient.

Mutaa is not an unrestrained connection without its legalised aspect. In Mutaa a woman has to devote herself wholly and solely to the man for the stipulated period and she is not free during the period to have sexual relation with any other man. She cannot enter into the next Mataa or Nikah without completing the period known as Iddat, which decides the parentage of the child if any, in the women. The issues born of Mutaa have the same right of inheritance as those of Nikah. Temporary marriage has not only been recognized by Islam but has also historically existed in various societies, even in pre-Islamic days and afterwards. "In Japan a girl may be hired for a temporary union, the duration of which is fixed by contract. This union often exists between Europeans and Japanese girls. "In Tibet, temporary marriages are contracted for sex months, one month or a week, perhaps a form of polyandry. Traders form temporary connections with women—a common custom wherever the caravan halts or markets are held."

These are not so different from the Mutaa except that it is not known whether the other obligations such as legitimacy and inheritance for the children are observed in such marriages or not. So Mutaa had not been so methodically legalised in any society as t is under the Shia law. In every country the problem of illicit relations of young people is becoming common. This fact is supported by Bertrand Russel, who says, "In recent years, however, even clergymen have become aware that neither men nor women invariably wait for marriage before experiencing sexual intercourse. Nevertheless, in America, in England, in Germany, in Scandinavia a great change has taken place since the war. Very many girls of respectable families have ceased to think it worth while to preserve their virginity, and young men, instead of finding an outlet with prostitutes have had affairs with girls of the kind whom, if they were richer, they would wish to marry."

Modern statistics reveal that there is a large percentage of illegitimate births due to unrestrained relations between young men and women. These figures of illegitimate children clearly show that there is a good percentage of illegal sexual union prevailing everywhere. These fatherless children create a social problem in every country, for they are not considered eligible for the same status as that of children born of a legal marriage. Such mothers also do not retain an honourable position in society. If such connections were to take place under the legalised from of Mutaa the issues would have also been quite legal and the mothers would have retained their status.

Again the system of modern education stretches over such a long period of life that the young people, although becoming mature, cannot be in a position to contract a permanent marriage. This period is crucial, for during this time biological urges being to operate and young people are very often led to immoral relations, or if they keep themselves celibate, have to suffer in health. In the same way the economic position of some people may not allow them to enter into a permanent marriage. There is also the rush of business travel in the modern age and people have to live away from their homes for long periods. For such people a temporary marriage becomes inevitable. From the statistics of various countries it is found that in some regions women exceed men in number and if each one is allowed only a single marriage a large percentage of women would remain unmarried. Hence this temporary marriage system would distribute those surplus women to get support and satisfaction through temporary marriages. In some countries the number of women is less than that of men and in such a case also the temporary marriage system will give a chance for married life to every male.

According to the findings of judge Ben B. Lindsey, who was for many years in charge of the Juvenile Court for Denver U.S.A., and thus had unrivalled opportunity for going deep into the facts, a new institution which he calls "companionate marriage" was proposed. His view was that "young people should be able to enter upon a new kinds of marriage, distinguished from ordinary marriage by three characteristics.

Firstly, that there should be for the time being no intention of having children and that, accordingly, the best available birth control information should be given to the young couple; secondly, that so long as there are no children and the wife is not pregnant a divorce should be possible by mutual consent and, thirdly, that in the event of a divorce the wife should not be entitled to alimony.

So the Islamic position is more reasonable than Judge Lindsey, who, under the stress of the circumstances and realities of modern life, was led to suggest companionate marriage in the 20th century, while Islam had suggested and legalised it thirteen hundred years earlier. Thus, Mutaa is a unique institution, as proved by the suggestion of the learned judge and further supported by Bertrand Russell, who says, "I have not the faintest doubt that Judgc Lindsey's proposal, if embodied in the law, would have a very beneficent influence, and that this influence would be such as all might agree to be a gain from a moral point of view." In fact, the unique idea of a Mutaa marriage was present in his mind in the solution of present day social evils. It is this uniqueness of the Mutaa marriage which appears desirable to both great thinkers, one of whom has suggested and the other supported a similar system. The greatest merit of Mutaa lies, in fact, in saving the temporary nature of marital ties from the evils of promiscuity in the interest of the progeny by placing paternity beyond dispute. Thus, Mutaa is a unique institution in the Shai religion as it has not been as yet legally recommended and accepted by the world at large, although the sociologists, moralists, philosophers and jurists of today feel the efficacy and thus the necessity of the same as a solution for social disorganization arising out of the sexual urges of man.

Since courtship and dating are alien notions the Shias of this region, settlement remains the only option open for the prospective couples to enter a socially sanctioned wedlock. The procedure of selection of the marriage partners is considered to be the most significant and important factor among Shias; they give every possible attention to this basic point. As described earlier, the marriages are performed generally between 'cousins' but this may not always be possible. In most cases, it is the elderly ladies of the families concerned who take the lead in the matter. They consider it their foremost duty to suggest marriage proposals for marriageable girls and boys. Other members of the family also keep on the lookout for suitable by young people.

The grand parents particularly, taken the greatest care to keep themselves well-informed about suitable boys and girls. When the elderly ladies of the two parties meet at some function or other the opportunity is available of the discuss the possibility of an alliance. As it is a family matter and previously contemplated, both parties give authority an elderly lady who settles a date for a talk between the families. This generally happens when the lead is taken by the elder people of the family.

Another procedure is through interested friends and relatives, especially when a suitable match is not available amongst near-relations. Friends and relatives often suggest the name to the guardians concerned and the process of investigation and settlements starts. In this way common friends and relatives are useful in the process of selection. The third procedure is by ascertaining a suitable match through servants, fruit and sweet vendors, barber's wife and the like who move among several families and are able to render service to various families.

In Western countries the procedure is quite deferent as the selection of mates is to a great extent mutual and direct. Girls as well as boys move freely in society and have opportunities to come into contact with and to get closely acquainted with each other. Co-education, professions and social gatherings, etc., afford favourable occasions. There is no question of the guardians taking the consent of the young people, but it is the young people themselves who inform their guardians of having settled a betrothal.

In present society, though the old role of the parents still prevails under the influence of Western education more and more, it is considered proper to take the consent of friends and cousins. This practice is becoming common.

Amongst Shias, it is considered indecent for a young man to choose a wife directly for himself. If he does so he informs his mother of other near female relatives of his wishes and if the guardians agree, the mother accompanied by some near relatives, calls on the mother of the girls and requests her for a matrimonial alliance. If the proposal is not acceptable to the girls mother, she gives an ambiguous reply, otherwise she consents after consultation with other members of the family. Amongst the Shias generally istikhara (meaning the will of God) is taken, which settles the fate of the alliance. This finally leads to the settlement of the marriage. If the istikhara is in favour, the mother of the girl asks the other party to perform the betrothal formalities.

Initiation of marriage proposal

The initiation of a marriage proposal as such is a very important item for it opens the way to negotiation and settlement. The main initiation starts, no doubt, with the guardians concerned but there are other people also connected with it e.g., relatives, friends and intermediaries. The initiation of a marriage in Western countries is different from ours, as they settle the marriage directly and the initiation is also direct. In India the initiation starts from the side of the girl, amongst the Hindus, but amongst the muslims it always start from the side of the boys.

Thus among the Shias also the marriage proposal is initiated by the guardians of the boy, either through correspondence or personal interview. The right to initiate a marriage by the mates themselves has been sanctioned any Islam. But in India it has become a social custom that usually the boys and girls do not initiate the proposals on their own. It is customary even now for the guardians to initiate the marriage proposals.

There is, however no had and fast rule in the religion as to which party should initiate the proposal, though generally the guardian of the boy take the lead in this respect and it is open to the guardian of the girl to accept of reject the proposal. In some cases it has also been observed that the proposal is not made directly by the guardians but through intermediaries. A marriage proposal from the girls side is considered to be humiliating or indecent and therefore is always avoided. But a change is perceptible in this connection. (During the last decade it has been the tendency of some of the educated and enlightened Shia guardians to take the consent of the mates before the initiation of marriage proposal). Respondents' education and sex and the degree to which they favoured initiation of marriage proposals by boys and girls themselves have been examined in this connection.

Negotiation starts after initiation through intermediaries and friends, and when concurrence has been reached in settlement, they become more and more defined and details are discussed and a day fixed for final settlement. It is the bridegroom's party that takes the initiative and makes the proposal for the marriage, but owing to the impact of Hindu culture and customs and the migration of a large number of suitable Shia young men to outside India, some times the bride's party takes the initiative and makes the proposal for the marriage. Thus the custom as it originally existed has undergone a change owing to the circumstances mentioned above.

As in initiation, so in negotiations, elderly ladies, mutual friends and close relatives play prominent role. Apart from them, a unique personality known as Mushatta was accustomed to play a great role in the marriage negotiations. A Mushatta is a working woman visiting well-to-do families to help young girls to complete their toilet, etc.

Because of their close associations and unchallenged access to different families and mixing with them, they used to gain close and deep knowledge of the status of the different families, the character of the individuals and their behavior. Such Mushattas are practically few now, but in the past amongst the erstwhile Muslim Estates and Zamindaries, they played a great role. They were, however, paid liberal sums as rewards for their services. The following table shows the role played by different people in the marriage negotiations.

On the details of the procedure in negotiations, it is worth mentioning that in some cases the guardians of the bride have been known to ask guardians of the bridegroom to transfer some immovable property such as a house, etc., in the name of bride, so that she becomes the owner of some immovable property from her husband's side.

Another condition which is also imposed in some cases is that the husband should pay Rs. 50 or Rs. 100 (Whatever amount is settled between the parties) as expenses of the pan dan (betel case) to the wife every month. This has nothing to do with other domestic expenses.

Istikhara and Imam-Zamin

Generally, Shias consider the negotiation complete after the ceremony of Istikhara. According to them, it is taking the consent of God for concluding a particular matter. Generally, the Mujtahid (Religious Head) obtain the consent of God with the help of a Tasbih (Rosary) and when the Istikhara is wajib (super affirmative) it is considered that the marriage between the parties should be finally settled.

The mother of the boy or some other near woman relative (if the mother is dead), accompanied by her female friends and relations, pays a visit to the house of the girl with sweets and Imam Zamin to see the girl immediately after Istikhara. The guardians of the girl accept the sweets and entertain them with refreshments.

In most cases the girl is adorned and the women members of the mother of the boy ties the Imam Zamin round the upper portion of the bride's right arm (a silver or gold coin wrapped in a silken cloth). This ceremony is called the Imam Zamin ceremony.

Mangni (Betrothal)

In some of the Shia families there is also the betrothal or mangni ceremony. In this ceremony, the female members of the boy's family visit the house of the girl, taking with them sweets, fruits and vegetables (according to the status of the boy's or girl's family). In some families even five to ten maunds of sweets are taken. The sweets are distributed among the relatives and friends of the girl's family. In return sweets, fruits and vegetables are sent to the boy's house and there also sweets are distributed among the relatives and friends of the boy's family. In some families at the Mangni ceremony, gold or silver rings are also exchanged. After this ceremony the marriage proposal is supposed to be finally settled.

Generally at the time of Imam Zamin or Mangni, the date for the marriage is settled by the guardians of the couple. Among the Shias, marriages mostly take place in the months of Rajah, Shaban, after the tenth of Id-ul-Zuha and the second half of Rabi-ul-Awwal. Moharrum is considered as an inauspicious occasion for marriage because of the tragedy of Karbala which took place in this month. Amongst the Shias the 'mourning period', is observed for 2 months and 8 days i.e., from the 1st. Moharrum upto the 8th of Rabi-ul-Awwal, the day when the female members of the family of the Holy prophet reached Madina after the tragedy of Karbala. Usually marriages do not take place in the month of Ramzan also, because people fast during this month. There are a very few cases in which marriage proposals were broken down after the ceremony of Istikhara.

4

Women in Society

The discrepancy between the "student" and "working woman" roles and the "family roles" of the woman is not caused, as can be seen from the above scale of priorities, by fundamental differences in the role expectations. To a great extent both sets of expectations run parallel to each other. Education is not only considered important for the personality development of a girl but it is at the same time functional for her marriage prospects. One of the most important criteria for the selection of a bride is, as B.V. Shah has found among college students in Gujarat, the education of the bride. In the beginning educational expectations and marriage expectation develop proportionally without conflicting with each other. However, there is a latent conflict in the educational expectation.

Women's education occupies a high position in the value system of the Indian middle classes and has a tendency, as all education in India, to do after the M.A. examination: "Do my Ph.D!" the same is true with regard to professional activities of the women. Many middle class families today expect of their unmarried daughters that they work and support the family. But for many educated Indian girls working is at the same time a means to acquire an independent social status.

We can locate the beginning of the role conflict situation of studying and working Indian women at around the 22nd year of her life. If a woman is still unmarried after this age, then with growing age and rising educational and professional status she is deviating more and more from the culturally prescribed norm of marriage. If she is married, then her extra familial roles come into conflict with the family roles.

Since more and more women are continuing study and work after marriage, as we shall see later, they inevitably land in this conflict situation. The most intense role conflicts of unmarried women will occur between their 25th and 30th years of life.

This individual striving after ever higher educational qualifications and after higher social status can prove to be disruptive to the established family order and lead to tensions between the woman and her main role senders. However, certain conditions must be fulfilled for that:

1. The unmarried woman must have already passed the age considered by society as "correct" marriage age. That is the case generally when she is older than 22 or 23 years.
2. Her educational qualification and social status must be so high that the possibilities of finding a "suitable" husband in the eligible groups are limited, because the woman should not be more educated and have a higher income that the man. This condition is usually fulfilled if the woman continues to study beyond the college level and does M.A., M.Sc,. etc. or Ph.D. and is in a high position. In many communities matriculation secondary school education up to the age of fifteen) is considered to be the optimal education for a girl.
3. The alternative of remaining unmarried is not accepted in the relevant communities and will provoke negative

sanctions. This is true of all Indian communities, even of those who allow women the possibility of religious celibacy like Jains, some Hindu sects, Christians and the Devadasi castes. An independent unmarried woman who is not living in religious celibacy is supposed to be an "immoral" woman and to lower the status of her family. She impairs, for example, the marriage prospects of her sisters and brothers.

For the married woman the variable age does not play a decisive role any more, but educational status and professional status do. If her education of her job position is better than that of her husband, the possibility of role conflicts grows.

In her case are added the contradictory expectations which she faces as housewife and mother on the one hand and as student and working woman on the other. One can imagine that the role conflicts of married women are most intensive in the first years of marriage when the children are small and not yet going to school.

Certain factors favour the deviant behaviour of studying and working women:

(a) In secondary schools and colleges certain political concepts and values derived from Western parliamentarian democracies are taught such as the idea of individual freedom, of equality, of basic human rights etc. At the same time the "traditional" Hindu values regarding the family roles of women are preserved and reinforced at all educational levels.

(b) The high prestige of education undermines the readiness of the family to impose strict sanctions. A father cannot easily marry away his studying daughter against her will, a husband who does not permit his wife to study is criticized.

(c) Many women students (also married ones) live in hostels. This segregation of the two spheres of life—family and studies—favours the develop-ment of deviant ideas and non-conforming behaviour, because "observability is a pre-condition of social control." In the case of working women this observability is reduced due to the separation between the family and the place of work.

(d) The present economic pressures not only induce women to strive for better education at the cost of their family roles but also weaken the readiness of fathers and husbands to insist on a strict fulfillment of these role expectations. Of course, they do pay lip-service to the traditional values but they allow their women in practice a broad margin of deviation. Thus a father of an unmarried studying or working daughter who is older than 25 years is of course unhappy, but he hopes on the other hand, that thus the problem of collecting a dowry for her marriage can be evaded or at least postponed for some time.

Role conflict situation of studying women is part of the modern ideology of progress that woman has the right to education and to equality of opportunity with men. Correspondingly, girls see in education the key to emancipation from many social compulsions. Thus in an investigation made by R. Ferris-Wiesinger among adolescent Hindu girls 34% declared that it is not absolutely necessary for a girl to marry, provided she has an education. The statement of one of the girls illustrates this view: "Now-a-days marriage is not absolutely necessary for a Hindu girl as it was in olden days when women were not educated. Today we can go to work and stand on our own two feet. We can earn and make a name for ourselves. We can remain single, independent and yet be happy."

What is astonishing in this statement is not only that Indian girls look at celibate life as a desirable alternative to marriage, but that they advocate such a life in the name of emancipatory goals. Male and female college students, whom M. Cormack studied also made similar general claims with reference to women's education. 95 per cent of the female students named education as the most important goal for women, and 88 per cent of them as well as 80 per cent of the male students considered education up to the college level as the optimal education for girls.

These general views on women's education and the positive attitude towards women taking to higher studies says, however, little about how this new cultural goal is realised within the existing family structures. Because side by side with this abstract postulate of women's education exists the view among means well as among women that the central function of a woman is her wife a mother role. Thus 90 per cent of the men and 88 per cent of the women students stated that the most important function of a woman is "to be a good wife and mother".

It seems that most of the students covered by this investigation were not at all aware of the incompatibility of their abstract claims with the social reality. According to this general view, women's education and her traditional family roles are easily reconcilable with one other, for education is considered to be functional for these roles.

However, women who have already finished their college education and are looking for employment show a more realistic attitude towards women's education, for they see education already in relation to other expectations of society. They know that education can be both functional and dysfunctional for a woman in the present Indian society. In a study which A. Ramanamma carried out among graduate working women in Poona only 5 per cent of the women advocated post-graduate studies for women, more than half said that women should study up to graduation only. More than a third of these women saw realistically that a woman with a higher education has difficulties in finding a more educated husband than herself and that a marriage in which the man is less educated than the woman is exposed to great stress.

This shows that the new cultural goal of women's education propagated in the name of progress can become within the existing social structure a conflict producing factor. These conflicts are different among married and unmarried women students, but they grow from the same structural roots:

(1) the irreversible and hierarchically defined relationship between husband and wife, according to which the wife should never be older, more educated or in a higher social position than the husband;

(2) the compelling obligation to marry, according to which an unmarried woman has no place in society.

If one compares the data on the expected and the actual marriage age as well as the educational qualification considered optimal for women with their actual educational qualifications, one can conclude that many women know the tensions and fears which result from the fact that they have high educational qualifications but are not yet married. Thus in Ramanamma's study 70 per cent of the women spoke in favour of a marriage before the age of 22, but only 54 per cent of the married women had themselves married before this age, 26 per cent had married only after the age of 25.

All these women were graduates, but only half of them considered graduation as the optimal educational qualification for women. for the unmarried woman who already has a B.A. or B.Sc. degree, is older than 22 or 23 and continues to study, further education has a negative effect on her marriage prospects; she is than in an objective conflict situation, it is immaterial whether she is conscious of it or not. Deviation from the ideal norm of marriageable age and educational qualification of women is perhaps more frequent than many attitude-studies make us believe. The question comes up, why these women, for whom their university degrees constitutes, in combination with advanced age, an obstacle to their marriage prospects, take up further studies and thus impair their marriage prospects still further.

Have these women solved the conflict between marriage and education by deciding in favour of education? Are they not conscious of the negative effects of education on marriage? Are higher studies an evasion of the questions from the family and society, which become ever more pressing? Is physical separation a means to reduce conflicts? Do they hope to ensure through a better educational qualification at least their economic and social status to such an extent that they can live which out a husband in case they do not marry ?

For the time being we must postpone this set of questions; we shall later try to find an answer to these questions through the analysis of individual cases. First we must examine the conflict-generation effect of education in the situation of the married woman.

It has already been pointed out that the higher educational status of the wife compared to that of the husband usually leads to problems in the marriage. That is why such marriages are rate. But the problem comes up also when a wife who has a lower educational qualification than her husband at the time of their marriage later begins to study once more and achieves an educational status higher than that of her husband.

As recent research has shown, marriage is by no means considered the end of the educational career of the middle-class woman in urban centres nowadays. Therefore the probability increases that wives finally become more educated than their husbands. Out of this fact certain tensions and conflicts must arise for the women concerned. N. Desai has examined 369 studying wives in Bombay. 75 of these women were regular students of the SNDT Women's University, 229 were external students of this university, and 65 were regular students of the Bombay University. For comparison and as a complement we shall draw on the results of the already mentioned study of Angara Ramanamma which she made in 1968 among 505 working graduate women of Poona. A. Ramanamma investigated above all the attitudes and problems of working women, but she also studied the educational status of these women.

The family situation has a much more dramatic significance for the studying woman than for the studying men. Her student role is dependent largely on the question whether she is married or not, whether she has children, whether she has taken up the study after a short or long period after marriage, whether she is the eldest or a younger daughter, whether she lives in a joint family or in a nuclear household, whether her family can afford to have enough servants or not.

All these factors of the family situation have a decisive significance for the woman in her student role, apart from the psychological and ideological factors, apart from the question whether the family is conservative or progressive, whether the mother in law is generous or nagging etc. The family situation of a married woman student is defined by the following factors. 1. socio-economic status, 2. type of family, 3. number of children, 4. presence or absence of domestic servants, 5. time lag between marriage and taking up studies.

The family situation of the studying wife depends above all on the economic position of the family. N. Desai has classified her sample in lower, middle and high income categories. The lower income goes up to Rs. 250, the middle income up to Rs. 750 and the higher income from Rs. 750 upwards. She found that only per cent of the women came from families of the lower income group, the majority of families belonged to the middle income group (59 per cent) and 28 per cent came from families of the higher income category, 15 per cent of them even from families with an income over Rs. 1000.

The husbands of these women were mostly employed in white collar professions. More than half of them worked in the services and 24 per cent in academic professions. Only a few were managers or businessmen. None of them was a worker.

The vast majority of the women came from higher castes (80 per cent) and the majority of their husbands were graduates. 22 per cent of the husbands were under-graduates. It is significant to note that these husbands were prepared to allow their wives a higher educational qualification than they themselves had obtained. These were men who mainly needed their wives' income to supplement their family incomes.

Thus the majority of these studying wives came from the educated urban middle class which has so far mainly profited from the educational facilities.

An important criterion for the actual burden of the studying wife is the size of the household. Desai reports that more than half of the examined married students lived in the "pure" type of nuclear household (15.22 per cent) i.e., in families which consisted of husband, wife and their children, 24.66 per cent lived in joint families and 12.2 per cent lived in expanded nuclear families (the couple, children and some relatives of the husband). On the basis of these data Neera Desai comes to the conclusion that the preponderance of the nuclear family type among these students is to be ascribed either to the "dead weight" of the joint family that does not allow married women to take up studies, or that the classical joint family type is becoming rare in the big cities. The data on the household size of the sample give us further information on the work load of the wives. 10 per cent came from 1-2 person households, were therefore widows or recently married women, 59.45 per cent came from 3-5 person households and the rest from bigger ones. In view of the fact that the wife in the nuclear household gets less help than the wife in the joint family it is all the more remarkable that a large number of wives from nuclear households show an urge for studies.

As in most societies, also in India it is expected of the mother that she herself nurses and looks after her children. 76.42 per cent of the married female students of the Bombay study, had children, 36.17 per cent of these mothers had one child, 39.01 per cent had two, 25 per cent had three or more children.

These findings warrant two conclusions 1. Presence of children is for the women of the middle class no obstacle to taking up studies. 2. These women, who have to fulfill at least three roles at the same time, execute their studies under much more difficulties and tensions than unmarried of childless women. This burden becomes heavier in those cases where the women, in addition to studying, also have a full time job, as was the case with 128 women; 104 of these working and studying women had children.

Now one could assume that only such mothers study whose children do not need constant care. The findings of the Bombay study do the studying mothers state that "nursing and feeding" belong to the main activities concerning their children. That means their children are still small. About as many mothers state that they prepare their children for school and help them in their home work. From this one can see that the majority of the studying mothers have children who still need their constant care.

In a society where millions of people are unemployed and where it is still possible to get servants for the household, the situation of the studying and working mother is different from that of her sisters in the western industrial societies. Middle-class families have generally at least on if not more servants. These servants are cooks, nannies, gardeners, drives, maidservants, watchmen and sweepers who perform the dirty jobs like cleaning of the W.C. and the bathroom.

The families of the lower middle class cannot naturally employ 3-5 servants, particularly because in the cities servants begin to demand higher wages. But the families of the lower middle class try to have at least one maidservant for the dirtier household work, even if on hourly basis or for half of the day. In N. Desai's study the number of servants in the families of studying wives is not explicitly assessed. However, to the question who looks after the children in their mothers' absence only about 16 per cent of the women said that a servant takes care of the children, about half of the women got help from some family members. Nevertheless, 78 women said that they had nobody to whom they could entrust their children.

The great majority of these women came from nuclear households. It is interesting to note that women from such families turn rather to the family of their origin than to their in-laws when they need help, although they belong to the husband's family of origin and her new family, which, according to the ideal type of the patrilocal family are to be almost completely broken, are again getting stronger today.

But the majority of studying mothers got help from the family into which they had married. Help from neighbours, creches of a baby-sitting system hardly exist. N. Desai points out correctly that "traditional sentiments are sustained more due to absence of modern facilities to look after the children of married women taking to education or going for earning rather than for their inherent value".

Whatever the attitude of women to wards traditional family solidarity may be, whether they tacitly decline the help of the mother-in-law or sister-in-law or not, there is no doubt that the traditional family ties help women to take up new roles outside the home. Here we encounter the paradox already hinted at earlier, that the prejudices against married women taking up studies are of course greater in the joint family than in the so-called nuclear family, that the nuclear family even encourages the women to study. But the practical preconditions for this double role are much more favourable in the joint family. That the women are quite conscious of this is shown by the fact that although most of the women live in nuclear households, 205 out of 369 consider the joint family as the ideal family type. The reasons given for the preference of the joint family are all of a utilitarian nature : sharing of the household work, children are always looked after, it is cheaper.

If we summarise the above results we can conclude that it is possible for Indian wives to study precisely because traditional feudal structures still exist both in the form of the joint family or in the joint family solidarity and in the form of the system of domestic servants. One can assume that with a breakdown of these structures women will have the same problems if they want to work as women in the West.

According to the social norm the educational career of the middle class woman to a close with the B.A. or B.Sc. examination, which is usually immediately followed by marriage. But we have seen that social reality does not conform to this norm any more and that even married women are crowding into the institutions of higher education in order to continue studies already begun before marriage or to begin their studies. Now the question arises at what point of time after marriage do they decide to take up higher studies. According to the experience in the West one would assume that a married woman can take up out-of-home activities only when the youngest child has left school and the home. That means after the conclusion of the so-called family cycle of the woman which is estimated according to latest research to last 20-25 years.

Married women students do not only deviate from the official Indian norm, but also from the western pattern. 60.4 per cent the women of the Bombay study had begun their higher education only after marriage, only 39.57 per cent had already studied before marriage. Still more informative is perhaps the fact that of the women who had begun their study before marriage, nevertheless one-third could continue to study without break after marriage.

Unfortunately, the study does not contain any facts regarding the time when the other two-thirds could come back to studies. However, of the women who began their studies after marriage, 8.07 per cent could begin immediately after or within the first year of marriage, 36.7 per cent had to wait up to about 6 years, and the rest, that is the majority, began to study only after the 7th year of marriage. The following table gives more information on the time lag between marriage and studies :

The marriage as such is no longer considered an obstacle to higher education of women and that the tendency exists to continue this education as early as possible after marriage is also shown by the results of the Poona study. Of the 255 married women of the sample more than 55 per cent had studied after marriage. It is significant that in the case of these women the time lag between marriage and studies generally lower than in the above table. Of the 129 women who studied after marriage 41 had begun already in the first year of marriage or had not discontinued their studies at all, 43 began to study in the second year of marriage, after the 3rd year of marriage the number of studying wives goes down and rises again only after the 9th year of marriage. The desire to take up higher studies is therefore, apparently strongest in the first 3 years after marriage, and after the 10th year of marriage. The steep fall in the number of studying wives after the third year of marriage can be understood as an indication that in the meantime small children are there, who need the mother.

After the analysis of the family situation we have to ask why married women take up or continue higher education. On the basis of the empirical data we can establish that among the women of the middle classes there exists a general interest in further education. Thus in the Ramanamma study in Poona 66 per cent of the working women expressed the desire for further education, but only 37 per cent were in a position to realise this desire.

The women of the Bombay study had demonstrated this desire by the fact that they had taken up further studies after marriage. The motives that were stated by the women of the two studies can be classified under the following categories:

1. Economic motives (professional training, possibility of earning an independent income);
2. Extension of knowledge personality development);
3. Enhancing social prestige through an academic degree;
4. Wish of the husband.

In both the studies the economic motive occupies the first place, 39 per cent of the women in Bombay mention economic considerations as the main reason for studying.

Among the women in Poona 35.1 per cent mention this motive. Women who are already working want to enhance their chances of promotion through further studies, others want to start a career and would like to prepare themselves for it.

As one would expect, economic reasons are found mostly among women whose husbands belong to the lower income groups (Rs. 251-500). The majority of the women in the Poona sample belonged to the middle and higher income categories (26 per cent : Rs. 601-1000, 31 per cent above Rs. 1000).

Also these women look at education mainly under the aspect of economic advantage. Further there seems to exist a relationship between the education and profession of the husband and the economic motive. Women whose husband possess a higher academic degree and are in higher positions look at education less from the point of view of economic gain.

In both the studies the motive of increases of knowledge and development of personality come second. In Bombay 38 per cent mentioned this motive, in Poona 32 per cent. The urge for knowledge as a purpose in itself is still prevalent among the middle classes. This motive is followed by the desire to enhance one's social prestige by academic degrees. In Bombay this goal is mentioned by 15 per cent of the women. In the Poona study it is not explicitly mentioned but could still have played a certain role, since academic titles and degrees have a very high prestige value in India.

In the case of a number of women it is clear that they took up their studies less on their own initiative than on the wish of their husbands. In Bombay 35 per cent said that their husbands wanted them to take up studies. In Poona 25 per cent of the married women stated that their husbands were interested in their higher education. This result may be interpreted in two ways :

1. Indian husbands are interested to have academically educated wives;
2. Indian women are dependent on the consent of their husbands in a matter like deciding on their further studies.

However, it is interesting to not that more than half of the women of the Desai study decided on their own to take up a further university course, in addition to marriage, family and partly also professional obligations. This fact is an indication of the urge of middle class women for higher education. On the other hand the fact that more than one-third of the women took up studies on the instance of their husbands could be an indication of changing patriarchal attitudes among Indian men N. Desai asks: "Does this mean that the Indian men are becoming liberal and progressive minded or are they realising that if their wives are deprived of higher education they would not be able to keep up with the changing times and environment?"

On the question why Indian husbands support higher education of their wives we get further information from an analysis of their attitudes towards the higher studies of their wife. Attitudes of Women towards the Burden of their Multiple Roles In the analysis of the conflict situation of the married female student the problem that deserves attention first is that of physical strain.

One of the most important duties of the Indian wife is "service" to her husband. Even in the joint family, where the mother-in-law manages the household and supervises the preparation of the males, the wife cooks for the husband; it is her duty to serve him during the meal, and since the food must always be served hot she runs to and fro between the kitchen and the dining room. She eats only when the husband has eaten his fill. To eat before the husband has eaten is unimaginable for most middle-class Indian women. Indian cooking is not only complicated, but is also extremely time-consuming, so that many women hardly come out of the kitchen. A simplification of the cooking habits would, however, encounter the resistance of men who are very spoilt in this point.

It is obvious that the wife has to "serve" her own children in the same selfless way as she serves her husband. Therefore, the physical burden of studying married women is considerable. 51.22 per cent of the women of the Bombay study came from nuclear families, 76-42 per cent had children, half of them toddlers, over 25 per cent of the mothers had nobody to whom they could entrust the children. Moreover, 128 of these 369 women were also working. That is why the majority of the married women student find only 1-2 hours' time for studying at home. Generally they can open a book only late in the evening or early in the morning or in the afternoon after finishing the domestic work.

That the husband helps in the household is still a rare thing. Of course almost all the women speak of the cooperative attitude of their husbands towards their studies. But most of them mean by that, the husband creates a "pleasant atmosphere", i.e. he does not stand in the way of their studies. The women are generally satisfied with this kind of "help"' although it seems that some men do give a helping hand to their wives in the household.

The burden due to the multiple roles in the case of the wife and mother who works and studies at the same time seems crushing. In the majority of the cases this role accumulation seems, however, not to lead to tensions and conflicts. 55 per cent of these women find the fulfilment of these role obligation "not difficult". They are satisfied with the triple in family, study and profession, because above all it gives them financial advantages and makes them economically independent of the husband. Those, however, who suffer from the pressure of the diverse demands complain primarily about physical exhaustion. It seems that the fact of physical strain is recognised, but inmost cases it does not led to psychological tensions. Many women feel it is a privilege to be able to study and work. For that they are prepared to accept any hardship. The psychological and nervous tensions which re caused by the double or triple roles result much more from the attitudes and reactions of the family than from the burden of work.

The majority of the women live in a family atmosphere, which is positively disposed towards their studies. Almost all women (98 per cent) speak of the cooperative attitude of their husbands. One can assume that many of these men support the study of their wives, because this way their own social prestige rises.

On the other hand they are also perhaps conscious that and educated wife raises the economic potential of the family. The women experience a little more opposition or indifference from the side of the parents-in-law, above all the mother-in-law. But it seems that the criticism of the parents-in-law hardly disturbs them.

They find it natural that they are against their study and do not bother much about their opinion. But it is a different case with the husband's attitude. Desai points out that the control of the parents-in-law over the married woman has weakened in favour of the control of the husband.

In her opinion the positive attitude of the husbands towards their wives' higher education does not allow the conclusion that Indian men have generally become liberal and progressive; she rather supposes that only those women can study whose husbands give them the permission. A woman can disregard the negative attitudes of the parents-in-law, but not of the husband. In urban nuclear households he is today the most important authority for the woman.

The worries of studying married women result therefore mainly from a feeling of guilt that they are unable to fulfil the demands of the multiple roles to the satisfaction of their husbands. It is remarkable that neither the criticism of the society against their out-of-home activity nor the lack of cooperation from the side of the parents-in-law and other family members give rise to similar strong fears and worries. By this it is confirmed that modern women fear the sanctions of traditional authority—the parents-in-law—less than those of the husband.

On the other hand they worry that they are not doing justice to the demands of their student role. The women of the Desai sample try hard to do justice to both the roles; in this process they expect of themselves, as it seems, an excessive degree of adaptation to the new situation, but almost nothing from the partners of their role set.

They do not dispute the claim of the husbands and the children on their unlimited traditional services. Above all they do not question anywhere the priority of the family roles of the woman. So they are torn between the demands of the multiple roles without rebelling against the one or the other.

Today it is impossible to project any one pattern that is likely to be most successful in the feature. The women who are middle-aged now were making their decisions in a different economic and social context form that which prevails today. Nevertheless, it is the purpose of this chapter to sift out the most successful patterns under a variety to historical and social conditions.

Our account begins with the historical trends in women's social roles, particularly their work and family life, since 1950. We then ask how these changes suggest a discernible life pattern of sequence of education, work experience, or marriage that has been more adaptive for women in recent experience, or marriage that has been more adaptive for women in recent years. If such a pattern can be identified, we ask whether its whether is success is likely to continue in the future.

Next we inquire into the types of family role system and work role system that have been most supportive of women's satisfaction and achievement.

Although many contextual factors such as social networks are also relevant, the links between work and family structure best enable a woman to fulfill herself? Which types of work environment are particularly conducive to her accomplishment? The dual-career family and flexible work arrangements have aroused particular interest. Each takes both family and employment into account.

Ultimately, lessons learned from life course studies and observations of family and employment have implications for practical programs. This chapter concludes with the social changes for reeducation and reentry that will help adult women return to the work place. The birthrate continued to fall, each year setting a new record low. By 1975 the fertility rate of women 15 to 44 years old was only half of what it had been twenty years earlier.

This decline, in turn coincided with a trend toward later marriages. By 1971 more than half of all women twenty years of age were single in contrast to only one-third in 1960, and the number of unmarried women in the 20-to-24 age bracket had climbed from 28 per cent in 1960 to 37 per cent a decade later.

Simultaneously, the greatest increase in the female labour occurred among younger women of childbearing age. The proportion of women working in the 20-to-24 years-old group increased from 50 per cent in 1964 to 61 per cent in 1973. Among college women in that age group the employment rate was 86 per cent. From 1959 through 1974 the employment rate of mothers with children under three more than doubled, from 15 to 31 per cent, and that for mothers of childrens three to five years old increased from 25 to 39 per cent.

Since 1970 every trend that Chafe mentioned has continued in essentially the same direction, and the proportion of women employed has increased by roughly 10 percentage points across ail age groups. The employment rate for women with children under six rose form 31 percent in 1970 to 42 percent in 1978. Of mothers with children under, 18, 40 per cent were employed in 1970 compared with 50 percent in 1978. By 1990 it is predicted that nearly 60 percent of women ages 35 to 54 will be in the labor force. Half of all mothers with children under six will be working, and the pattern of wife at home will fit only one-fourth of the 44 million women who are expected to be married and living with their children.

By comparison women's family roles in 1990 are expected to show a less striking change. The proportion of women aged 16-54 who are married with husband present will rise only slightly form 60 percent in 1978 to 66 percent in 1990 with a corresponding drop in the proportion of never married (from 26 to 20 percent) and little change in the category of " other ever-married" who represent about 13 percent in both periods. The average size of family will continue to decline from 3.6 in 1970 to roughly 3.0 in 1990. The proportion of married of ever-married women aged 16-54 with 1 children present or with very young children with hold constant. There will be a slight increase in proportion of women with children aged 6-17-from 27 percent of all women in the 16-54 age group in 1978 to 32 percent in 1990.

The upshot of these two trends-rising employment and continued family involvements is that a different mix in women's work and family roles will become increasingly evident. Change in the number of earners per family is an example. In 1950 only about one-third, (36 percent) of all families had two earners or more. By 1975 the proportion had grown to nearly half because of the great increase in participation in the labor force by married women.

An important question for the future is whether these changes will last. At the moment there are two contrasting views on the subject. One views is that the economic situation is about change drastically and with it will come a return to traditional attitudes. The other views is that structural and attitudinal changes have already been institutionalized and will not easily be-reversed.

The economist Richard Easterlin expects that as economic prospects for the smaller birth cohorts of the 1960s improve during the 1980s, women will marry earlier, have children sooner, and then withdraw from the labour force. He reasons that young males income relative to older males will improve, and that wife's income will no longer be so much needed for the family to live at the standard to which it aspires. As a result, more of the wife's time and effort will go into rearing and other family work.

An opposite prediction comes from demographer Valerie Kincade Oppenheimer. She concedes that the "bay bust" generation born in the 1960s will experience better times, but she takes issue with Easterlin. Oppenheimer particular questions the wife's predicted withdrawal from the labor force. She believes that young men's "life cycle squeeze" (between heavy financial obligations and limited earning power) will instead continue and that current adaptations such as wives work and postponement of childbearing will also continue. These patterns have already been institutionalized. There is now an expectation that wives will take paid employment.

Moreover, current wage scales for young men take the two-earner family into account. Wages are lower not only because of recent large birth cohorts entering the labor force but also because of job competition form young women in the labour force but also because of job competition from young women in the same cohorts. It is no clear that employers in the future will in fact face any imperative to raise salaries, given demographic changes alone.

Even before future developments unfold, it is possible to assess the actual normative changes that have occurred. There is a clear trend toward greater acceptance of women's employment and achievements outside the home. Each successive generation of women has participated in the labour force at a higher rate than its predecessors. So great is the change that it seems hardly likely to be reversed by demographic or economic cycles.

The place of work in the face cycle has also shifted. Women born before 1900 worked when they were young adults, then withdrew for the rest of their lives. Women born between 1900 and 1930 worked briefly, withdrew to family activity, and then in some instances reentered the work force in middle age. Among younger women particularly those born since the Depression, the interrupted pattern no longer holds. Instead, women's age curve of participation in the labor force is becoming ever more similar to that of man, with a gradual rise occurring during young adulthood and little sign of withdrawal until retirement age.

Explanation of these striking patterns requires more than a cyclical demographic or economic theory. Women are now built into the economy in clerical or professional occupations. The pattern is common to all the Western industrial nations. Concentrated in a few occupations (low level sales, high level clerical. etc.), their earnings average only 60 percent of men's Industrial economies evidently share certain structural features that systematically impose these patterns. Only in those countries such as Belgium and the Federal Republic of Germany, where the service sector is somewhat smaller relative to agriculture and manufacturing, does the rate of women's participation in the labor force fall much lower than the 45-50 percent rate that is typical of the United States, the United Kingdom, and Canada.

Evidently may families need two earners, especially in times of employment uncertainty. A longitudinal study of 5000 American families reveals that one-third of all primary breadwinners were out of work at some point between 1968 and 1976. In addition, nearly two-thirds of all employed females in America in 1978 were single, widowed divorced, separated, or had a husband who earned less than $10,000 in 1977. Under such circumstances, a family need for a wife's earning ability is a key factor in rising rates of participation by women in the labour force.

Yet women's family roles also exert pressures the negatively shape the typical patterns of female employment. Women enter a much narrower range of occupations than men. More than one-third are in clerical occupations alone, and these and other female-typed jobs are typically underpaid and over crowed. One hypothesis is that typical women's jobs can be more easily combined with family responsibilities. Some occupations like teaching or library work offer scheduling advantages. Others such as clerical work can be centered and reentered with minimum obsolescence of skills. But the penalties to women are lower remuneration and less opportunity for advancement.

Thus, structural features of the industrial economy have built women into the labor force. But also have changes in attitudes. All the major surveys on sex-role attitudes reports the same trend-a movement in the direction of more egalitarian beliefs. Gallup polls and other surveys have inquired since 1937 whether the respondent would vote for a woman president. There has been a steady upward trend in the percentage agreeing, from roughly one-third in 1937 to 80 percent in 1978. Similarly, even if she had a husband capable of supporting her, rose from only 20 percent in 1938 to 55 percent in 1969 and 75 percent in 1978.

Other more detailed surveys have inquired the desirability of the traditional sex division of labor within the family the consequences of maternal employment for children's welfare, and the rights of men and women in the labor force. Mason. Czajka, and Arber compared the results of five surveys conducted between 1964 and 1974 and showed that attitudes had moved in an egalitarian direction on all three dimensions. As time went on fewer people believed in strict sex-typed roles. Fewer thought that a preschools child would suffer if the mother worked, and more believed that a woman should have exactly the same job opportunities as a man. By 1977 a New York Times-CBS poll reported that more Americans believed in marriage in which partner could share the tasks of breadwinner and homemaker (47 percent) than those who preferred the traditional marriage (43 percent) in which the husband was exclusively a provider and the wife was exclusively homemaker and mother. The Detroit Area Studies documented a related shift: In 1963 than a third of the respondents disagreed with the statement that "most important decisions of family life should be made by the man of the house." Generally speaking liberal attitudes were more frequent in three groups-the young, the educated, and in those families where women were already working. These were presumably the groups who were most likely to benefit under new conditions.

Actual living arrangements, however, are not perfectly correlated with changes in attitudes. People may believe that couples are more satisfied who share homemaking and bread-winning roles, but this does not ensure implementation of these principles in their own lives. Research to date, in fact shows that husbands have been slower to share household tasks than changing ideology might suggest. Duncan and Duncan, for example were unable to discover much change in the number of tasks that they shared. Yet behavioural changes have certainly occurred in the work place. The changes in women's employment are in fact so dramatic that economists conclude that rewards for women's continuous work participation are out-weighing the rewards for work in the home. It may be that the higher opportunity cost for home work in recent years has lowered fertility and stimulated a search for shortcuts in cleaning, cooking and laundry. Greater use of outside services has perhaps kept the marital division of labor from responding more than it might have.

In addition, rather than a major revision of sex roles, it may be that the structure of the family is changing to provide for what Ryan has called "a disengagement of the sexes". Within the American home "male and female teeter on a delicate imbalance of power" an outside the home "wide margins of inequity separate the sexes in the labor force." single-parent households now constitute 15 percent of all households whereas the number of single-person households has doubled from about 10 percent of all households in 1950 to 20 percent in 1976.

These changes have not come together to form a new integrated model of work and family life. No single path to adulthood, no one pattern for the middle years can be recommended over all others. Nevertheless, it is possible to trace three emerging patterns. The first is a new picture of women's life cycle. The second appears in the experimental division of labor between home and work place. A third is the changing national consciousness and new policy frontier that increasingly assumes egalitarian sex roles.

Changing theories

Women's changing work patterns naturally put a strain on

traditional expectations of what a woman's life should be like. Even today, high school counselors frequently note that many girls still primarily look to marriage as their chief career goal. Such young women ignore the present reality that some women will ever marry. Perhaps as many as one-third will be separated or divorced. Most women will face at least 30 more years of life after their last child leaves home; and on the average, wives will outlive their husbands by as many as 10 or 15 years. If young women today are still not fully prepared were even less prepared. In fact, it is probably true that despite feminism and related changes, each age cohort of women since 1900 has at first modeled its life in terms of the traditional ideal-a brief period of work outside the home, then marriage and insurance policy against emergency or disaster than for an occupation that is to be expected.

Now all this changing. Some time during the 1970s the norm "tipped" from the previously dominant pattern in which mothers were homemakers to a new pattern in which a majority are employed. The change was particularly noticeable in the suburbs among the college educated. This quiet revolution produced unfamiliar problems. Women were no longer available to save as den mothers for the Cub Scouts or to work at the church rummage sale. But at the same time, as middle-aged women entering the work force, the women found that their training was inadequate or too general and diffuse. They frequently could not find jobs commensurate with their education and intelligence. Relative to their husbands, many of them had fallen behind because of years out of the force, lack of graduate, work, or lack of special professional training.

Women in this transitional age group thus particularly disadvantaged because they had grown up with the ideals of their mothers generation but had to live with a different reality. The question for the future thus became a question of the ideal life cycle. How can present generations of young women face the major life events (education, marriage, births, moves employment) and negotiate a path that results in a good life? This is the great unspoken quandary for young women are caught between two worlds, the feminine mystique of their mother's generation and the feminist mystique of their own. Young women want both career success and family intimacy.

So far as we know there is no one authority who has come up with an answer. Past experience doesn't give much to go on, and the research results are complex and confusing. Past negative experience of middle-aged and older women do not automatically reveal an obverse set of positive developmental steps that each young woman should try in the future. Levinson's and Vaillant's theories based on men are no more helpful. The only alternative seems to be induction from piecemeal findings about women. One asks what factors contribute to life satisfaction or career success. What decisions of life events and what timing patterns stand in the way?

A new model of the life course is emerging for women as well as for men. Its structure, rather than holding out a single optimum sequence of life events, is characterized by several possible options, all viable and all potentially capable of giving satisfaction. The significance of this new model of the life course is that it is peculiarly adapted to conditions of modern society. It recognizes a number of individual variations. It accounts for flexibility, redirection, and multiple possible combinations of timing and sequence. It implies that versatility and freedom of choice are to be valued. By the same token, it suggests that certain other patterns should be avoided, particularly those like very early childbearing or school leaving. Such patterns close opinions and decrease adaptability late on. In my opinion, women who live in such a complex society as our own would do well to have a complex and flexible model before them rather than to believe in marrying and living happily ever after, or to follow simple stairstep guides to maturity. It is fortuitous that a new image of the life course is rising just when the inadequacies of the old model are becoming fully apparent.

One imagines that the people who preserve maximum adaptability and choice are those most happy and at peace with themselves. The unhappy ones, the sick ones, must be those so bound by constraint, stress and duty that they feel helpless and without hope. Considerable support for this interpretation comes from available research on women's mental health. Gittentag and Salasin and Belle suggest that a sense of helplessness underlies many cases of depression in women. The women who are particularly vulnerable to depression are heads of a single-parent family, have poor education, have responsibility for young children, and at the same time are working but at low wages. A British study of women and depression likewise shows that it is the women subject to high stress and precipitating events (four times as many working-class women as middle-classes women) who become to depressed. Thus it is the persons who have at lot of responsibility but very little help in meeting strain who are more likely to be unhappy or develop symptoms. Several other pieces of evidence support his conclusion.

In the national survey on quality of American life, Campbell, Converse, and Rodgers discovered that the highest levels of dissatisfaction appeared in mothers with young children. It was the young married who were still childless and the older married whose children had left home who seemed the happiest. An earlier report by Norval Glenn based on four national surveys also showed that mothers whose children have left home report somewhat greater happiness. The highest rate of psychiatric and physical symptoms occurs in women who have greatest care-taking responsibilities, especially those married women with young children and those divorced, separated, or widowed women with dependents.

Significantly, however, it is not simply the amount of stress of burden that accounts for low satisfaction or high rates illness. There are in addition certain internal and contextual factors that make some individuals more vulnerable than others. Some are persons with shaky inner resources, such as women in the British study who had lost a mother before the age of 11 and presumably were emotionally more vulnerable as a result. Others are lacking a friend or relative who can help out. This may take the form of living arrangements such as the single-parent family where the nurturer is peculiarly alone. Or the more vulnerable may lack a confidant-or may be in a marriage relationship without intimacy-and thus be more likely to experience depression.

A third factors in women's vulnerability to illness is employment. Brown and Harris found in the British study that employed women subject to high stress or low companionship were about half as likely to succumb to depression as the women who were not employed. Yet Deborah Belle observed in a study of Boston women that frequently the depressed are those heading single-parent families, who have poor education, and who are working at low-paid jobs. Employment perhaps work as an antidote to depression when it creates options, gives some leverage against the demands of the nurturant roles, and open up a new source of social contact and stimulation. Otherwise, it simply adds to total drag. Evidently the employed women in Camberwell, England, gained immunity to symptoms through the options created by multiple roles instead of the hazards of role overload that burdened the poor Massachusetts women. Not just any type of employment is an antidote to depression, but the type of work that supplies adequate earnings, rewards competence, and generally reinforces a sense of self-direction and personal control does seem to be such an antidote. Conditions to promote women's health apparently require a balance between nurturant and productive roles. This is true not only in the help and resources that such roles generate but also in the role demands they make on the women herself.

For protection against depression a woman need confidants and emotional support as well as income and material resources. Gratification comes from ties to other as well as from work. Until now we have tended to focus on either nurturance or productive work without taking the question of trade-offs into account. The result had been a statistical and rhetorical game of showing whether married women were happier than single women, or employed women happier than housewives.

The results of these comparisons have been ambiguous, however, because married people generally report higher satisfaction than the single, windowed, divorced or separated, But working women report fewer symptoms than housewives. And single women report greater satisfaction with their life than married women.

What we believe this all adds up to is that we are just beginning to formulate a new ideal of health and happiness for adult women. In the early stages of the recent feminist movement. Women discovered the costs they had paid for concentrating on the nurturant role to the detriment of their work lives and their sense of competence and power. Then a research tradition developed that showed the value of a sense of competence to women. Current studies of women in the middle years hark back to this initial insight.

It is almost a cliche now for people who work long hours at demanding jobs, aware of what they are missing in terms with family, long talks with friends, concerts, and all kinds of opportunities for leisure, to express the sentiment that "there is more to life than work". The problem is that life without productive work is terrible.

Now, however, a new generation of women has come of age who were imbued with the work and achievement ethic and immunized against the feminine mystique. Like Linda Sexton "caught between two worlds." They ask how they will find intimacy and connectedness to others. They have their careers; but when will they marry, and will they have children? The second wave of the new women's movements is thus concerned with the rediscovery of nurturant roles and values. Now the question for the individual is how to negotiate the life course to have it all.

Even more than the studies of mental health, the research on status attainment considers what order of life events may be most conducive to a satisfying and successful life. While psychologists have measured mental health and life situations conducive to it, sociologists have measured who gets ahead. Do women move up the educational and career ladders the way men do? Do they attain the same levels of achievement? If not, why not? These questions have implications for the ideal life course. Ultimately they can be used to answer whether there is an optimum of education, marriage childbearing and employment that will maximize the chances for a woman's health and happiness.

First, we must face up to a challenging conceptual and empirical question. What are the major timing patterns, and which one are associated with the best outcome? Glen Elder has defined a career as " a patterned sequence of movements and events. "Using this definition, several topologies are possible. An Australian sociologist, Christabel Young, categorizes women's career like Mendelian genetic types. She develops several temporal sequences that combine working or not working with different stages of the family life cycle. Our of eight possible role sequences, the five most common are never working (NNN), working only before having a family (YNN), beginning work after children are in school (NNY), working except when the children are of preschool age (YNY), and continuous working (YYY).

A more universal typology (not defined ın terms of family life cycle) has been developed by Mary Corcoran to characterize the work histories of women in the Five Thousand American Family Study. Her findings concisely convey not only the difference between men's and women's career patterns but also the frequency with which each pattern is found among women themselves. Perhaps most surprising about these findings is that the continuous work pattern that is most frequent among them men is also the most frequent among the women, even though the proportion who worked continuously is about 1½-times greater for men and the average time they have worked is several years longer. Another surprising findings is that the differences in men's and women's work pattern do not account for the 40 percent difference in their earnings. Can we then say whether the order and time of life events has any effect on life outcomes?

When all is said and done, given our current research findings, two themes stand out. One points to the normative sequences of major lie events and the costs of deviaing fro them. The other emphasizes the complexity of timing, the variety of individual life-styles, and the constantly changing social backdrop. Rather than costs of deviation, this second type of research shows the multiple possible routes to satisfaction. A great deal of research has shown that people pay a price for deviating markedly from the normal path or the normal pace. Among men, for, example, Hogan has shown that such a disruption in timing as caused by the draft and military service is associated with higher rates of marital disruption later in life. An issue of comparable importance for women is early marriage or child bearing, since numerous studies demonstrate negative consequences. The woman who bears a child very early (before the age of 20 or before or during the first year of marriage) is more likely so suffer a marital breakup, gain limited work experience, foreshorten her education, and become dependent on welfare. Similarly early marriage is more likely to be associated with poorer marriage financial status later no, restricted education, and a heavy burden of child care. Being late in marriage and childbearing also has its costs. In a small pilot study in western Massachusetts Alice Rossi found that women who had larger families and later childbearing had more "again symptoms". They wanted to be a lot younger or to die sooner, and generally they were more dissatisfied than women whose childbearing and occurred at the usual age.

Yet against this evidence of poorer outcomes associated with "off-time" patterns must be weighted other findings that fail so show any great difference for women who do things one way as compared with those who do them another. It is at all clear, for example that work discontinuities hurt women's occupational status or earnings all that much. This curious finding appears in Corcoran's analysis of women's work histories in the Five Thousand Family Study. It also appears in results from the National Longitudinal Surveys of women analyzed by Sandell and Shapiro who found little evidence that women's work discontinuities had a negative effect. Instead, the large earnings gap between men and women holds even for the never-married women who presumably have experienced continuous work histories like those of men.

Moreover life outcomes appear to be determined as much by "tastes" and values (toward a career, further education, or having children) as by the opening or closing of doors that are triggered by the order and timing of life events. At least, this is what we get out of some complicated findings on the relation between participation in the labor force and fertility. Researchers have been trying to answer a question that goes something like this: Does having babies make a woman less likely to participate in the labor force, or women's attitudes and values. If mothering is important to her and if she rates herself high as a mother, a woman will continue to have children even it she is in the labor force. On the other hand, if she has a high initial commitment to a career, she will shape a life-style that ultimately leads to a decision have few or no children.

To complicate matters, further there appears to be a reciprocal relationship between and certain life events. Using data from the National Longitudinal Survey (NLS) sample of younger women (aged 19-29 in 1973). Spitze and Waite discovered that a woman's first marriage lowers her preference for paid (market) work by 10 to 20 percentage points, especially if it occurs in the 14-23 age bracket. The first birth, however, raises preference for market work form 10 to 15 percent, especially in the younger age groups of 16 to 27. Divorce also raises preference for paid work by 20 to 30 percentage points. Spitze and Waite clearly imply that, although life choices are shaped by previously held values and attitudes, actual experiences in turn give rise to some what different values with experience that perhaps makes the most sense out of the relativity of outcomes observed in women's lives. Daiels and Weingartern studied the timing of parenthood and found that parents who had their children later (after the age of 27) experienced certain costs as a result-such as being less youthful flexible, and energetic than younger parents, but older parents also expressed satisfaction that they were more secure and established when their children were born. Younger parents, on the other hand, were glad for their vitality and flexibility but regretted the financial strain and the educational sacrifice the older parents had not experienced. Evidently, both major temporal alternatives can net roughly equal amounts, although different kinds of satisfaction.

Much the same point emerges from a study of women's career paths. Perun and Bielby studied 41 married women with doctorates who were born between 1893 and 1906. Among these women they found three types of accommodation to major life events. Pattern I marriage then receiving the doctorate; Pattern II, work for the doctorate, then marriage and Pattern III, simultaneous marriage and work for the doctorate. Some women had children and others did not. When these women's attainments were examined at age 60 few difference could be found either in the status of the institution at which they were employed or in their academic rank. Women with children were employed at institutions of slightly lower rank. Women with children were employed at institutions of slightly lower rank. When the sample was divided into two groups, one with and the other without children, no difference could be found within groups between those who had followed the three different sequential patterns.

How shall we put together these rich and puzzling finding on status attainment? There appear to be costs for deviation from the normal expectable life course, but satisfaction can also be attained through any one of several other possible routes. Neither fact invalidates the other, it is a theoretical challenge to find an over arching conceptual umbrella that makes sense out of both. Such a framework is now in process of development.

All living systems exhibits two processes in the course of change and development. One is differentiation, specialization, and increasing complexity in their component parts. The other is integration and greater interdependence among the specialized parts. The traditions of life-span research on women reflect both of these tendencies. Efforts to delineate an optimum timing pattern are related to the differentiation tendency; significant lie events are enumerated, critical turning points are recognized, and a pattern of optimum development is identified. Skepticism about optimum pattern appears in theories that emphasize integration. Significant life events are also noted in these theories, but they are more likely to be observed according to the way they fir a sequential pattern rather than as being on or off schedule. This second type of research celebrates the number of possible sequential orders or events and emphasizes the variety of combinations that can integrate the whole life course and give it unity.

The crossover them is the result of both these tendencies. Crossover in sex roles holds that both women and men can usefully perform many tasks that once were primarily assigned to the opposite sex. Crossover in age roles suggests that developmental task and significant life events can be taken up at a number of possible different points in the life cycle without undue harm, we find both of these crossover themes throughout contemporary research on the changing roles of women. They did not emerge, until the society had become sufficiently specialized so that actual age and sex crossovers could occur. Then social changes were reflected in research and theory.

Generally speaking the differentiation theme appeared in refined stage theories based on a few individuals and the crossover theme emerged from research on large heterogeneous populations. The crossover theme, in my opinion, however, could not emerge until refined developmental tasks had been described by the stage theorists.

In Childhood and Society Erikson charted eight major stages of life. Heavily influenced by his work. Levinson, Gould, and Vaillant gave highly detailed accounts of the middle years. In The Seasons in a Man's Life Levinson described an early adult era (with three distinct phases), a middle adult era (with another three phases) and a late adult era. Such intellectual refinements had not been necessary in simpler colonial and rural society where persons hardly spoke of adulthood other than to distinguish manhood from childhood and old age. Now in our post-industrial era, we are refining our categories of knowledge to explore the psychological frontiers of adulthood.

One important discovery during this historical transition was that gross deviations in timing that limited the very complexity of future prospects were in themselves harmful. Thus, very early childbearing and the resulting truncated education and poor job opportunities were out of keeping with a rapidly changing and complex society. Individuals caught in this pattern could not respond flexibly and adaptively to the complicated labor conditions or personal circumstances that they were likely to face.

An unexpected consequence of these refinements, however, was that they made explicit the developmental tasks to be accomplished, and in the process individuals discovered that such takes were not necessarily linked to age but could be taken up in any one of several possible orders, with far more complex opportunities for mixing and matching activities then any one "ideal" normal expectable life course could possible encompass. While stage theorists continued to propound the idea of an optimum life course, other social scientists began to claim that some important life events were " age-independent". Because some major life events are unexpected or un-wanted there they be no particular expectable order to timing of adult development.

Pearlin finds that developmental issues very immensely according to a person's socioeconomic location. In research on both middle and working class Americans. Fiske cannot find evidence to support stage theory. Targ notes that the current theories built on male experience of middle age frequently do not fit women, in part because the theories fail to recognize the unexpected events such as divorce, employment, or unemployment that heavily influence many women's lives.

Those studies of women's work and fertility histories that fail to find a difference in attainment that can be attributed to the patterning of life events thus fit the skeptical school of theories of the life span. They recognize the complex society but drew a different lesson. They discover myriad possible combinations of developmental tasks and life events. Perun and Bielby's discovery that academic women could achieve in any one of several ways at home in this tradition. So also Daniels and Weigarten's balanced findings on the advantages of early and late parenthood.

In addition, social roles have changed to reflect increasing complexity and crossover. Tasks have become more differentiated within each sex role. Such women's jobs as cooking or child are have been specialized and rationalized so that they can be done by others. Men's jobs that required greater physical strength have also become more specialized because machinery has taken over some of the heaviest work. As a result, it is now much easier to move across the sex-role boundaries. Men can cook; women can operate power machinery. Quite naturally these change are also being reflected in theories of the life course. Writes such as Gutmann and Brim has commented on the "unisex of later life". In their middle years, men discover the nurturant aspects of their personality that may have been suppressed in the fight to establish a career. Women, on the other hand, discover their long-delayed desire for assertion and achievement. These theories recognize sex-role crossover in the middle stages of the life course.

At the same time official recognition is growing of the possibilities for what we call "age crossover". Education and employment programs for women take into account the various possible life schedules in which women engage. They may have their children early or late, enter the job market, drop out and reenter, or remain continuously. They may finish their education before establishing a family or getting a job, or they may drop out and continue later: As the variety of patterns gains further acceptance, the challenge to policy makers, educational institutions, and corporations will be to devise programs that meet such a diverse range of needs.

Changing ideas about the typical life cycle of women have affected family structure. No longer is it taken for granted that women's primary takes to be the home marker and child tender while men earn the money and "bring home the bacon". Instead, what appears to be happening in very major industrial society is a redefinition of men's and women's roles. Change is in the direction of greater equality and sharing in parenting, housekeeping and making money. The new patterns correspond with greater interpenetration between the worlds of work and family life. They also illustrate crossover in the family roles of women and men.

Recent books and articles on family life indicate a remarkable convergence on a new more egalitarian from that Young and Willmott have labeled "the symmetrical family" On the basis of a study of 2600 London families surveyed in 1970, Young and Willmott theorized that family structure had passed through several broad states of development that corresponded with the preindustrial area, family activity and economic activity were joined; the whole family worked at the tasks that supported them. The husband and primary authority both as major producer and head of the family. With the onset of the industrial revolution, the patriarchal family was replaced by the nineteenth—century Victorian ideal. The work place was separate from family activity. The husband was the primary breadwinner, and the wife was in charge of the children and the domestic front. In the twentieth century, a third major type of family has appeared. With an advanced industrial economy, even more specialized jobs, and household conveniences, the symmetrical family, found among blue-collar workers and professionals alike is the result of increasing interpenetration of work and family life. Both husband and wife typically work outside the home, both also share in household tasks. However, the division of labor is still skewed toward greater responsibility of the husband as income producer and the wife as housekeeper and care giver.

Sociological studies form a number of countries reinforce this outline of the emerging symmetrical family. A pilot program in Sweden tries to encourage this type of role sharing by expanding the repertories of men and women so that each, by incorporating elements of the provider, parent and citizen roles, can become more a " whole person" and realize the goal of sex equality. Dual-career families in Great Britain are the subject of a major study by Rapoport and Rapoport. Gronseth analyses the relationship of work-sharing couples that face two-career couples in the United States. Lein describes American families "in the middle" (working class and lower middle classes) who arrange their work time in order to share responsibilities for child care.

In the United States an ever larger number of families include working wives. In 1979 families with both a husband and wife in the labor force made up 41 percent of all husband-wife families, a larger single block than any other form. Families with husbands only in the labour constituted 34 percent. The remaining 12 percent of husband-wife families have a wife only in the labor force, no employed member, or some other combination.

Why is the dual-worker family becoming so widespread? Sociologically. The symmetrical family has advantages in a complex and rapidly changing society such as our own because it promotes flexibility and adaptability far better than traditional forms, which dictate rigid role segregation between husband and wife. If husband and wife can substitute for each other, whether in breadwinning or child tending, they are better able to respond to unforeseen circumstances such as loss of health or income, failure in school or work, or some threat to the local economy.

This new type of couples is still likely, however, to put primary emphasis on the husband's job as a basis for choosing residential location or timing major family events. The wife's role more often involves the compromises that keep the family flexible. This perhaps accounts for two penalties that fall on working women: lower pay and a heavier combined burden of paid work and housework.

An international time study by Szalai extended into Belgium, Bulgaria, Czechoslovakia, France, East and West Germany, Hungary, peru, Poland the United States, the USSR, and Yugoslavia and collected data from 30,000 respondents. Perhaps most telling was the consistent finding that after their contributions to the household employed men still had 50 percent more leisure than the employed women. An earlier time study in the United States by Walker showed the same pattern Women performed more family work than the employed women. An earlier time study in the United States by Walker showed the same pattern. Women performed more family work than men-4.8 hours a day for married women employed 30 or more hours a week as compared with 1.6 hours for the employed men who were married to working wives. A recent study by Pleck and Rustad using time budget data from a national survey shows considerable improvement in this picture. Husbands of employed women have doubled the time they give to help around the home (from 1.6 hours in the Walker study to 3.8 hours per day). Still working wives, family work (6.9 hours per day) is significantly more than their husbands-almost twice as much. This degree of inequality is a definite improvement, however, over the 3:1 ratio reported by Walker 10 years earlier.

Have these trends toward role sharing and equality now stabilized? Or will the improvement continue in the future? Our guess is that additional forward movement is still likely, although perhaps at a slower rate.

Perhaps the central of women's family roles is that traditional ways need not prevail but can be examined critically and be changed to accommodate people's needs and desires. Nowhere is this more evident than in child care. Among dual-career families, there is a belief that parenting arrangements are most satisfying when they are chosen, are the best possible available under the circumstances, and have clear-cut standards and goals, This new attitude has fostered discovery of men's capacity for parenting, a new willingness for women and men to share more responsibility for child care, and a search for outside supports (day care, cooperative community arrangement, etc.) that will somewhat lighten the traditional burden on the mother.

The father's important role in child development is a relatively recent topic for research. Numerous studies have examined the potentially harmful effects of father absence. More recently there has been an effort to document that father absence. More recently there has been an effort to document that fathers can ably care four young children, even newborns. In addition there is growing evidence that more active participation in child care is both gratifying and beneficial to the fathers themselves.

Certainly it is a boon to women if they can call on their husband for relief from the intense demands for care that young children can make. Piotrowski'e sensitive account of one young mother's days spent with her three preschool children suggests the welcome change that a father can provide when the baby is crying, the mother is tired, and each of the other children also needs care and attention. Under such circumstances the father relieves the tension; he is not so caught up with other competing concerns like cooking and the housework. Nor has he the accumulation of a whole day's demands, frustrations, and fatigue when he faces the particular moment at hand. There is a great advantage to be gained from an ideology of parenting and a practical schedule for child care than allow as much sharing as possible.

When children are a little older, they also can be encouraged to help. In their study of dual-career families, the Rapoports discovered that al-though there was a good deal of variation in parental roles, all the families expected help from their children.

In the current movement toward egalitarian sex roles, we wouldn't be surprised if more progress were made in sharing child care than housework. Children do offer gratification; they cannot be neglected. Using national time study data, Pleck in fact discovered that husbands of working wives spent 2.7 more hours per week in child care than husbands of non working wives and only 1.8 hours more per week in housework. Other national surveys have shown that the personal rewards of a good marriage and family are actually through to be nearly twice as important for happiness as a interesting job.

Besides more sharing, husbands and wives now also use more outside facilities-formal day care, informal child care, after school programs, and so on. Between 1964 and 1974 the proportion of all children three to five years old who were enrolled in nursery school and kindergarten rose from one-quarter to nearly half. Of all the care arrangements used for children under six between 1965 and 1971, only one-quarter was provided outside homes in a day-care center or other such arrangement. This compares with a third of all families who have day care in their homes provides by a father or other relative. Another quarter arrange care in their homes to be given by a combination of relatives or nonrelatives. The remaining fraction (17 percent) are cared for in another person's home. Whether existing facilities are adequate is a large and unanswered question. Certainly the women's movement and child advocacy groups have shown a sustained interest in providing sufficient high-quality care. Similar interest in adequate child-care programs has surfaced in other advanced industrial nations, and the trend seems likely to continue.

Despite parental role sharing and development of child-care programs outside the family, a familiar asymmetry nevertheless characterizes male and female roles. Increasingly the observers of two-worker families appear to question whether it will ever be otherwise. Pleck voices the dilemma:

> In the past, with some stress, one breadwinner in the family could follow the male work model. In the present, with more stress, one breadwinner could emphasize work and another breadwinner plan an ancillary, less-demanding work role. But it is doubtful whether large numbers of families can function with both partners following the male work model. For both spouses to adopt the male worm model families would have to stop having children, or else household and child care services would have to be provided on a scale hitherto unprecedented. Without one or the other, two-role living by both men and women will require a new work role model and for men an expanded family role.

In the meantime, we wait to see the future, it does seem likely that men will participate more in child rearing, and women will seek their help especially if they are also employed. Yet at the same time women will continue to have a larger role in child tending. It will probably be much as Ferber and Huber have shown in presently the case with men and women who received their Ph. D. after 1958. Highly educated women in professional careers in the future will likely have fewer children than their male counterparts. Such is the difficulty of working out a new work-family role system; the opportunity costs for rearing children will still be largely determined by the value of a mother's time.

Equal sharing of housework in the future is also problematic. The rule of one of the Rapoports dual-career families seems the ideal direction in which others should follow: When there is family work to do, no one sits down until the work is finished and everyone can sit down. American time budget studies however, show that employed women are still doing roughly twice as much housework (32.6 hours per week) as their employed husbands (11.4 hours per week). Why is this the case, the what is the likely trend in the future?

Researchers have been surprised that since the 1920s housewives time spent in household work has not diminished but actually increased. Vanek found that non-employed women spent 55 hours a week in family work in 1965-1966 compared with 52 hours a week reported by housewives in 1925-1926 before compared with 52 hours a week reported by housewives in 1925-1926 before the widespread introduction of the refrigerator and automatic washing machine. Standards apparently rose: The addition more time was apparently spent in child care because of the increasing emphasis on mothering, and perhaps also because of absence of older children or others who could help. By contrast, the employed wives spent only about half as much time on family work-26 hours. They evidently had to " cut corners" accept messier houses and perhaps eat out more. The difference did not result from more help by their husbands or from workers in their households.

There is ample evidence that men resist taking on household chores even when their wives are employed. But Lein and Pleck attribute the reason to men's feeling that their primary work on behalf of the family is in the breadwinner role. Resistance to housework protects the primary of their obligation to the provider role: At times it may also be an expression of a stubborn wish that their wives don't have to work.

Given this bottleneck that slows men's acceptance of responsibility for household chores, several alternative nevertheless are possible. Chief among them are household conveniences and outside help. Numerous technological advances have streamlined laundry: wash and wear clothing, the automatic washer and dryer, a dependable water supply and plumbing Cooking is easier because of convenience foods, the refrigerator, freezer and other mechanical devices for food preparation. Children can eat their lunches in school. Until devices for food preparation. Children can eat their lunches in school. Until high rates of inflation many families frequently ate out. There is still the cleaning, but some families have their children help with vacuuming, dusting, and yard work when they are old enough. Cleaning services visit those who can afford them. In the meantime there is a slow but steady change in the ideology surrounding men's household work. A husband taking clothes out of the dryer gets pictured in Newsweek. Gerlad Ford, president of the United States, was know to cook his own breakfasts. The young professional family in which both work are a fashionable symbol of new age-the advanced, affluent, egalitarian couple who combine personal liberation with responsibility for others. These changes are not yet widespread, however. Some older couples are set in their sex-typed mold. Some younger couples are making do as firemen and keypunch operators, not at all glamorous managerial or professional pair who can afford day care, dinners out, and a cleaning service.

Yet hopeful of more crossover in household roles of men and women come from a variety of quarters. It is claimed that doing things around the home is good for men, helps them to relax and get in touch with their feelings. The middle-aged companionate marriage actually allows the relationship is in some cases less preoccupied with his work, and takes a larger part in housework., especially after he has retired. Role theories suggest there may be a value to role expansion and role accumulation, so that a woman, rather than being depleted by employment may return to her household chores with greater energy and efficiency and also be able to resist the endless demands that would be made on her if homemaking were her only role. One recent study even reports a significant decline in the amount of time women spend in family care, 6.6 hours less per week in 1975 than in 1965. Finally, new generations are coming along. The boys now required to take home economics in the junior high schools will presumably feel more comfortable doing household work as adults. Those around them, including the women they marry, will have a stake in reinforcing their confidence and sense of worth as they help with family work in the future.

These changes in child care and housework are predicated on the idea that women's increasing participation in the labor force is beneficial to families and should be accommodated wherever possible. Indeed, one of the striking themes of the two-worker family is how important the woman's contribution is to its economic well-being. Families need the woman's income. This is particularly true if a divorce or separation occurs; the woman's work, rather than alimony or child support, is what keeps a woman and her children afloat. Even in the intact families unemployment of the major breadwinner is such a common occurrence that the wife's income is badly needed to tide the family over. Lein's working family study of 14 dual-worker families in the Boston area found that every family had experienced at least one layoff of either husband or wife in the recession following 1972-1973. Husband tremendously valued a wife's contribution when her wages helped keep the family income up to the standard they desired.

Yet in the face of this powerful reason to encourage married women's employment, all the evidence points to a strong tendency or the husband's employment, all the evidence point to a strong tendency for the husband's work to take precedence. Even in the professional dual-career families where the ideology of equality is presumably strongest, Homstrom found that the wives accommodated to their husbands' work to take precedence. Even in the professional dual-careers more than vice versa when deciding where to live. In a study of women and men with the Ph.D. degree Ferber and Huber found that women were more likely to permit their location to be determined by their spouse's career, even though negative career effects on the woman's eventual employment usually followed.

Perhaps as Pleck suggested, it is difficult to realize full equality when both male and female follow the male work-role model. In order to maintain some flexibility, at last one of the pair must be able to adjust and compromise. They only other solution is to gain room or flexibility in both persons' work roles though adjustable works schedules and other devices. We examine these possibilities in the following consideration of changing work roles.

The most important single strategy for restructuring work has bee the manipulation of scheduling through such devices as part-time jobs, flexible hours, provisions for parental leave, and the like. Between 1948 and 1976 the proportion of part-time workers increased substantially, going from one-fifth to one-third of all women workers and from 9 to 15 percent of all men workers. Flexible hours drew considerable attention as another major means of accommodating work to family life, and in the late 1970s one estimate reported at least 300,000 workers known to be presently so employed. The value of women's part-time work was recognized in many quarters and took on certain glamorous possibilities, particularly for the professional or managerial woman. Bell pictured the accountant who retires from a large firm of auditors but continuous to take a few select clients, and the security analyst operations researcher, or market specialist who works at her former firm as a two-or three-day-a-week consultant and has more time at home with her children. Bell states: "For them, the status of part-time carries none of the stigma, low skills, undependability or lack of motivation attributed to part-time workers at low-income levels."

Gradually, also, the part-time concept expanded. Rather than refer only to women (who make up roughly 70 percent of all part-time workers), social visionaries began to see the possibilities in part-time work or men as well—the students, the retired, and those in the middle years who wish more time with their families. Calls for maternity leaves were transformed into the broader language of "parental leave." The advanced ideas found in Sweden seemed to point the way. Employment services were to help demolish sex barriers in the labor market, train males for "female" jobs, protect the desires of women working part-time who wished to work more, an gain a shorter working day or both men ad women.

Practical details on the dynamics and effects of such changes surfaced in accounts of women who shared part-time professional jobs such as teaching, in research on couples who shared a single academic or professional job, and on couples who each worked part-time but sometimes at different jobs. By all accounts, these joint experiments in part-time work had excellent effect on the family life of the participants: Their roles were less sex typed, marital intimacy increased, ad child care was easier and more satisfying. What was not so clear were the negative effects, but there were some. One was reduced financial gains. Another was the tendency or the part-time job to expand so that each individual was doing much more work than was being paid for. A third disadvantage—especially in high-status occupations in which full time is equate with professionalism and part time with a casual attitude—was the low self-esteem that each part-time person eventually had to confront. Finally, it was difficult to regularize part-time appointments, have them be paid for on a pro-rated basis, and carry pro-rated fringe benefits. Employers were usually afraid to "set a precedent."

At the present moment, part-time work and flexible working hours seem to have only a tenuous place in American working life. They are most common in a few industries (finance, banking, insurance) an among a few occupations (waitresses, cooks, teachers, health workers). Part-time work still carries the dangers of low pay, poor opportunities to gain seniority, and high turnover. Even it may be good for families under optimum conditions, what likelihood is there that it will spread? And in the long run, what are its prospects for the future work roles of adult women?

The current interest in part-time work is indicative, we believe, of a process that will help bring about greater sex-role crossover in the work place. Experiments with scheduling are essentially signs of a further differentiation of work roles in which desecrate bundles of tasks can be moved around and combined in new ways. Discovery that a job can be performed by two part-time people is antecedent to this differentiation process. Such re-arrangements cannot occur without sufficient rationality and objectivity to list the job duties and requirements discretely and recognize that they can either be subdivided or be shared with another equally quilted person. When such a breakdown of global attributes has been made, the ascriptive qualities of being a male (able to work full time) or a female (likely to be vulnerable to family demands and to work part time) become less relevant. Thus crossover and equality are facilitated.

Such changes in work demands have obvious implications for family life. A woman's interest in a career in a career can be accommodated more easily. So can a man's interest if he is not fully wrapped up in his work and if he ways more time with his family. The rigidity of work schedules is relaxed somewhat, and family demands can more easily be met as they arise. Instead of having or full-time worker who follows the male work model, and one flexible worker whose job is secondary, both workers reach an intermediate level of commitment to work and responsiveness to family needs.

Ultimately, the part-time idea has implications for the relative priority of work and family life in the larger society as well as in the lives of individuals. In their study of job-sharing couples, Arkin and Dobrovsky reported a finding consistent with that of the Rapoports. Occupation for these couples, rather than being a primary source of fulfillment, is either equal to or less important than family and other sources of fulfillment, is either equal to or less important then family and other sources of fulfillment. It is my own hunch that women's equality will not be fully realized until this balanced ideal of relationship and achievement is writ large in the interaction of work and family life. It will be manifest when women see their competence of work as important as intimacy and family life, and when men see close personal ties and family work as important as their occupations and career success. At the moment the realization of this ideal seems a long way off. Women and men still differentiate their primary responsibilities asymmetrically. Yet change is in the direction of a more similar constellation of future duties and rewards.

No more dramatic evidence of social change in women's work and family roles can be found than in the crescendo to concern for the so-called displaced homemaker. This is a person who has devoted her adult work life to care of family and home and then finds herself economically dependent by loss of a spouse through death or divorce or the maturity of her children (which makes her no longer eligible to receive the child benefits to which she was formerly entitled). Concern for the displaced homemaker whether she be a middle-class woman threatened by poverty who suddenly must head a single-parent family or a welfare mother whose children have grown, is indicative of two broad converging trends in modern society.

One relates to the increasing likelihood of divorce, the other stems a growing expectation that women cannot (as traditionally expected) depend on others for economic support but must be able to support themselves and their children if the need arises.

The term displaced homemaker first appeared in 1974 as a result of a special task force of the National Organization of Women headed by Tish Sommers and Laurie Shields. They defined and publicized the problem of women's dependency and vulnerability if they were suddenly "displaced" from their usual role as full-time homemakers and could no longer depend on a husband or Aid to Families of Dependent Child (AFDC) for economic support. Sommers and Shields proposed counseling services, continuing and vocational education, job placement, and living stipends to tide women over and eventually help them to reenter the work world and become self-supporting.

Their naming of the problem was soon followed by a series of legislative efforts by Representative Yvonne Braithwaite Burke and Senator Birch Bayh that eventually resulted in funding and programs for displaced homemakers under the 1979 amendments to the Comprehensive Employment and Training Act (CETA). Six demonstration projects for retraining CETA-eligible (low income) displaced homemakers. 40 years of age or older, were set up throughout the United States. Experience to date in the Boston area has shown remarkable success in training and placing the low-income inner-city women enrolled in the program. The women are strongly motivated to be, economically independent and have tackled verbal and mathematical deficiencies, participated regularly in daily training and counseling sessions, and eagerly pushed job opportunities.

For suburban displaced homemakers who are not eligible under CETA, the tasks of retraining and reentry are somewhat different. Very little financial support is available for community services, counseling, and job placement for this group. Yet the problems are still very real: Even women will college degrees who have been out of the labor force 25 or 30 years are frequently so depressed when faced with a sudden status change as a result of separation or divorce that they fail to respond even to those outreach efforts that community agencies do make.

In other countries such as East Germany and the Scandinavian nations, policies on behalf women's retraining, labour force recently and promotions have long been more comprehensive and explicit than in the United States.

In the United States over the last decade, however, there has been remarkable change in the direction of actual programs and behavior. Such change indicates increased male and female involvement in both work and the family. The displaced homemaker movement is merely one manifestation of this trend; it excites the interest of both liberals who believe in egalitarian sex roles and conservatives who want to get women off welfare and into the work place.

In addition, in the popular mind there is growing interest in other topics such as continuing education, career change, and ethic of personal growth and change throughout the life course. All these developments have lessened the stereotyped roles of both age and sex that are applied to men and women over a whole lifetime. It is now increasingly being recognized that children do grow up, that women need not and should not plan for a single role that is solely concerned around mothering. At the same time, men may wish to retire early, explore another career or seek education in another field. The new flexible model of the life course and family division of labor now makes these activities possible.

5

Women's Employment

In urban labour market women workers were the victims of gender-based discrimination. In the labour market they faced employment, wage and occupational segregation. But before entering the labour market they were victims of the human-capital discrimination. In other words, women as workers were already operating in stratified and segmented labour market and were likely to be exposed to greater vulnerability in the future than in the past.

The new economic policy measures were announced by the Government of India in 1991, essentially in the wake of the debt crisis the country faced. They were a part of the "structural adjustment policy package" accepted by many developed and developing countries in the face of debt crisis and changing global economic situation in the late seventies and the eighties. International attention in the eighties was focused on financial crisis and economic adjustment rather than on poverty related issues.

As for the labour markets the main objective was to improve efficiency and make production cost-effective. The process was expected to re-allocate resources to reflect their relative scarcities. Persistent high levels of unemployment were to be accepted as an unavoidable evil under the policy.

The acceptance of the "structural adjustment policy" in 1991 was the first step towards liberalization of the Indian economy. Starting with changes in trade and industrial policy, the government subsequently has pursued the liberalization policy through a number of measures announced from time to time. The new trade and industrial policy package is expected to make Indian manufacturing competitive and responsive to changing national and international demand. It is also expected to being relative prices of labour and capital in conformity with their relative supplies. Going by the experience of other countries, liberalization trade and industry, under certain conditions, in the medium and long run could be expected to increase the demand for labour in general and that for female labour in particular. The process would reduce under utilization of labour and hasten the shift of employment away from agriculture initiated in the seventies.

In the light of the changes in the female employment in the 1980s in urban India argues that the pursuit of structural adjustment policies, in the short run, is likely to affect adversely not only the nature of female employment but also their job access in the light of emerging complex labour processes. Women are likely to be exploited much more in the near future than in the past and may be forced to devise diverse survival strategies. To reduce the adverse impact in the short run, there is a need to understand the emerging process of job access since these processes would control female labour force participation. This understanding would go a long way in taking steps that could reduce women's exploitation in the labour market if not eliminating it altogether.

There are two major sources of data no female employment in India, the decennial population Census and the quinquennial employment and unemployment survey rounds of the NSSO. Both, but the Census more than the other, under enumerate female workers. Comparable data from the Census over the eighties and that from NSSO over the last two decades lends somewhat support to the claim that the urban work force in India is getting feminized over the years.

The process was occurring through increased female participation and faster growth of female relatively to male employment. The NSSO data on labour absorption by industries in the non-farm sector revealed that in the eighties women were entering manufacturing in a big way, a phenomenon which is evident also in the date from the Annual Survey of Industries. The ASI data also supplied explanation for the phenomenon. A woman earned 62 per cent of the male wage in 1971 but only 38 per cent of it in 1983-84. No wonder female employment increased absolutely and relatively over the years.

The structural adjustment policy package entails deflation, devaluation, deregulation and decentralization. All these measures are likely to affect the volume and nature of employment in urban India. Deflationary policies would help the government reduce fiscal deficit. Devaluation and result in a better allocation of available resources. The policy package together is designed to open up the Indian economy to global competition.

The new policies where market mechanism and cost competitiveness get high priority have often been accompanied by radical changes in labour relations in most parts of the world. Since cost competitiveness is of utmost significance, adherence to labour market regulations in the form of labour and social rights, objective of redistributive welfare state, poverty alleviation and universal social security have received much less attention of the governments in the 1980s than in the past. Role of the state in expected to be minimal. Consequently in almost all countries that accepted the policy, formal regulations in the form of labour and social rights, which governed the working of labour markets, have eroded.

In some, the legislation continues to exist but it was less effective in reality, partially because it was not implemented but more so because it was systematically by passed by employers. It is important to understand how the changes in the macro-level policies would affect the female labour market both in the long-run and the short-run. More importantly we should visualize the kind of labour processes that are likely to emerge in the labour market which would control the female labour force participation.

If we go by the experience elsewhere in South Fast Asia and China, demand for female labour in urban India could be expected to increase over a span of a decade or so. Female participation rates too would rise eventually and the Indian economy could be expected to again high rates of growth like those attained in countries which accepted the Strategy. As elsewhere the strategy would increase per capita incomes and bring about a decline in the poverty ratios much faster than in the past.

But this encouraging picture of the long-run should not blind us. In the short-run the policies are likely to affect adversely to affect adversely the nature of female employment. Deflationary polices may force many poor women in urban India to fend for themselves as self-employed in the labour. Devaluation with trade liberalization could be expected to increases demand for female labour in the export industries, but the kind of employment offered would be both insecure and low paid. Most importantly, women are likely to be exposed to working conditions that are hazardous to their health . Deregulation and decent realization of domestic industrial production together would create flexible female labour which is intermittently employed, mostly on low wages. Nearly 55 per cent of female workers in urban India were illiterate and together with those with education upto primary level, comprised three fourths of the total female workers in 1987-88. Given the low levels of education of the workers, with limited options left, women will be forced to accept either the 'precarious" jobs which the labour market offers or be tied down to hobs which permit them to combine house work with work.

Precarious forms of work that create insecurity of income and employment and expose women to many forms of abuse are new to women in India. This kind of employment exists even now but its extent is likely to increase in future.

In the past, precarious jobs have ranged from temporary, casual, part-time to home-based wage work. They have taken the form of disguised or invisible work of helpers and unpaid family workers. Very often poor women take to menial kind of self-employment as petty traders or vendors and even as rag-pickets. The need to earn forced women to accept work that was poorly paid and demanded long working hours.

And yet such acceptance was in fact a survival strategy which they accepted given the limited options under the circumstances in which they accepted given the limited option under the circumstances in which they found themselves. The diverse nature of economic activity in the past gave rise to exploitative relationships within and outside the household. We could say that the severity of these exploitative relationships could be expected to increase over time considering the kind of jobs which labour market may offer to women in future.

Jobs which are likely to be offered to women who enter the labour market could be best described as follows:

(i) these jobs are likely to have short time horizons or would be non-permanent in status, they could be temporary, casual or contract jobs;

(ii) since these jobs are non-permanent it implies that they would be irregular and intermittent and would create insecurity of income;

(iii) in these jobs women would have no control either over their working conditions or their wages of the pace of work as all these factors would be controlled by others like employers, jobbers or contractors; and

(iv) these jobs would not only lie outside the purview of labour legislation but also would not enjoy the protection of family, community or caste which women could get as helpers or unpaid family workers in agricultural or artisan households.

The emerging female labour market indicates clearly that women working therein would be victims of discrimination and unfair labour practices to a greater extent than in the past. But despite the precariousness of the work, with its instability, insecurity and social and economic vulnerability, the women given their poverty and lack of skills would have very little option by to tolerate exploitation. The meagre incomes they get would be precious for their own and for their family's survival since they form substantial proportions of their equally low family/household incomes. More importantly, as the future labour market would offer wage work to women, certain complex labour processes could be expected to emerge which would control both women's participation and their job access.

To understand these it is necessary to see micro-level evidence on the nature of urban markets, how they function in reality and what kind of factors control workers' access to jobs offered in the labour market.

Urban labour markets in India as elsewhere depict inequality. Depending upon the productively differentials between occupations, and the endowments of workers, wages differ between workers/sectors and occupations. Very often workers with similar abilities receive different incomes as a result of labour market discrimination. But worse still, wage differentials areas because jobs are not equally accessible to all workers alike since urban labour markets in India are stratified or segmented.

Deshpande's study of Bombay and that of Coimbatore by Harriss and others highlighted another important dimension of how urban labour markets functioned in reality. They show that stratification and segmentation was reflected in the mechanism of job access. Though there were no formal restriction to entry into any particular sub-market, informal barriers could be inferred from the characteristics of workers working in each sub-market. Allocation of workers to each sub-market was determined by availability of information and help, educational qualifications and also the selection processes adopted by employers.

But information regarding jobs and source help in getting them were by far the most important factors that determined where a worker would ultimately work. "Particularist" sources of information like family, casts, community/village or personal contacts made certain occupations or sectors preserves of specific castes or groups of communities. These dominated as sources of job information compared to formal sources like employment exchanges and new paper advertisements in job access. Employers generally selected workers who were trainable, not necessarily those who were already trained. Personal contracts acted as means of controlling labour market access and perhaps a way of screening and rationing jobs. But they in turn created obligations either financial or social.

There was very little mobility between sub-markets; once a worker entered one of them, he was doomed to remain there during most of his working life. This was true of occupations too. Though there was some horizontal mobility within the sector/occupation, very little vertical mobility was evident.

The particularistic processes reflected the importance of social institutions like kinship, caste and community in the Indian society. The most important was the finding that due to these processes some groups of workers who were "vulnerable" were condemned to be vulnerable. Women form one such vulnerable group and therefore it is crucial to know how they have access to job information and who helps them get jobs.

Though both the studies noted earlier give data on source of information and help in job access, only one of them, Deshpande's study of Bombay, provides the data by sex. Further, these data are available for workers in two of the three sectors, namely, causal and factory sector covered in the study but not for those who worked in small establishments. It would therefore be important to understand these data to visualize what kind of labour processes could be expected to dominate in future and control women's access to jobs.

Deshpande's study carried out in 1974-76 covered over 6100 workers working in the factory sector, small establishments and casual sector in Bombay. We would be restricting here to 2937 workers working in factories and 1104 causal workers covered in the study. Women formed 6 per cent of the workers in the factory sector while 18 per cent of them were in the casual sector.

At survey, data were collected on the number of jobs held by each worker and source of information was enumerated for each job held by the worker. Irrespective of the sector of employment job mobility was higher amongst men than women. Secondly, formal sources of information were less important than "particularist" for both the sexes but more so for those working in the casual sector, where less than 2 per cent of the male workers while none of the female workers reported getting jobs through either advertisements or employment exchange.

Information about better paid jobs of the factory sector was available to both males and females but more so to the females largely through relatives and friends. Friends comprised of caste fellows, persons belonging to the same community or persons coming from the same village.

A larger proportion of jobs held by men than women working in factories, were acquired by their own efforts or through personal contracts. Curiously enough, the source identified as "others" which included jobbers/contractors did not emerge as an important source of information in the factory sector.

Pattern of hobs held by casual male workers by source of information did not differ much from the pattern observed earlier for their counterparts in the factory sector. But the pattern of job access for women in the casual sector differed both from that reported by males working within the sector but more importantly from that reported by women working within the factory sector.

Nearly half, 44 per cent of the jobs held by these women had been acquired through information that was passed on through a person working in the same profession. This was not so for men for whom barely 6 per cent of the jobs were so acquired.

Relatives and friends were far less important as source of information to women than men working as casual workers. It was precisely in this respect that their pattern of job access differed from women who worked in the factory sector.

Casual women workers depended more both on their fellow workers and their own efforts and much less on relatives and friends than women working in the factory sector for access to job information.

In other words, information regarding better paid factory jobs for women was not easily available to all women in Bombay labour market. Rather it was restricted to an exclusive group who had friend/relatives working already in factories. Interestingly enough, even in the mid-seventies, job information through contractors/jobbers was acquired much more by women in the casual than in the factory sector.

Workers, both male and female in the factory sector, were helped largely by relatives and friends in getting jobs, though many reported getting them through their own effort.

In the casual sector, however, once job information was available, workers had to fend for themselves though workers in the same profession did provide some help. Family, kith and kin relationships were much stronger in case of women employed in factories than for those working in the casual sector.

Unlike men, friends were more important than relatives to women in the casual sector in giving job information. While women working in construction depended to a great extent on contractors, those in trade and commerce had to fend for themselves, while those in service occupations were drawn into them by others working in the same occupation.

Bombay Labour Market study covered self-employed women in the casual sector working in service but does not provide date on job access separately for them. Harriss' study reveals that most self-employed (male and female workers together) reported being in the current occupation either because it was their family occupation or because they had worked as employees in a similar business. Employed mostly in menial jobs, they struggled through their own efforts to earn their daily bread.

Analysis of this micro-level evidence on hob access suggests that the extent of segmentation in urban labour markets is not likely to decline in future. The emerging future labour markets would be more segmented and stratified than in the past. The relative importance to "formal" sources in job access would decline further. The existing 'Particularist" sources would because more important than in the past but in addition contractors/subcontractors and jobbers would emerge as important source of job access. These change are in fact implicit in the changes in the labour market which the adjustment policies entail.

As a part of deflationary policies, if subsidies on essential commodities are reduced, poor women, both those working for wages and others working as self-employed, would be forced to work harder and for longer hours at home or outside to be able to provide the same bare essential needs for the family to survive. Apart from affecting those already in the labour market, deflationary policies may draw more women from poor households in the urban labour market. Ill-equipped as they are to compete with others in the labour market they are likely to over crowd such activities like petty trade or small-scale production or rag-picking which are already precarious. This is turn is likely to reduce incomes of all who are involved in such activities forcing each one to struggle harder.

Trade liberalization along with deregulation and decentralization of domestic industry is likely to make certain forms of employer/employee relationships more important in the future than in the past. These changes would determine access to hob information women have in future. Women working on wages either in small manufacturing units in the export or domestic sector out-side their houses or others who get work at home on piece rate would find that their dependence on middle men like contractors/jobbers would increase. This is inevitable because production would no more be carried out under one roof.

Women would be getting work at the mercy of these middlemen. And there could division of production process itself. This entails insecurity of employment and therefore income; though in addition other forms of abuse cannot be ruled out. In fact this situation may force women not only to accept low wages but make them reluctant even to form unions. Their weak bargaining position would make them victims of wages and other forms of exploitation.

Women working in traditional occupations at home, even in the past, were exploited both by sellers of raw materials and buyers of their finished products. Some of them may in future join the ranks of women who work as home-based workers in manufacturing and be victims of exploitative practices of middlemen. Others may survive in these dead-end jobs which offer no future. They would have very little option to change their occupation and would be forced to devise continually new strategies for sheer survival.

The kind of exploitative relationship between women who need income and therefor work and others like employers or contractors who need their labour are implicit in the work patterns that are likely to merge in future. They are to some extent inevitable because we saw earlier that a disproportionately large share of women in the casual sector reported getting jobs through either their own effort or their follow workers. Their own weak bargaining position and that of others in similar occupations is likely to make them extremely vulnerable. Employers in small manufacturing units, the middlemen and contractors, traders of raw materials and others who buy their output, persons lending them credit (including those sanctioning it through formal sources) and others who may lend them equipment at home to work with, all are likely to exploit poor women in the labour market because of their precarious position. Despite the awareness of these exploitative practices. Women would have no control over the work they do, the number of hours such work demands and the remuneration such work brings in. Clinging to these precarious forms of work would be the sole survival strategy they would be left with.

Social scientists working in the field of women's studies in India have very often tried to draw attention of policy makers to "invisibility" of women workers in the conventional labour force statistics. It must be emphasized that apart from missing and uncounted omen workers, our conventional data on employment status which classifies workers as employers, employees, own-account workers and unpaid family workers, does not capture the diverse relationships which exist today between workers, traders, employers and middlemen. These relationship arise because when production gets decentralized, workers are distributed over space.

Under the new economic policies, importance of such relationships is likely to increase. Each women worker would be dealt with by an employer or a contractor in her individual capacity. In the process, given the weak bargaining position of the women workers in general their interests are likely to be sacrificed. Data on these intricate relationships are hard to come by. They are not yet collected routinely by any official agency. If collected, they would go a log way in suggesting policies which could reduce exploitation of not eliminating it altogether. To this we turn to the next section.

A large majority of the urban women were forced to work because of their poverty. Their economic deprivation forced them to accept precarious jobs. These jobs displayed certain bad characteristics like low pay, bad working conditions, long hours of work, insecurity and exposure to health hazards. The last probably was the most dangerous. International experience revealed that after a short working span women employed in Sun-Rise industries, which grew in the export processing zones in South Asia, found it difficult to continue in some of these occupations because they often developed physical disabilities like, poor eyesight and backaches. Worst still they could not be re-employed elsewhere because of this physical damage. And yet poor women could not be expected to give up their meager incomes since the option they had was to remain at home and have no income. Their participation in labour market and the exploitation accompanying it was in fact survival strategy which they were forced to accept.

The vulnerability which poor women as workers experience is likely to increase in future because of the informal production and distribution relationships which would emerge with adjustment policies. Employers in core production units would not employ their workers directly. Rather a chain of intermediaries consisting of contractors, sub-contractors, traders and the like who would deal with individual workers separately. Personalized relationships would become more important than in the past. Insecurity of employment and fear of losing the job and awareness of their weak position in the labour market forced women at SEEPZ in Bombay to report that they are not very keen on joining trade unions. Shara of such workers in urban female work force would increase over the time.

In a sense, the measures adopted to liberalize and globalize the Indian economy has thrown up a challenge to the trade union movement in India. In the post-independence period the strong trade union movement succeeded in pressurizing the government to give industrial and other workers in the organized sector protective labour legislation and social security benefits. Under the changed economic scenario, very little of the protective legislation would be applicable to the growing flexible work force consisting of women among others. Given the objective of doing away with sickness in industry and with less protection given to producers and workers, unions would be forced to accept that they are unable to defend interests of workers in the organized sectors any more.

Most of the these unions performed rather well their role of promoting the interests of their members in the organized sector. But in the past they have failed to protect the interests of a much bigger segment of workers who belong to the informal sector of the Indian economy. This cannot continue in future. Ever for sheer survival unions would have to turn to the workers in the informal sector who are physically strewn over space and victims of exploitation. This is not to say that the unorganized workers were totally neglected in the past. But unfortunately such efforts have been few. More importantly it must be noted that trade unions which tried to protect interests of workers in general did not take up problems of women workers per se. Barring a few social security measures most other protective labour legislation was applicable to women not because they were women but because they formed a segment of the organized sector workers.

It must be noted that activist groups working at the grass-roots level have made immense contribution by taking up both economic and social issues that confront women. Taking into account the kind of future labour/employer/contractor relationships, activists would be forced to innovate ways and means by which individual women workers distributed over space are brought together through trade-union-like organization. These organizations could be social in character, but they would essentially provide women opportunity to share their experiences, views and problems with others who are similarly placed. The real challenge lies in empowering these women with awareness and a sense of confidence that together they can fight exploitation. Some of the experiences of grass-roots level activists are encouraging indeed. This makes one feel that women are not destined to be doomed.

NGO's have played an important role in protecting interests of women workers in the informal sector. They could be expected to take over the role of intermediaries who are likely to become important in future production processes. This may help women get the income that is due to them. Micro-level evidence suggests that very often NGOs were unable to give home-based sub-contract workers, work on continuous basis though the workers reported their availability for work. True attempts may have to be made by the government to strengthen NGOs as alternative institutions to intermediaries both in production and distribution. More importantly, NGOs and similar agencies would do good to make women aware of their strength which could emerge essentially by their collective effort after sharing their individual experiences with others in similar situations. The emerging women's organizations would not be unions per se but union-like organizations formed through women's own initiative to fight exploitation.

To sum up, the structural adjustment policy package is not a panacea for all ills that exist today. Going by the experience of other countries, especially in South Asia, it could be expected to increase the demand for female labour faster than in the past, offer diverse employment opportunities in the non-farm sector and thereby widen women's occupational choice and reduce their poverty to some extent. In this sense the change should be regarded as an improvement. But these changes are essentially long run changes. In the short run women are likely to be exposed to exploitation both in the labour market and within the household. The former kind of exploitation which essentially is the consequences of their weak bargaining position in the labour market could be reduced through efforts of both NGOs and activists. But the latter would require a change in the attitudes and values in the society and are difficult to materialize in the short run. And yet, even though women are victims of exploitation in the labour market and at home they themselves would be prepared to put up with it because their meager income is vital for their own and their family's survival. This precarious situation of the majority of the women workers in India is a challenge to established union, activists and NGOs alike. The ingenuity of these agencies would lie in their devising and innovating union-like organizations which would enable and empower women to fight for their own cause.

Now, the main question before us is 'did economic development lead to marginalisation of female workers in India?' The second question posed here is, 'how the structural adjustment will affect the employment opportunities of female workers in India?'

The status of women and its contribution to social and economic development largely depends on the availability of employment opportunities for women. In spite of serious efforts of the state to improve the status of women in India, it continues to be unsatisfactory.

The Female Marginalisation (FM) in its generic from contends that the process of industrialisation and economic development are accompanied by marginalisation of women in the production process. The Marxists argue the FM is inherent in the organisation of capitalist production and use of Labour. It is capitalism and patriarchal organisation of society which result in confinement of women to homes and to inferior occupations. The divorce between production and reproduction under capitalism on the one hand and existence of multistructuralist society give rise to segregation and marginalisation of production while, others try to seek explanations in terms of economic, social and cultural fabric of a particular society. Empirical evidence to FM thesis shows an erosion of traditional female role as such and exclusion of women from industrial employment. That is why, the testing of hypothesis becomes difficult. FM can be verified on the basis of following visible dimensions:

(1) FM can mean exclusion of women from productive employment which can be observed either as decline in overall work participation rates of women or diminution in their share in wage and salaried employment;

(2) FM can also mean segregation of women workers in certain specific jobs which are low in occupational hierarchy and less rewarding and low in status and increasing exclusion of either sex from a particular function;

(3) FM may be manifested in concentration of majority of women workers in the marginal occupations, industries and sectors of employment. For example, concentration of women in the informal sectors or in unpaid occupations;

(4) FM may also mean economic inequality reflected through gender wage differentials and casualisaion of female labour force.

It is not necessary that the dimensions of FM have to manifest in order to prove FM thesis. Scott observes that the dimensions outlined above are not different aspects of a single phenomenon. The manifestation of a particular dimension depends upon the stage of economic development. For example, in the initial stage of industrialisation, the first dimension may manifest itself, whereas, in the advanced industrial societies, there may overall increase in participation rates of women accompanied by occupational segregation or feminisation of occupation. India is predominantly an agrarian economy. The primary sector accounts for nearly 35 per cent of GDP and employs 65 per cent of the main workers. Over the period, the share of non-agriculture sector in GDP has increased but its share in total employment is less than proportionate. It is because the modern sector in India exhibits similar patterns as that of developed countries in economic growth without generating much employment.

Women's employment in India has been analysed in the following inter-connected dimensions: (i) work participation rates; (ii) status of employment; and (iii) economic sectors of employment.

Status of employment

Employment by status shows that between 1972 and 1988, the share of women in self-employment and in regular employment has declined. Contrarily, the share of women in casual employment has increased in rural and urban areas. In other words, female employment in India is getting increasingly casualised. This is mainly on account of two reasons. First, in order to avoid provision of maternity and other social and economic benefits etc., the employers recruit women as casual workers. Second, with the increase in the sub-contracting of the production process, the employment in general and that of women in particular is being gradually transferred from the organised to unorganised sector.

The census data makes distinction between Main and Marginal Workers. Marginal workers have been defined as those who have to worked for a major part of the preceding year. In 1991 census, women account for only 16.03 per cent of the total main workers in India. However, women account for 84 per cent of the total female marginal plus non-workers together 80.18 per cent in rural areas and 91.85 per cent in urban areas are women. This again shows a typical nature of female employment in India.

It is generally argued that women in India show reluctance to enter in the labour force, that is why, their participation rates are low. This argument holds good, if unemployment among women is negligible or at lest is lower as compared to men. However, the available estimates of female unemployment are contrary.

Nearly 80 per cent of the women workers in India are concentrated in agricultural activities. The major shift in women employment in this sector is form agriculture labour category to cultivators. The cultivator in Indian census means either an employer or family worker engaged in cultivation. The women in Indian context belong mainly to the latter category. It is thus obvious that the status of women between three census periods has marginally shifted from agriculture worker to unpaid family worker. But the share of men in this sector has declined. This may partly be due to migration of males from rural areas to urban areas.

The share of men declined in the household industries while that of women increased between 1971 and 1981 and declined between 1981 and 1991. In non-household industries, the share of men shows improvement between 1971 and 1981 and a decline between 1981 and 1991. The share of women in non-household industry improved during the three Census; periods. The share of women in relatively better paying jab in transport, storage and communication sector shows a decline, while their share in other services after registering a decline shows a marginal increase in the last census period.

The Census evidence points that there are marginal changes in women's employment by sectors whatever be the magnitude of these changes. The evidence suggests that women are sliding down to low paying or unpaid work. Even in the higher paying sector the advancement of women is rather slow as compared to men.

Many studies analysing the pattern of women's employment in the manufacturing industries have shown that women are being excluded from most skilled jobs and are concentrated in lower paid jobs and industries. The empirical evidence shows that there is a plausible ground to argue for a validation of female marginalisation thesis in India. In other words, the overall economic development has increasingly excluded women from productive employment; pushed them into marginal occupations and increasingly casualised women in terms of employment.

The modern technology has always favoured capital and not the labour. The capital has become cheaper than before and this is justified on the ground that industries need technological upgradation. This ultimately will increases the demand for skilled labour of qualitatively new type. Economic restructuring aims at production restructuring and, in turn, involves labour restricting.

Such increase in demand as might arise for the least skilled job where workers would be further exploited as in the case of women in textile and garment industry. Since women have fewer skills as compared to men, it is likely that men may gain in terms of employment in the labour restructuring process. This may result in increased exclusion of women from the production process.

Presently, most of the developing countries are focusing their attention on 'Human Led Development'.

6

Development of Women

National Commission of Women Act, suggested that a survey or study be taken up to assess the participation of women in the different areas supported by the Government. On the basis of the survey positive action should be taken to motivate and encourage talented women in various aspects of culture. Women should be enabled to make their contribution through better opportunities for securing training cultural education research etc. In the training schemes for conservation of cultural property, women should be given equal opportunity. Technical courses (for instance, for Museum staff) should have larger participation of women trainees.

The commission advised that space for women artists in galleries and museums should be enhanced. Augmentation of teaching positions for women in institutions of art and culture was warranted. To enhance the contribution if women to culture, managerial administrative and decision-making posts should be made available to women in an equitable manner.

The Commission urged that Government's grant awarding policies should be modified to give adequate opportunities to women. Award panels should have greater representation of women. Proposals from women applicants for grants should be specifically invited. Women should get a fair share of grants-in-aid, project grants findings for research projects fellowships etc., meant for support of art and culture.

The provision under section 16 of the NCW Act applies to all the Ministers/Departments of government of India Concerned with women's issues such as Home Affairs, Health & Family, Welfare, Education, Culture, Social Welfare Agriculture, Labour, Urban Development, Rural Development, Information & Broadcasting Environment & forests etc. These Minister/Department should also consult NCW for all major policy matters affecting women.

Women's cells in ministries/Public sector undertakings

Women's Cells to monitor the schemes for women were setup some years ago in the Ministries of Labour, Industry, Rural Development and Science & Technology.

The National Perspective plan for women had recommended that the planning Commission and each ministry/ Department should have a women's Cell. Pursuant thereto, women's cells were set up in several Ministries and Departments. A special unit was also set up in the planning Commission. The Commission called for information regarding the role and activities of women's Cells since their setting up from all the concerned Ministries/Departments. The feedback indicated that most of the Cells were dormant and many of them were not even aware of their scope and functions.

Recognising the need to activities Women's Cells to define their role and functions and to promote exchange of ideas and information among the cells, the Commission convened a meeting of senior officers of the concerned

Ministries/Departments and representatives of SCOPE (Standing Conference of Public Sector Enterprises), WIPs (Women in Public Sector) etc. Pursuant to the deliberations a sub-committee was set up to prepare guidelines for Women's Cells. The sub-Committee consisted of representatives of the Commission as well as the Ministers of Finance, rural Development and the Department of Women & Child Development.

After considering the suggestions of the subcommittee, the Commission issued guidelines for women's Cells, which included *inter alia* the following:

(a) The Departments as well as Public Sector Undertakings and autonomous bodies under their control, should set up women Cells in their organisations within a specific period (three months or so).

(b) The women's Cells should review the plan schemes and other programmes of the Department/ PSU concerned and ensure that wherever possible the aspect of women's development is promoted through these schemes component exists in a scheme, it should be periodically monitored to ensure proper implementation.

(c) Other schemes/programmes a my be examined and wherever feasible, a component for women's development be introduced in the activity by getting the schemes amended suitably.

(d) the concerned Department/PSU should collect basic information and data regarding employment of women in the organisation employment of women in the organisation, their educational status and other relevant data. Further the Guidelines indicated that these cells should promote (i) an all round develop-ment of women employees of the Ministries/Departments/Organisations and (2) the developments of the male as well as female employees through non-formal/adult education health care family care assistance training for skill formation etc.

Women and the electronic media

Social scientists acknowledge that planning for women's advancement cannot success unless supported by an awareness generation programme covering all sections of the population. The reason is that women's empowerment is inexorably task is to root out gender bias and implant positive attitudes in the hearts and minds of men and women and children so that the family and the society would endorse and participate in the planning process for women's advancement.

Till recently, the means to achieve attitudinal changes in society were indeed limited. The traditional modes of communication had a limited outreach, besides being not cost effective. In the last decade the communication revolution has opened up a magic door to reach millions of people through the electronic media's audio and audio-visual network of satellite transmission. It is as though the benighted path of women can now be illuminated by the flood lights of communication technology.

The dream of luminous electronic media dispelling darkness is unfortunately, not coming true for women. The reality is that often the electronic media are reinforcing traditional stereo-types which have kept women shackled or beaming denigrations and negative portrayals detrimental to the women's cause. Even when positive projections of women are a attempted in some programmes these are negated by counter messages which cause "crossed wires" and confusion in the minds of the viewers.

After surveying the dismal scenario of glaring gender bias of the electronic media and recognizing the immense potential of the media to effectively promote gender equality the Commission decided to organise a workshop on "gender Perspective for the Electronic Media".

Prior to the holding of the Workshop, an advocacy group of media experts and social activists completed a monitoring study if television programmes of Doordarshan in 5 cities i.e., Bombay, Calcutta, Bangalore, Hyderabad and Delhi. This study made a content analysis of TV programmes over a specific period. The study revealed vividly the kind of sex roles, trivialization and media stereotyping that women were victims of in several programmes.

The most common images put out are of the self-effacing and timorous wife, the foul seductress, the despicable vamp etc. The transmissions aimed primarily at women (e.g. the afternoon programme) revealed an obsession with marriage, home, cooking etc. perpetuating the notion of women's limited range of interests. Even the so-called "socially concerned" serials betray camouflaged prejudices and regressive tendencies. In the news and current affairs programmes women news-makers are left out and considered unfit to be included in panel discussions.

The recommended which emerged from the Workshop are summarised below:-

(i) The Government and in particular doordarshan should review and modify the present practices regarding the portrayal of women on the electronic media and evolve a policy which reflects the responsibility and role of the media for women's development in the country.

(ii) To evolve policy shifts based on actual data and analysis of relevant information the Ministry of Information and

Broadcasting should promote research to comprehend the preferences and preconceived notions among the audience, especially the women, on gender portrayals on TAV and also to gauge audience response to the different kinds of portrayals.

(iii) The outcome of research could be examined in consultation with the National Commission for Women and professionals with expertise on gender issues, in order to formulate the long-term objectives of media policy.

(iv) Revised guidelines for the media may be prepared to move away from gender stereotyping, to eliminate negative portrayal of women and to strengthen positive portrayal.

(v) The Ministry of Information & Broadcasting may consider constituting annual awards to producers/ Directors who contribute positively to promote women's development through media programmes.

(vi) Efforts should be made to set up a strong data base regarding gender sensitive professionals and institutions. A resource directory of experts and institutions could be prepared either by the Ministry or by the Commission.

(vii) Urgent action may be taken to sensitive media officials and professionals on gender issues. For this purpose, training modules may be developed with the help of national training institutes and the Commission.

The Commission is taking follow -up action on the output of the workshop.

Women and the Print Media

On women's issues and concerns, the multidimensional and crucial roles played by the print media are well-known. Our newspaper and magazines have been taking up pivotal issues concerning women, and could often provoke a national debate, for instance on the rights of Muslim women and Christian women as illustrated in the case of Ms Shah Bano and of MS. Mary Roy; on the custodial crimes on women and the need for more stringent penal laws as in the Mathura rape case; on the contraceptive conundrum which has been agitating women activists; on the menace of sale of minor girls in the guise of marriage of foreign national, etc. Interventions in bringing to the fore various aspects of the issues under debate and have facilitated lobbying by NGOs and experts for changes in public policies and legislation.

Another dimension of media intervention is illustrated by the recent case of Saathin of Bhateri in which the Commission and Women's Organisations could not have mobilized public opinion and official response so effectively as to overcome the immense clout of the culprits and their supporters.

In several other instances also, the unstinted media support was largely instrumental in securing justice for individual women victims.

During the period report the Commission took up a small project to monitor and analyses the qualitative and quantitative content of coverage of women issues by the newspaper. It is envisaged that after completing the exercise the commission could interact with editors and media professionals regarding measures to enhance the quantitative coverage of women's issues in the print media.

Evaluation of "the progress of the development of women under the Union and any State" is one of the statutory functions assigned to the Commission under section 10 (1) of the National Commission for Women Act, 1990. The task, obviously, is a stupendous one.

Plan strategies for women's education

The economic and social returns for education of women are, on the whole greater than those of men. By educating women, as is well-known a country can reduce poverty, improve productivity, ease population pressure and offer its children a better future. During the very first decade of planning a National Committee on Women's Education was set up which submitted its report in 1959. Based on the recommendations of this Committee, schemes like "Condensed Courses of Education for Adult Women", "Bal Sevika Training" etc., were introduced in the Third Five Year Plan. In order to remove the persisting vast disparities between education and literacy levels of males and females, special incentives for girls like free text books mid-day meals, uniforms and attendance scholarships were included in the education programmes in the fifth plan. The sixth Plan, following the report of the Committee on Status of Women in India, recognised the need to promote Balwadi/ Creches to enable elder girls to devote time to schooling and to appoint lady teachers in order to attract girls to schools in rural areas. The adult education programme was also strengthened during the Sixth plan.

The seventh plan strategy for education included revision of school curricula to remove gender bias and accorded priority to enrolment of girls in formal and non-formal education courses. Education was made free for girls at the elementary stage. Early childhood education centres were set up as adjuncts to primary/ middle schools in order to help older girls attend the schools while their younger siblings were taken care of by these centres. Teachers training programme was given a boost and open learning system including correspondence courses was expanded. Promotion of technical and vocational education among girls was effected through expansion of women polytechnics and vocational training institutes.

Participation of women and girls in sports was encouraged by instituting sports scholarships for girls.

Women are progressing faster than men in the field of education

The educational scene, as it emerged at the end of the eighties, clearly showed that girls are progressing faster than boys and though much remains to be a achieved there has been a positive impetus to girls education. The literacy rate of females in the age group of 7 years and above was recorded by 1991 census at 39.19 percent against 64.20 percent for males. The corresponding rates for 1981 were 29.85 and 56.50 respectively.

Thus the increase in literacy rate during the decade 1981-91 among females is higher compared to males. The male literates increased by 42.41 percent and female literates increased by 63.56 percent. The male female differential came down from about 26.55 percentage points in 1981 to 25.01 points in 1991. The six ratio among literates increased from 491 in 1981 to 564 in 1991.

Women-headed households

Recent studies have indicated that about 30 per cent of rural households are headed by come on account of male migration to urban areas neglect or abandonment. These women-headed households generally survive on minimum income levels.

Legal provisions meant for protecting interests of female workers have, by and large, not been availed of by women. The minimum Wages Act is not being implemented effectively and women are not paid equal wages for equal work-Moreover the Act does not benefit women in the unorganised sectors who form a large proportion of women workers.

Trends in female employment

During the decade 1981-91, the percentage of female workers both main and marginal, has increased in rural as well as urban areas. Percentage of marginal workers among males, on the other hand has declined in rural as well as urban areas. The obvious reason for increased visibility in work participation rates of females could be improved canvassing during the 1991 census. The improvements are noticeable in occupational categories of "cultivators", trade and commence" and "other services" There are 9 state and Union Territories where the female work participation declined during the decade. The sharpest decline was noted in Arunachal Pradesh i.e., from 45.67 percent in 1981 to 37.49 percent in 1991. The work participation for females in Punjab which was the lowest of all states in 1981 fell down further in 1991 from 6.17 to 4.40.

During the same period, increase has been noted in the category of cultivators by 1.13 percentages points within the female workers. The proportion of female agricultural labourers declined by 1.41 percentage points. It is quite contrary to the position in the previous decade when proportion of agricultural labour had increased in the female labour force. A decline is also observed in the proportion of female workers engaged in household industries and construction. Women workers are being represented in lager proportion in "order services" as well as in "trade and commerce".

Women in unorganised sectors

According to "Shram Shakti"—Report of the National Commission on Self employed women and Women in Informal Sectors—the women in the unorganised sectors are the "weakest link in labour statistics." The Conventional classification of workers and their contribution to the economy reduces the poor labouring women as marginal workers little recognition of their contribution to the national economy. Broadly speaking this group includes those who are outside the pale of the organised sector. They include all those poor women who are engaged as:-

— the home-based producers including artisans and piece rate workers paid and unpaid voluntary labourers;

— petty vendors and hawkers who do not hire labour but take the assistance of family members.

— contract labour and sub-contract labour.

— provides of services like washer-women, scavengers and domestic helpers.

— those doing manual who like construction labour working in agriculture and other primary sectors.

The proportion of women in the female work force engaged in the unorganised sector is estimated to be 90 per cent. The workers in these occupations suffer from high incidence of casualisation. "The incidence of casual wages workers agricultural and construction workers amongst females ranges from 75 per cent to 96 per cent of the total female wage earners."

According to an ILO report, the informal sector comprises units producing very small scale goods and services involving little or on capital using a low level of productivity and generally yielding very low and irregular incomes. These units are mostly unregistered and the workers receive little or on legal protection, But the sector is continuously growing.

Women belonging to scheduled caste communities

The Scheduled Caste women have continued to toil in the

lowest rung of the social order in the Indian society. They have been relegated to lower status compared to men within the Scheduled Caste groups who themselves are placed at the lowest level in the society. The Scheduled Caste women therefore constitute the most distressed and poverty stricken section of the Hindu Society.

According to 1991 census, the Scheduled Castes numbering 138.22 million constitute 16.48 percent of the total population. The females form 47 percent of the Scheduled Castes population. The sex ratio among Scheduled Castes is 922 which is less than that for the total population. The fall in their sex ratio during 1981-91 was also more than that of the total population. From 932, the sex ratio for Scheduled Castes fell to 922 whereas for the total population this ratio fell from 935 (Excluding Assam and J & K) to 927.

The Scheduled Caste women a re generally invisible workers. the official statistics categories them as non-workers. They work mostly as agriculture labour, plantation, workers mine workers construction workers, washer women, rag pickers, vendors bidi workers etc. More than 90 percent are confined to unorganised sector. The main problems faced by then are lack of regular employment low wages discrimination in ages ad lack of social security as workers.

In the "mining and quarrying" sectors, the Scheduled Caste women are in general working as contract or casual labour. The wages they receive are extremely low compared to the wages of regular employees. Lately, there has been a decline in the number of regular employees among Scheduled Caste women and the number of casual/contract has been increasing. The labour laws are hardly implemented for these workers. bonded labour is still practised in a number of States.

In the household sector, the Scheduled Caste women are generally engaged alongwith other family members in traditional activities such as handloom weaving flaying and tanning and bamboo work, etc. The main problems faced by them are lack of access to raw material market, credit modern technology and skill training and lack of storage and transport facilities.

In urban areas, although both men and women are engaged in sweeping and sweeping and scavenging work, men are generally employed by municipalities and other civic authorities. The women's earnings are extremely low and work remains insecure. Majority of women are employed as domestic workers and have to work of for long hours without any protective legislation for them. Other activities which the Scheduled Caste women are engaged in are vending and hawking, small animal rearing specially pigs chickens and goats, rag picking and bidi making.

Women belonging to scheduled tribe communities

The Scheduled Tribes numbering 76.76 million constitute 8.08 percent of the population according to 1991 census. In 1981, Scheduled Tribes constituted 6.82 percent of the total population. The heterogeneous nature of the tribal socio-economic situation makes to difficult to generalise the status of women in tribal societies. The sex ratio among scheduled Tribes is 972 against 923 for non-Scheduled Castes/Tribes population. For 1981, the sex ratio for Scheduled Tribes was recorded as 983. This indicates a sharp fall during the decade, which is more than that in the non SC/ST population where it fell from 930 to 923. In urban population of the Scheduled Tribes the sex ratio has significantly risen from 912 to 922. The fall in the sex ratio during the decade is thus mainly in the rural population from 988 it fell down to 976. However the sex ratio among Scheduled Tribes is still higher than t hat of Scheduled Castes and the general population.

Literacy rates of Scheduled Tribe Women a re extremely low. As per 1991 census, the literacy rate among Scheduled Tribe was only 29.60 percent and that of female among than 18.19 percent. Rajasthan had only 4.42 percent literate Scheduled Tribe females the next higher being Andhra 'Pradesh with a female rate of 8.68 percent. In rural areas where the majority of the Scheduled tribe population lives the Scheduled Tribe female literacy was only 6.18 in 1981 as compared to 20.85 percent in the general population. It was even less than one percent or nearing zero in certain areas. There is also a very wide gap in the literacy levels of males and females among the STs compared to rest of the population.

Gender Gap in the enrolment ratio of Scheduled Tribes is higher than that of Scheduled Castes.

The enrolment ratio of ST boys for 1991-92 is 125.63 at primary level and half down steeply to less than half (nearly 43 percent) i.e. 54.11 at the middle level. but in the case of girls the fall is much steeper, i.e. from 82.59 to 27.28 which is almost one third of the enrolment ratio at primary level. It is rather interesting to note that enrolment ratio at primary level for ST boys is higher than that of the Scheduled Caste as well as the general population, but at the middle level, the enrolment ratio of ST boys is even less than that of SC boys.

The decadal growth of literacy rate during 1971-81 shows that for ST women, the percentage growth has been much higher than that of women of all communities excluding SCs STs-being 65.72 and 32.27 respectively. The main reason for low achievements of ST women in the education field is their extreme poverty which ties them down to their households, perpetuating their ignorance and black of aspiration to improve their status.

The employment position of ST women shoes that majority of them work at subsistence level, as agricultural labourers, construction workers or gathering fuel, fodder and water for survival/. Being mostly forest dwellers they traditionally depend on forest for survival. They have been suffering immensely on account of deforestation and reservation of forest land etc. The traditional economic sources having mostly labourers which is the most vulnerable group.

According to 1981 census, more than 13 percent of ST women workers are employed in marginal occupations and 58.68 per cent are non-workers. However these figures do not take into account majority of the types of economic activities in which ST Women are employed. Most of these are related to family occupation like agriculture animal husbandry forestry weaving construction labour and cottage industry. The women's contribution getting merged with those of the families becomes invisible. Wages for ST women are generally low and go supplement the family income.

Suggestions for improving the status of women in backward groups.

In order to improve the literacy and educational level of Scheduled Caste/Tribe women it is essential that they are relieved of their household drudgery. The major reasons for Scheduled Caste girls dropping out of their schools are poverty and lack of supporting services available to them in the prevalent social system. The responsibilities of girls in the household have to be reduced to the minimum through provision of creches drinking water sources fuel and fodder within easy reach of these girls which would go a long way in relieving them from drudgery of domestic work for participating in development activities.

— due to low levels of nourishment available to the Scheduled Caste women, they suffer from various types of problems relating to malnutrition. Their general debility and occupational health problems result in constant ill health. It is necessary to focus attention on the occupational health problems associated with the working environment of the Scheduled Caste women.

— it is imperative under the Tribal sub-plan approach special attention is given to programmes for the Scheduled Tribe women including education health economic development transfer of appropriate technologies and supportive services. the integrated Rural Development Programme (IRDP) and other poverty alleviation programmes where coverage of SC/ST families are specified, should accord due priority to SC/ST women and not be restricted to men. Implementation of land reforms suitable programmes for freed bonded labour and economic support structure including credit marketing and supply of raw material are most essential for the development of tribal women.

— special attention is necessary for improving the lot of the Devadasis. Apart from generation of awareness among the Devadasis against the age old evil system and superstition regarding dedication to Goddess Yellamma, it would be important to pay attention to an overall development of the region where the system is prevalent. Provision of Ashram schools for their children and training for the Devadasis in remunerative vocations would go a long way in alleviating the suffering of Devadasis. For this purpose reservation in training institutes may be made for them.

Index

Ali, Aruna Asaf, 56
All India Women's Conference (AIWC), 32
Anti-Price-Rise movement, 55
Anti-war movement, 3

Bal Sevika Training, 296
Bengali Muslim community, 195
Bombay Labour Market, 277
British im-perialism, 31
Bureau-cratic organizations, 2

Centrifugal forces, 198
Committee on the Status of Women (CSWI), 58
Communist Party of India (CPI), 12
Communist Party of India Marxist (CPM), 22
Communist Party of India Marxist-Leninist (CPML), 22
Community participation, 9
Criminal procedure Code, 149

Decentralized structure, 1
Deflationary policies, 270
Deflationary policies, 278
Democratic Women's Association, 51
Devaluation, 270
Dowry Prohibition Act, 48

Electronic media, 292
Empowerment organizations, 16
Empowerment wing, 15
Equal Remuneration Act, 43

Female agricultural labour, 71
Female infanti-cide, 146
Female Marginalisation (FM), 284
Fundamentalists, 29

Gandhi Indira, 41
Green revolution, 20
Group autonomy, 7

Home-based workers, 279
Household drudgery, 303

Indian Administrative Service (I.A.S.), 68
Indian Foreign Service (IFS), 68
Indian Union Muslim League (IUML), 157
Indian women's Movement, 7
Integrated Rural Development Programme (IRDP), 304
Istikhara, 211

Labour legislation, 281
Labour markets, 268
Legitimize movements, 6
Liberalization, 271

Mahila Dakshata Samiti, 12
Material transactions, 178
Movement organizations, 4
Muslim customs, 147
Muslim fundamentalism, 30
Mutaa marriage, 201

New Education Policy, 46
New social movement, 6
Non-party organizations, 21

Obscurantism, 153
Occupational segregation, 268
Oswal woman, 169

Physical termination, 183
Political empowerment, 26
Purdah, 164

Respect-avoidance, 196
Roy, Mary, 295
Russell, Bertrand, 206

Scheduled Caste women, 300
Shram Shakti, 298
Social pathology, 6
Social scientists, 280

Tebhaga movement, 34
Temporary marriage, 205
Traditional stereotypes, 292

Women Act, National Commission of, 189
Women's India Association (WIA), 32
Women's India Association (WIA), 32

Young Women's Christian Association, (YMCA), 12